Novel Institutions

Edinburgh Critical Studies in Victorian Culture
Series Editor: Julian Wolfreys

For a complete list of titles published visit the Edinburgh Critical Studies in Victorian Culture web page at
www.edinburghuniversitypress.com/series/ECVC

Also Available:
Victoriographies – A Journal of Nineteenth-Century Writing, 1790–1914, edited by Diane Piccitto and
Patricia Pulham
ISSN: 2044-2416
www.eupjournals.com/vic

Novel Institutions

Anachronism, Irish Novels and
Nineteenth-Century Realism

Mary L. Mullen

EDINBURGH
University Press

Edinburgh University Press is one of the leading university presses in the UK. We publish academic books and journals in our selected subject areas across the humanities and social sciences, combining cutting-edge scholarship with high editorial and production values to produce academic works of lasting importance. For more information visit our website: edinburghuniversitypress.com

Edinburgh University Press Ltd
The Tun – Holyrood Road, 12(2f) Jackson's Entry, Edinburgh EH8 8PJ

Typeset in 11/13 Adobe Sabon by
IDSUK (DataConnection) Ltd, and
printed and bound in Great Britain.

A CIP record for this book is available from the British Library

ISBN 978 1 4744 5324 0 (hardback)
ISBN 978 1 4744 5326 4 (webready PDF)
ISBN 978 1 4744 5327 1 (epub)

Contents

Series Editor's Preface

'Victorian' is a term, at once indicative of a strongly determined concept and an often notoriously vague notion, emptied of all meaningful content by the many journalistic misconceptions that persist about the inhabitants and cultures of the British Isles and Victoria's Empire in the nineteenth century. As such, it has become a byword for the assumption of various, often contradictory habits of thought, belief, behaviour and perceptions. Victorian studies and studies in nineteenth-century literature and culture have, from their institutional inception, questioned narrowness of presumption, pushed at the limits of the nominal definition, and sought to question the very grounds on which the unreflective perception of the so-called Victorian has been built; and so they continue to do. Victorian and nineteenth-century studies of literature and culture maintain a breadth and diversity of interest, of focus and inquiry, in an interrogative and intellectually open-minded and challenging manner, which are equal to the exploration and inquisitiveness of its subjects. Many of the questions asked by scholars and researchers of the innumerable productions of nineteenth-century society actively put into suspension the clichés and stereotypes of 'Victorianism', whether the approach has been sustained by historical, scientific, philosophical, empirical, ideological or theoretical concerns; indeed, it would be incorrect to assume that each of these approaches to the idea of the Victorian has been, or has remained, in the main exclusive, sealed off from the interests and engagements of other approaches. A vital interdisciplinarity has been pursued and embraced, for the most part, even as there has been contest and debate amongst Victorianists, pursued with as much fervour as the affirmative exploration between different disciplines and differing epistemologies put to work in the service of reading the nineteenth century.

Edinburgh Critical Studies in Victorian Culture aims to take up both the debates and the inventive approaches and departures from convention that studies in the nineteenth century have witnessed for the last half century at least. Aiming to maintain a 'Victorian' (in the most positive sense of that motif) spirit of inquiry, the series' purpose is to continue and augment the cross-fertilisation of interdisciplinary approaches, and to offer, in addition, a number of timely and untimely revisions of Victorian literature, culture, history and identity. At the same time, the series will ask questions concerning what has been missed or improperly received, misread, or not read at all, in order to present a multifaceted and heterogeneous kaleidoscope of representations. Drawing on the most provocative, thoughtful and original research, the series will seek to prod at the notion of the 'Victorian', and in so doing, principally through theoretically and epistemologically sophisticated close readings of the historicity of literature and culture in the nineteenth century, to offer the reader provocative insights into a world that is at once overly familiar and irreducibly different, other and strange. Working from original sources, primary documents and recent interdisciplinary theoretical models, Edinburgh Critical Studies in Victorian Culture seeks not simply to push at the boundaries of research in the nineteenth century, but also to inaugurate the persistent erasure and provisional, strategic redrawing of those borders.

Julian Wolfreys

Acknowledgements

Many of the ideas in this book result from my struggles within institutions, but this book exists because institutions helped ensure that it had a future. A fellowship at the Moore Institute at the National University of Ireland, Galway allowed me to conduct the necessary research for Chapter 2 and to present work from the project. I am grateful to Villanova University's writing centre, especially Mary Beth Simmons and Liz Mathews, for hosting such well-organised faculty writing retreats and consulting on Chapter 5. Maria Klecko and Kristen Sieranski were invaluable research assistants. The students in my two 'Institutional Fictions' seminars at Villanova helped me refine my ideas by grappling with some of the questions that shape this book and sharing their own insights about institutions. A summer research fellowship from Villanova allowed me to complete a draft of the manuscript, its Subvention of Publication Program provided money to hire an indexer, and a professional development grant enabled me to host a manuscript workshop with my dream team of readers – Nora Hanson, Nathan Hensley and Amy Martin – whose generous reading, thoughtful discussion and ethical orientation to the profession transformed and energised this project. I cannot thank Nora, Nathan and Amy enough for their critical engagement and example. Thank you to Ersev Ersoy, Michelle Houston and Julian Wolfreys at Edinburgh University Press for their support of this book and guidance throughout the publication process.

This book has benefited from many readers. Ted Martin, Heather Warren-Crow, Roger McNamara and Elaine Freedgood read very early drafts of the introduction. More recently, the Delaware Valley British Studies group, hosted by Seth Koven and Lynn Hollen Lees, offered crucial feedback – special thanks to Rachel Buurma and Evan Radcliffe for their participation in that meeting. Along the way, Sarah Townsend, Megan Ward, Chelsea Phillips and Jacob

Jewusiak provided incredibly useful thoughts on individual chapters. Kyoko Takanashi's enthusiasm, as well as her expertise on institutions, spurred me on in the final stages. At Villanova, the English department's junior faculty research group – Joe Drury, Travis Foster, Brooke Hunter, Kamran Javadizadeh and Yumi Lee – offered such smart feedback. Throughout, Beth Coggin Womack and Alisha Walters were indispensable interlocutors: providing thoughts on the book while creating a lovely community of writing and thinking in West Philadelphia. Jeanette Tran, a dear friend, offered wisdom on drafts and so much more. Ereck Jarvis, who has taught me about the wonder of voluntary association, was one of the project's first and best readers: his thinking has made this project possible. Editing chapters, Michelle Niemann made the most stressful time of writing become fun: I am so grateful for her professional expertise. Thank you to the anonymous readers for Edinburgh University Press who engaged with the project in such thoughtful ways.

I owe so much to the many mentors and friends who have shaped this project. Most crucially, Caroline Levine, who has taught me so much about writing, thinking and being in the world: I feel very lucky to have worked with her and to be able to continue to think with her. Susan Bernstein, Mario Ortiz-Robles, Terry Kelley and Mary Trotter were fantastic dissertation committee members (and so much more) and Lynn Keller, Sara Guyer and Susan Friedman taught me about navigating institutions. At Madison, the Middle Modernity Group was an institutional formation that was also communal: I am grateful for all of the people who helped shape those meetings and who continue to shape my experience of the profession, especially Jesse Oak Taylor. At UW-Milwaukee, I learned so much from Nigel Rothfels, who knows that particular institution better than anyone. Kristie Hamilton, Ted Martin, Annie McClanahan, Caitjan Gainty and Sukanya Banerjee (and so many others!) offered key support. At Texas Tech, Jen Shelton's willingness to think creatively about – and put work into – institutions, transformed my career. At Villanova, I have learned so much from everyone in the English department and Center for Irish Studies, but Jean Lutes and Megan Quigley deserve special acknowledgement for their mentorship – I know I can ask them the difficult questions; Travis Foster for providing so many lifelines; Brooke Hunter for her friendship; Kamran Javadizadeh for heartening office chats; Lauren Shohet and Joe Drury for feedback on the proposal; Heather Hicks and Joseph Lennon for their leadership; and Brooke Erdman and Sharon Rose-Davis for their support. I will always be inspired by and grateful to Lisa Lowe, whose intelligence about institutions at Tufts University made it possible for me to do my job at Villanova. Elaine Freedgood's unparalleled example has motivated me to fight the good fight, even when it is exhausting. Sara Maurer, my brilliant undergraduate professor, generously invited me to share part of this project at Notre Dame. Sarah Allison, Elaine Auyong, Carolyn Betensky, Emma Francis, Walt Hunter, Lindsay Turner, Tom Church, Craig Willse, Josh Freker and Renee Fox also deserve many thanks for their friendship, guidance and inspiration. Thank you to my parents, Barb and Marty Mullen, and to Mary and Dan Hooley for their encouragement.

Finally, my unending love and gratitude to Matt Hooley: our relationship in and across institutions, while not always easy, has made the process of writing this book so much better. Your uncompromising vision helps me to imagine otherwise and your humour and fierce intelligence makes life with you a joy.

Portions of Chapter 5 were first published in *Victoriographies* under the title 'Untimely Development, Ugly History: *A Drama in Muslin* and the Rejection of National-Historical Time' in 2013. Hal Sedgwick and Jonathan Goldberg generously granted permission to reprint a sentence from Eve Kosofsky Sedgwick's 'Queer and Now' as the epigraph to the introduction.

Introduction

'The depressing thing about the Christmas season – isn't it? – is that it's the time when all the institutions are speaking with one voice.'[1]

The Circumlocution Office, one of Charles Dickens's most famous institutional targets, is a mass of contradictions. Run by the Barnacle family, the office is both the vestige of an old aristocratic government structure – 'a school for gentlemen' – and a modern bureaucratic machine.[2] It is a physical site – when Arthur Clennam ventures to the office, he finds himself sitting in a series of waiting rooms – as well as an ever-expanding mode of perception that casts 'its shining influence through the whole of the official proceedings'.[3] Emphasising the office's diffuse influence, Dickens writes, 'Whatever was required to be done, the Circumlocution Office was beforehand with all the public departments in the art of perceiving – HOW NOT TO DO IT.'[4]

But although the Circumlocution Office is difficult to pin down, its logic is not. The office delimits political possibilities by organising time. Integrating diverse people and organisational forms into a shared temporality and singular path – what the young Barnacle calls 'a groove' – it actively extends present social arrangements into the future.[5] As Dickens writes, it 'went on mechanically, every day, keeping this wonderful, all-sufficient wheel of statesmanship, How not to do it, in motion.'[6] Always 'in motion', it never brings people 'nearer to an end'.[7] Instead, it teaches people to accept the institution as the only possible 'end'. In the face of a seemingly all-consuming, future-oriented temporality, those who refuse to get into the 'groove' of the institution 'grew tired, got dead beat, got lamed, got their backs broken, died off, gave it up, went in for other games'.[8] The constant motion of the institution to maintain itself exhausts alternative political possibilities: people either accept the Circumlocution Office's vision of the future or learn to let it alone.

Dickens suggests that the Circumlocution Office endures in part because it produces a profoundly divided response: people either consider it to be 'a flagrant nuisance' and try to escape it or see it as 'a heaven-born institution, that had an absolute right do whatever it liked'.[9] The same divided response to institutions has long shaped the field of Victorian studies. Considering institutions to be key social forms in a larger disciplinary landscape, Foucauldian critics such as D. A. Miller and Nancy Armstrong chronicle how distinct institutions such as the police, the law, the family, the novel work together to establish an all-pervasive system of social control.[10] For them, cultural institutions like the novel extend disciplinary power by dramatising what readers most desire: an escape from carceral institutions. Edward Said is similarly critical, claiming that nineteenth-century British novels 'keep the empire more or less in place' precisely because they function as cultural institutions that direct attention away from imperial networks.[11] But recently critics such as Amanda Anderson, Bruce Robbins and Lauren Goodlad have taken an opposite approach, associating liberal institutions with the development of character or even 'the common good'.[12] For Robbins, Foucault's account of power is no longer pragmatic: because Foucault views institutions as part of larger networks of power, he does not provide the necessary language to defend public institutions in an era of privatisation.[13] Working to defend liberal institutions from Foucauldian and postcolonial critique, these critics advocate for the future that institutions imagine.

Novel Institutions offers a new understanding of the politics of institutions through an attention to temporality, arguing that institutions acquire political authority by organising time. Institutions become the horizon for future imagining because they allow multiple historical temporalities within the present to be brought onto a shared and singular path. But that does not mean that we must embrace institutional time, as scholars who support liberal institutions claim, or are doomed to subject ourselves to disciplinary rhythms, as Foucauldian scholars argue: we can inhabit institutions without accepting the future that they imagine. Institutions constrain social relations in the present and limit our sense of political possibilities in the future, but they never entirely suppress alternative political possibilities. Anachronisms – out-of-date characters, obsolete practices, untimely chronologies – inspire what Roderick Ferguson calls 'visions that are in the institution but not of it'.[14] In nineteenth-century Britain, the term anachronism referred to chronological errors, confused chronologies in speech or writing, and the state of being out of date – either too late or too early for the contemporary moment. But even then, anachronism was not simply a discrete form – an identifiable historical error – it always expressed a relationship with the chronology that produced it.[15] Anachronisms function as visible sites of dislocation that call what counts as history into question by distinguishing between institutional and historical time.

Anachronisms restore historicity to institutions by insisting that the future that the institution works to secure is not the only possible future. In *Little Dorrit*, the inventor Daniel Doyce rejects the Circumlocution Office's narrow vision of the future by holding onto an idea of truth that predates his confrontation with the bureaucratic department. Despite the office's best efforts to insist that there is no future for his invention, Doyce 'could not forget the old design of so many years'.[16] His sense of broader historical possibilities cannot be exhausted; he possesses 'a calm knowledge that what was true must remain true, in spite of all the Barnacles'.[17] Doyce, more than anyone, understands the deadly effects of the Circumlocution Office as he tries and fails to get his invention approved, but he maintains his conviction that his 'old design' will be realised. In doing so, he expresses what Ashon Crawley calls 'an otherwise relation to organization', a relationship to institutions that reconfigures institutional time.[18] In Ireland and Irish novels, these otherwise relations to organisation are even more pronounced because of Ireland's colonial history. British rule in Ireland depended upon a dual strategy of assimilation and exclusion: Britain violently integrated Ireland into British institutions while continuing to treat Irish people as what Amy Martin calls a 'colonized and alien population'.[19] But although Britain imposed institutions on Ireland that cut Irish people off from the past, constrained their social relations in the present and taught them to imagine an imperial future, Irish people could not forget what they already knew: that institutions shape but cannot entirely define historical or political possibilities. Arguing that English and Irish realist novels encourage such 'otherwise possibilities' through anachronisms, *Novel Institutions* contends that although we cannot escape institutions, we can refuse their erasure of history.[20]

Institutions are durable social formations that structure social life, limit the scope of politics and mediate how people understand history. They include social organisations with material buildings such as schools, prisons, the workhouse, churches but also what Emile Durkheim calls 'social facts': things such as laws, customs, norms that exceed the individual but necessarily constrain individual behaviour.[21] Institutions are distinguished from more fluid modes of social organisation by what Herbert Spencer calls their 'instinct of self-preservation' – the fact that they endure over time, changing without ceding power or authority.[22]

Studying this temporal logic rather than distinct institutions, *Novel Institutions* focuses on what I call modern institutionalism – a discourse that understands institutions as markers of modernity on the one hand, and horizons of futurity on the other.[23] Modern institutionalism is a social theory that manifests itself as a temporal structure. It distinguishes between modern institutional subjects and supposedly backward people who cannot be easily assimilated into institutions. It also delimits futurity by defining political and social life through institutions and thus extending existing institutional arrangements into the future. Modern institutionalism encourages a form of historicism that social scientists call 'path dependency', which claims that organisations make decisions at 'critical junctures' and that subsequent developments reinforce these decisions.[24] Path dependency explains why institutions begin to feel inevitable: they insist that the existing institutional path is the only legitimate way to understand the present and imagine the future.

Novel Institutions turns to the realist novel – the most institutional of literary forms – to point us to ways of inhabiting institutions while rejecting institutional time. Realism is a literary mode that seeks to represent everyday life through thick description, references to the real world and a focus on the ordinary rather than the extraordinary. It is notoriously difficult to define – established accounts of realism include gothic novels like Mary Shelley's *Frankenstein* (1818); historical romances like Walter Scott's *Waverley* (1814); sensational novels like Wilkie Collins's *The Moonstone* (1868); even fantasy novels like Lewis Carroll's *Alice's Adventures in Wonderland* (1865).[25] The difficulty deciding which novels are and are not realist is partly institutional: because realism is so important to the field of Victorian studies, scholars sometimes conflate the Victorian novel with realism, often in ways that minimise the importance of novels published outside of England.[26] But I suggest that realism's slipperiness also results from the contradictions at the heart of realist form.[27] Like institutions, realist novels mediate social life through a set of formal conventions and informal expectations – they describe existing social arrangements in order to extend them into the future. But their descriptions of the world as it is also express how the world could be otherwise. In realist novels, representing how characters inhabit institutions means encountering alternative temporalities, envisioning otherwise possibilities. Focusing on these contradictions, *Novel Institutions* approaches realism not as a stable set of texts or even a coherent genre, but rather as a formal dynamic at work in canonical, metropolitan realist novels but more visible in novels written at a distance from England and at odds with British imperial institutions, such as Irish novels.

Realist novels often describe distinct institutions: think of Lowood Institution, the charitable school that Jane Eyre attends in *Jane Eyre* (1847), Hiram's Hospital, the almshouse that creates narrative tension in *The Warden* (1855), the workhouse where Oliver asks for more food in *Oliver Twist* (1838) or the presence of the police in Irish novels like Emily Lawless's *Hurrish* (1886). But realist novels more forcefully engage with modern institutionalism, that is, the social theory that upholds institutions' temporal logic, through their narrative temporalities. Realist novels integrate diverse characters and readers into a shared institutional temporality through their visions of the future. They organise, order and regulate the historical world, often arriving at resolutions grounded in institutions such as marriage or the nation-state. However, realist novels' representation of a heterogeneous present moment – of anachronisms that do not fit within the existing institutional order – highlight the political possibilities that result from the uncertainty and discordance of the present. Anachronisms push against social consensus and imagine the future otherwise.

Nineteenth-century thinkers like John Stuart Mill, Herbert Spencer, Harriet Martineau, John Mitchel and Thomas Carlyle chronicled the growing impulse to define both modernity and futurity through institutions in their essays.[28] But while nonfiction diagnoses the problems and possibilities of institutionalism, realist novels dramatise them. As realist novels move between the shared time of institutions and the heterogeneous historical time of anachronisms in their narratives, they show how modern institutionalism depends upon contradictions. Although modern institutionalism works to control historical time and stabilise an imperial future in the present, institutions cultivate lived relationships that maintain a sense of historical difference. These contradictions suggest that although institutions act as forms, they also foster relationships that undermine the stability of these forms. Realist novels both extend the ideology of the British empire and undermine it; they consolidate heteropatriarchal domestic institutions and unsettle them; they establish boundaries for the nation-state and exceed them. Thus, *Novel Institutions* turns to realist novels to understand the politics of institutions because time in realist novels is political: in these novels, shared institutional time delimits who is included in the present and who can shape the future while anachronisms express historical and social relationships that exceed institutions.

The dynamic between the shared time of modern institutionalism and the unruly politics of anachronism is most visible in colonial locations where defining modernity and futurity through institutions sought to justify British imperial rule. *Novel Institutions* thus focuses on nineteenth-century Ireland and rethinks both the politics of institutions and the politics of British realism through an attention to nineteenth-century Irish realist novels. In Ireland, British colonial practices make the violence of modern institutionalism explicit: imagining a shared future through colonial institutions meant loss. Loss of life – after all, the Famine was a crucial moment in British institutional consolidation – but also the loss of other modes of social organisation, other ways of communicating, other visions of the future. Precisely because the violence of modern institutionalism is so visible in Ireland, so too are the anachronisms that insist that institutional time is not historical time, that the future institutions imagine is not the only possible future. We cannot understand British realism without considering Irish realism, not only because Irish novels shaped English realist novels, but also because Irish realist novels insist that institutional time is not neutral or merely disciplinary: it structures empire. The explicit formal, temporal and political divisions in Irish realist novels, and the way in which these novels connect modern institutionalism to empire, allow us to rethink the form and politics of British realism. Rather than being anomalous, these Irish novels highlight realism's contradictory movement between shared institutional time and anachronisms, upholding modern institutionalism and imagining otherwise.

Unnecessary Anachronisms

The measurement of time was increasingly standardised in the nineteenth century through the spread of railroads and telegraphs, but the politics of time was not. Establishing uniform, shared time served empire by creating what Anne McClintock calls 'anachronistic space' where 'imperial progress across the space of empire is figured as a journey backward in time to an anachronistic moment of prehistory'.[29] Think of H. Rider Haggard's imperial romance, *She*, which is structured through this temporal asymmetry: the characters travel from culture to nature as they leave modern university life in

Cambridge to seek a ruined city in Africa. In these imperial discourses, anachronistic colonial spaces require institutional interventions to become modern. But I suggest that the proliferation of anachronisms in both imperial and anti-colonial discourses also draws attention to heterogeneous temporalities that cut across the imperial, future-oriented temporality of institutions. Similar to what Raymond Williams calls the 'residual' and the 'emergent' – active cultural processes that suggest enduring social forms or new possibilities within dominant cultural structures – anachronisms are sites where the 'complex interrelations' within and across social structures become visible.[30] Thus anachronisms are produced by power relations on one hand, and disrupt structures of power on the other.

The metric of necessity has constrained anachronism's disruptive potential, however, both in the nineteenth century and in our own theoretical practices. Georg Lukács, for instance, famously articulates the importance of 'necessary anachronisms', or chronological mistakes that elucidate historical development and express 'the given historical relationship'.[31] For Lukács, such anachronisms are 'necessary' in two senses: they are unavoidable, and they help clarify historical relationships by using knowledge from the present to enhance representations of the past. But what is 'the given historical relationship'? Lukács suggests that it is 'the *necessary prehistory* of the present' which allows readers to grasp the totality of history.[32] I suggest, however, that necessary anachronisms reinforce a far more narrow narrative of history that has been institutionalised. Clarifying the 'given historical relationship' actually projects the present both into the past and the future.

Modern institutionalism makes certain anachronisms appear necessary while making other anachronisms appear as mere errors to avoid. Take, for instance, an 1803 review of the Scottish novel *St Clair of the Isles: Or, the Outlaws of Barra, a Scottish Tradition*, which legitimates anachronisms because they mediate the otherwise insurmountable gaps of cultural and historical distance. Describing how the novel uses contemporary manners and language to describe Scotland in the fifteenth century, the review concludes: 'This is a kind of anachronism, however, which it would be idle to represent in a heinous light, when the genuine language of the country could not be understood by an Englishman, nor the unvarnished manners of the times tolerated by a modern.'[33] Here, anachronisms are necessary insofar as they confirm the assumptions of the contemporary, metropolitan, English reader. Instead of providing a sense of historical change, they foster smug comfort in the here and now – English

readers do not need to know Scotland's 'genuine language' or toler-
ate backward behaviours from the past.

Necessary anachronisms define who counts as a political agent
and a historical subject in terms of institutions, relegating particular
social groups to the past. They often depend on what Johannes Fabian
calls 'a denial of coevalness', or the refusal to see certain social and
ethnic groups as contemporaries.[34] Walter Scott's *Waverley* (1814),
which Lukács celebrates, suggests that integration into the British
state is the only future for Scotland by describing a Highland gentleman as 'a relic of primitive simplicity' rather than a contemporary to
Edward Waverley.[35] In Charles Dickens's *Our Mutual Friend* (1865),
the Jewish Mr. Riah steals 'through the streets in his ancient dress,
like the ghost of a departed Time'.[36] Unleashing the gothic elements
of the novel only to map them onto a specific ethnic and religious
group, this sentence equates Jewishness with ghosts of the past rather
than people in the present. Women were also often represented as
belated in relation to their male contemporaries – as Rhoda Nunn
tells Everand Barfoot at the end of *The Odd Women* (1893), 'It is
difficult you see, for me to keep pace with you.'[37]

While necessary anachronisms elucidate historical development,
what I call 'unnecessary anachronisms' reveal historical relationships that fail to cohere as institutionalised development. In realist
novels, unnecessary anachronisms are just as pervasive as necessary
ones: they show the discordant paces of historical change, propel the
reader backward to 'useless' pasts that do not continue into the present, and reveal ruptures within institutionalised narratives. Instead
of reinforcing the necessity of a single, continuous line of development where the present emerges from the past, these anachronisms
question the extent to which historical narratives depend upon a predetermined but exclusionary sense of what is necessary to achieve the
future. For instance, as I argue in Chapter 5, George Moore deliberately centres the character of Esther Waters in his novel of English
life not because she represents ongoing historical change but because
she challenges it: in an era of literacy, she remains illiterate; in an era
of secularisation, she tries 'to live like the Early Christians'.[38]

In attending to the political effects of both necessary and unnecessary anachronisms, I draw on recent work in postcolonial and
queer theory that interrogates the assumption that anachronisms are
merely errors to avoid.[39] In the field of postcolonial theory, Dipesh
Chakrabarty shows that anachronisms' supposed necessity emerges
in relation to established institutional practices and methodologies.
He suggests that history, as it is institutionalised in the university,

depends on 'our capacity to deploy the historicist or ethnographic mode of viewing that involves a sense of anachronism in order to convert objects, institutions, and practices with which we have lived relationships into relics of other times'.[40] Understanding anachronisms to result from Western historicist methods helpfully reveals how institutions distinguish between necessary and unnecessary anachronisms: what is necessary emerges from dominant institutionalised practices, while subaltern people and subaltern practices appear unnecessary. Ultimately, for Chakrabarty, necessary anachronisms – like homogeneous time itself – exclude particular people, practices and methodologies from history.

Taking up the claim that homogeneous historical time excludes social groups, scholars of queer theory have begun to think about the political possibilities of anachronisms that are not legitimated by and do not legitimate dominant institutions. These unnecessary anachronisms cultivate queer time that, in the words of Jack Halberstam, 'offers an alternative framework for the theorisation of disqualified and anticanonical knowledges of queer practices'.[41] In other words, precisely because anachronisms are unnecessary and undermine modern institutionalism, they offer a framework for thinking differently. Of course, not all unnecessary anachronisms are queer – that is, they do not always resist heteronormativity by creating what Eve Kosofsky Sedgwick calls an 'open mesh of possibilities' of gender and sexuality.[42] But by shifting the framework towards disqualified knowledges, anachronisms can foster relationships that push against institutions and the futurity they promise.[43]

Unnecessary anachronisms allow us to imagine both history and politics otherwise. As scholars such as Ashon Crawley, Kandice Chuh and Elizabeth Povinelli indicate, imagining otherwise does not mean seeing institutions through new perspectives or working to create more inclusive social structures; it requires 'undoing' existing social structures and rethinking what constitutes the social, political and historical.[44] The concept of 'otherwise' thus acknowledges the violence of existing social arrangements – how their very coherence suppresses other ways of knowing, other forms of social relation, other modes of history, other approaches to politics. But it also recognises the forms of social life, which are already present, that enable the undoing of this coherence: performance, Black sociality, dissensus, embodied potentiality and, as I argue, anachronism. Although institutions are conditions of possibility, other possibilities always exist. Thinking otherwise in relation to nineteenth-century England and Ireland means acknowledging how our relations to the past often work to ensure that the violence of Victorian liberalism lives on in our twenty-first-century present. But it also allows us to think beyond flawed Victorian social forms and avoid extending them into the future. At odds with institutional time, unnecessary anachronisms insist on the importance of social relationality as opposed to social reproduction as they expand political possibilities and encourage a nonlinear, heterogeneous understanding of historical time.

Realist novels contain both necessary and unnecessary anachronisms; they represent existing social arrangements and open up otherwise possibilities. Some emerge from the novel's narrative anachronies that return to pasts that do not continue into the novel's present, while some are anti-developmental counter-narratives that challenge the novel's linear plotting. Narrative anachrony refers to the temporal discordance between the story (the plot) and the discourse (the narration of the plot). Gérard Genette describes the various forms of narrative anachrony: prolepsis (the anticipation of events that have not yet occurred within the story), analepsis (a retrospection that extends beyond the time of the story) and metalepsis (the collision of the time of the story and the time of the discourse).[45] These anachronies are part and parcel of the realist novel's narrative form: think of *Waverley*'s 'Tis sixty years since', *Jane Eyre*'s metaleptic address, 'Reader, I married him,' or *Adam Bede*'s famous reflection on realism that collapses the temporal distance between reader and narrator as it jumps to a future moment when the narrator talks to Adam Bede 'in his old age'.[46] Realist novels manage temporal distance in ways that suggest historical time is heterogeneous rather than singular or shared.

Narrative anachronies create anachronisms that foster relationships across time even as they often highlight historical change. The temporal distance between the story and the discourse draws attention to pasts that do not continue into the present – anachronistic people, practices and modes of social organisation that modern institutionalism eradicates. George Eliot's provincial realism, for instance, uses metalepsis to mark institutional changes. In *Adam Bede*, the narrator interrupts the narrative to distinguish between the 'old-fashioned' Methodist who believes in miracles, and the 'modern type' of Methodist who reads 'quarterly reviews and attends in chapels with pillared porticoes'.[47] Although the narrator differentiates between these two forms of Methodism in part to suggest the inevitability of institutional rationalisation – religious belief gives way to codified practices – the strange temporality of this metaleptic address, where the present tense of the narrator and reader collide, pushes against this sense of historical inevitability. Metalepsis imagines historical connections across time that remain at odds with the narrative of institutional development over time.

Anachronisms also emerge through anti-developmental counternarratives that question the assumption that time must be put to use to achieve a given future. Scholars tend to associate such counternarratives with various subgenres distinguished from mainstream realism, such as queer narratives of development and the female, modernist and colonial versions of the *Bildungsroman*.[48] Focusing on narratives of queer children and musing on the queerness of childhood, Kathryn Bond Stockton catalogues the strange temporalities of queer narratives of development: temporal lags, sideways growth, 'backward birth'.[49] In turn, Jed Esty's theory of the colonial *Bildungsroman* probes the unruly temporalities of novels of development set in colonial locations. Arguing that these novels pair development with anti-development through the trope of 'frozen youth', he suggests that their formal resistance to linear progression registers their distance from the imperial centre.[50] Studies of the modernist *Bildungsroman* indicate that these narratives of untimely growth and failed maturation are not just queer or colonial. As Sarah Townsend argues, such modernist narratives work 'to forestall . . . realism's assimilatory developmental arc'.[51] Such accounts offer different reasons for nonlinear temporalities and failed growth – queer resistance to normative development, colonial underdevelopment, modernist aesthetics – but they tend to agree that canonical realism represents linear, normative growth that ends in institutional assimilation.

By contrast, I suggest that realism's contradictory dynamic itself counters development through anachronisms that create anti-developmental narratives. Take, for instance, the eccentric Miss Havisham, whose development stops with her watches and clocks at 'twenty minutes to nine' – the time she was to be married.[52] No longer desiring to keep pace with the times, Miss Havisham embraces stasis as she watches herself decay with her house. The less radical Miss Thorne from *Barchester Towers* (1857), who refuses to read modern quarterlies or contemporary newspapers, is another apposite example, as is *New Grub Street*'s Alfred Yule, who 'was living in a past age; his literary ideals were formed on the study of Boswell'.[53] In Elizabeth Gaskell's *Cranford* (1853), this refusal to develop becomes the central narrative rather than a counter-narrative or subplot. Tracing the habits and customs of old-fashioned women in a provincial town, the novel functions as what Megan Ward calls 'a litany of small moments scheduled for endless repetition'.[54] Such an emphasis on stasis rather than growth, repetition rather than development, reorients modern institutionalism's emphasis on futurity towards the political possibilities that result from attending to a discordant present.

Because of these multivalent temporalities, I argue that realism's historicism paradoxically results from its anachronisms.[55] Although realist novels aestheticise an imperialist narrative where England is both a stable site of modernity and the future that the colonial peripheries should achieve, they also represent anachronisms that explode this historical narrative in favour of a more capacious historicism. Anachronism in all its forms – a denial of coevalness, a 'useless' past that does not continue into the present and a resistance to development – is at the heart of nineteenth-century realist narrative, fostering relationships of difference that lead us to question our assumptions about realism as it has been institutionalised.

Realism's Institutions

In many ways, focusing on realism in a book about anachronisms is counter-intuitive: critics more frequently associate temporal disjunctions in nineteenth-century narrative with the gothic, romance, sensation fiction, stories of time travel or even ethnography.[56] Picture *Dracula* (1897) and *She* (1887), where Dracula and Ayesha threaten modern Britain precisely because they live beyond their historical moment, or *Lady Audley's Secret* (1862), where George Talboys's disappearance disrupts the lazy monotony of Robert Audley's life, encouraging him to begin a 'backward investigation' into origins and antecedents.[57] In turn, *News from Nowhere* (1890) represents the future as a return to the past. The nineteenth-century protagonist travels forward in time to a future utopia, but nevertheless feels 'as if I were alive in the fourteenth century'.[58] In Ireland, nineteenth-century ethnography depended upon temporal asychronicity, or temporal distance between the culture being studied and the culture studying it. A. C. Haddon, for instance, begins his 1893 study of the Aran Islands by noting the modernity of the islanders, only to focus entirely on 'survivals': the traditions, antiquities and practices that endure.[59] Despite the prevalence of anachronisms in a wide range of nineteenth-century narrative forms, I focus on realism because of its centrality within the discipline of literary studies: its importance to histories of the novel, canon formations and postcolonial theory.[60]

After all, realism's importance is not merely literary; it is also institutional. As the dominant form of nineteenth-century writing, realism carries important institutional weight both in the nineteenth century and in our twenty-first-century present. It is 'the generic centre of canonical judgments about the novel as form, against which other modes of prose fiction are measured', as David Lloyd argues.[61] Literary histories that narrate the rise of the novel tend to focus on the rise of realism, representing other novelistic forms as minor or even anachronistic. Because of the dominance of realism within Victorian studies, I suggest that we need to consider how the institutionalised practices of literary study mediate our approaches to realism.

As literary scholars narrate the rise of the novel, they separate English realist novels from Irish ones, failing to show how both novel traditions dynamically move between shared time and anachronisms. Although Victorian studies scholars have recently emphasised realism's cosmopolitanism, transatlanticism and global reach, the importance of Irish realism to English realist novels of the period remains unstudied. Irish studies scholars compound this problem by emphasising how nineteenth-century Irish novels differ from English realist novels of the period. Associating English realism with consensus, integration, and homogeneous, empty time, they claim that the nineteenth-century Irish novel represents contradictions instead of consensus, discordance instead of integration and anachronism instead of homogeneous time.[62] In contrast, *Novel Institutions* argues that nineteenth-century Irish realism is exemplary rather than anomalous: its explicit divisions between anachronisms and institutions make these same divisions visible in canonical British novels.

In Irish realism, anachronisms are prevalent and readily apparent because of the violence of modern institutionalism in Ireland. *Castle Rackrent* (1800) moves between the fictional editor's emphasis on futurity and the Irish narrator's reanimation of the past, producing a narrative that, as Patrick O'Malley suggests, looks both forward and backward, remembers and forgets as it depicts the Act of Union as a 'temporal crisis'.[63] The narrator of *Knocknagow; or the Homes of Tipperary* (1873) distinguishes between the 'dead Past' and the 'living Present' only to declare, 'The "living Present?" And the "dead Past?" We hold that the Past is the more living of the two, sometimes.'[64] Given these explicit anachronisms, Terry Eagleton claims that literary representations of Irish history stubbornly refuse the 'symbolic order of modern historical time'.[65] According to Eagleton, English realism creates a stable, continuous chronology that merges past and present into a harmonious whole, while Irish novels create an uneasy and uneven movement between past and present, nature and culture. The strange temporalities of nineteenth-century Irish novels, for Eagleton, show that Irish writers fail to reproduce realism and instead become successful modernists: they refuse totalising aesthetics.

By contrast, I argue that the Irish novel's supposed failure of form makes visible the ways in which realism is a form of failure. Realism is a contradictory dynamic rather than a stable, coherent form. Mikhail Bakhtin is useful here, suggesting that the novel is a polyglot form defined through competing centripetal and centrifugal forces. Bakhtin suggests that although novels seek to 'predict and influence the real future', they are defined through 'eternal re-thinking and re-evaluating'.[66] In other words, the novel works to centre its narrative *as* the future while also opening itself to the centrifugal forces of the historical present that unsettle the stability of this future.

More recently, scholars suggest that even canonical realist novels produce a divided rather than a uniform landscape. Alex Woloch challenges the assumption that all characters become integrated into a single temporal plane by defining realism through the tension between the one (central characters with interiors and psychological depth) and the many (minor characters whose exteriors populate the social world).[67] He argues that minor characters embed social stratification into the realist form as he suggests that realism depends upon tension, contradiction and difference rather than integration. In turn, Fredric Jameson argues that realism moves between two temporalities as he reads realist antinomies: the unfolding temporality associated with narrative and history, and atemporal, ahistorical presence – what he calls 'the realm of affect'.[68] Such approaches to realism indicate that the Irish novel actually intensifies characteristics of British realism by failing to integrate plot and politics or to establish homogeneous, empty time.

Given this scholarship that highlights realism's divided time, the question remains, why is there such an emphasis on the failure of Irish realism in Irish studies? And why are Irish novels so neglected in Victorian studies? I argue that contemporary institutional practices mediate our approach to realism in ways that obscure realism's inherent transnationalism. In the field of Irish Studies, where James Joyce and W. B. Yeats loom large, nineteenth-century Irish novels are either understood as proto-modernist precursors to novels like *Ulysses* or aesthetic failures that should be read for political and historical reasons as opposed to literary ones. Yeats's self-conscious institution building in the midst of the Irish Literary Revival encouraged such readings of the Irish novelists who preceded him. His anthologies of

Irish writing and contributions to ongoing debates about the 'best Irish books' establish a tradition of Irish writing, only to suggest that the best is yet to come. His 1895 review of Irish prose writers, for instance, ends with an appeal to a still unrealised future, saying that Irish writers 'may hope some day, in the maturity of our traditions; to fashion out of the world about us, and the things our fathers have told us, a new ritual for the builders of peoples, the imperishable moods'.[69] The implication is that in the nineteenth-century present in which Yeats writes, Irish literary traditions are still immature, still unformed, still need to be institutionalised.

The growth of Irish studies programmes in the 1980s led to more scholarship on nineteenth-century Irish novels, but often extended Yeats's criticism of these novels. Irish studies critics tend to accept Yeats's vision of the Irish literary canon, and often favour poetry and drama as opposed to prose, modernism as opposed to realism.[70] Studies of nineteenth-century Irish realism thus often become studies of failure as scholars ask why there is not an Irish *Middlemarch* only to explain the political, historical and formal reasons for Irish realism's failure.[71] In turn, the transnational nature of Irish realism – the fact that these novels represented Ireland but were often published by British publishers and often addressed a British reading public – encourages some scholars to approach these novels as part of a British colonial project.[72] They see nineteenth-century Irish realism as an 'imported form'[73] characterised by a 'crisis of representation' rather than a native cultural production.[74] Only recently have scholars like Claire Connolly and Derek Hand pushed against these institutional practices in order to question the narrative of failed Irish realism. Although these scholars recover the importance of the nineteenth-century Irish novel, the relationship between Irish and English realism remains unexplored.

The critical neglect of Irish realism within Victorian studies also results from institutional practices. The scholars who have recently highlighted realism's transnational scope challenge the assumption that realism is a national form without questioning its inherently national canon.[75] Realism's worldliness is found to inhere in the very novels that were previously understood to be national. In turn, scholars interested in 'peripheral realisms' tend to focus on the disparate realisms that flourish in modernist and contemporary fiction rather than the peripheral forms of realism within the Victorian period. Tracing the institutional history that has led to 'a new realist turn', or the re-embrace of realism by writers and critics alike, Jed Esty and Colleen Lye often reinforce the distance between the Victorian and modernist periods even as they unsettle the aesthetic distinctions between realism and modernism.[76] These periodising moves, combined with Irish studies scholars' understanding of Irish novels as proto-modernist precursors, suggest that nineteenth-century Irish realism is an untimely literary mode. It is more likely to be discussed in modernist studies than Victorian studies.

One of the central claims of *Novel Institutions* is that nation-based literary histories – whether English histories that ignore the Irish realist novel altogether, or Irish histories that approach Irish realism as a strange variant of English realism – obscure how nineteenth-century British realism was shaped by seemingly minor novels from the periphery. Like the anachronisms that proliferate in realist fictions, minor novels that appear at odds with mainstream definitions of realism unsettle institutional consensus.[77] In fact, many of the novels that seem minor in the twenty-first century were actually foundational to establishing realism's contradictory formal characteristics. Thus, *Novel Institutions* focuses on Irish novels to conclude that peripheral realism is not always minor and is not simply a modernist phenomenon. As I argue in the first chapter, Maria Edgeworth's *Castle Rackrent* inaugurates a nineteenth-century realist tradition divided between institutional and anachronistic aesthetics precisely because it represents traditional Irish practices as it considers how the Act of Union will further integrate Ireland into British institutions.

Although I demonstrate how both English and Irish realist novels move between the shared time of institutions and the heterogeneous temporalities of anachronism, that does not necessarily mean that they always share a politics. Elizabeth Gaskell's *North and South* (1855), for example, excludes Irish people from futural imagining by representing them as an anachronistic race, even as the novel otherwise celebrates the multiple temporalities at work within the English nation.[78] Writing shortly before the Famine, Thomas Carlyle concludes, 'The time has come when the Irish population must either be improved a little, or else exterminated.'[79] Carlyle's two options – improvement and extermination – demonstrate how representing Irish people as anachronisms contributed to their political oppression and legitimated England's response to the Famine, which led to massive human and cultural loss. Even Matthew Arnold's *On the Study of Celtic Literature* (1867) suggests that Celtic languages are only valuable insofar as they are dead objects of the past to study rather than living languages to use. Using Welsh language and literature to signify all Celtic literature, he declares, 'The sooner the

Welsh language disappears as an instrument of the practical, political, social life of Wales, the better; the better for England, the better for Wales itself.'[80] Even as English realist novels like *North and South* assert the value of undermining institutional consensus through tradition, orality and reimagining social and historical relations, they still often fail to recognise the Irish as modern political subjects. They, like Carlyle and Arnold, violently exclude Irish people from the present and future, even as they reimagine social and historical relationships within England. Thus, although anachronisms in English realism disrupt particular forms of modern institutionalism, they often still exclude colonial subjects, like the Irish, from their vision of modernity and the future they imagine.

Modern Institutionalism

Arriving at Lowood Institution, Jane Eyre puzzles over the inscription on the stone tablet above the door, pondering 'the signification of "Institution"'.[81] She tells the reader, 'I read these words over and over again: I felt that an explanation belonged to them, and was unable fully to penetrate their import.'[82] The novel invites the reader to ponder these words with Jane and interrupts the narrative to include the complete inscription:

LOWOOD INSTITUTION
THIS PORTION WAS REBUILT A.D. – , BY NAOMI BROCKLEHURST,
OF BROCKLEHURST HALL, IN THIS COUNTY.
'Let your light so shine before men that they may see
your good works, and glorify your Father
which is in heaven'. – ST. MATT. v. 16.[83]

This inscription, coupled with the narrative interruption, encourages an understanding of institutions as spatial forms – imposing, 'church-like' buildings.[84] But it also raises questions about time. Although the inscription refers to 'Lowood Institution' as a whole, it actually commemorates the recent rebuilding of a schoolroom and dormitory. The institution appears as if it has always been there, but it is actually built and 'rebuilt' over time. And, as Jane suggests, the connection between 'the first words and the verse of Scripture' – the name of the institution and its ideology – requires interpretation.[85] Jane's reflection on the meaning of the word 'institution' as well as the words of the inscription suggests that institutions cannot be understood entirely through their material structures; their meanings need to be penetrated, uncovered, revealed. This passage demonstrates that understanding the full meaning and political effects of the social concept 'institution' requires not just information but also time.

This scene in *Jane Eyre* moves between representing a single institution and reflecting on the larger social theory of modern institutionalism. The particular features of Lowood Institution can be easily identified: it is a charity school for orphans managed by the Brocklehurst family. Modern institutionalism – the broader idea implied as Jane seeks to understand 'the signification of "Institution"' – is more difficult to grasp because it suggests a temporal structure as well as a discrete spatial form. Jane learns about institutionalism throughout the narrative: not only through her experience adapting to the rules and systems at Lowood, but also as she contemplates marrying Mr Rochester only to realise that they cannot legally wed. Tempted by Mr Rochester's pleas to live with him as if they were married, Jane finds strength in 'laws and principles' precisely because they are 'preconceived opinions, foregone determinations'.[86] The 'laws and principles' that Jane draws upon to steel her resolve are not entirely specified, but their temporality is: their future is already known. Their 'foregone determinations' encourage her to shift from her past and present with Mr Rochester to a future sanctioned by institutions. As these scenes from *Jane Eyre* demonstrate, realist novels engage with both institutions and institutionalism as they explore the power that inheres in enclosed material structures as well as the social and temporal forms that underwrite that power.

In order to advance a theory of institutionalism, *Novel Institutions* focuses on three related characteristics of institutions: their endurance over time, reduction of uncertainty and legitimation of social consensus. Political scientists, sociologists and organisational theorists celebrate these aspects of institutions: they allow patterns to emerge that enable them to predict political and social trajectories.[87] But social consensus often functions as a form of what Manu Vimalassery, Juliana Hu Pegues and Aloysha Goldstein call 'colonial unknowing'.[88] Reducing uncertainty means reproducing ways of thinking that make it more difficult to understand the dynamic complexities of racial, capitalist and colonial formations and, instead, extending these formations into the future. When institutions become the primary realm of political action and the horizon of future imagining, 'decolonization is named as either impossible or unreasonable'.[89]

Studying modern institutionalism in the specific context of nineteenth-century England and Ireland demonstrates how modern institutionalism is distinctly imperial: it is a mode of reproducing Englishness elsewhere. Ireland's apparent lack of modern institutions and the Irish people's supposed inability to think in terms of abstract institutions justified British control. Questioning British governance of Ireland, John Stuart Mill points to England's narrow institutional thinking: 'We had got a set of institutions of our own, which we thought suited us – whose imperfections we were, at any rate, used to: we, or our ruling classes, thought, that there could be no boon to any country equal to that of imparting these institutions to her.'[90] British policy in Ireland sought to transform traditional Irish customs and practices into modern British institutions. In *Castle Rackrent*, for instance, the narrative traces the shift from 'honour', which suggests traditional customs grounded in personal relationships, to 'law', which suggests impersonal procedures.[91] When the reproduction of such institutions failed, English people invariably blamed the 'backward' Irish national character rather than the institutions themselves.[92]

When modernity is defined through institutions, England becomes a known future for the periphery – the future that places like Ireland need to achieve in order to become modern.[93] The national tale's marriage plot is a fantasy of such futurity, uniting England and Ireland through the institution of marriage and thus symbolically modernising Ireland through British institutionalism. The devastating losses of the Great Famine show the implicit violence of such fantasies. As Joe Cleary, David Lloyd and Michael Rubenstein argue, the Famine was not simply a natural event, but rather part of a larger process of 'colonial modernization' that violently eradicated traditional forms of social organisation.[94] John Mitchel, the Irish nationalist who sought to popularise an understanding of the Famine as an act of genocide, famously portrays it as a self-conscious project of British institutional consolidation. Adopting Dickensian language, Mitchel declares that Ireland has been 'strangled by red tape' as he suggests that British institutions imagine the future in ways that legitimate destruction in Ireland.[95]

And yet, England depended upon colonies, like Ireland, to develop new institutions.[96] According to Sara Maurer, Ireland was a place 'where all British citizens could read the British state's potential for power over everyday life'.[97] Ireland's national system of education, founded forty years before England's, is another English 'modernising experiment' that began in a colony and then travelled to the metropole.[98] Such contradictions between Ireland's 'backwardness' and its all-too-rapid process of modernisation reveal what David Lloyd calls 'forms of unevenness' that disrupt the linear logic of modernisation.[99] These 'forms of unevenness' emphasise how institutions' reproductive logic obscures historical realities. Modern institutionalism imagines institutions as portable (they can be exported to and imported from colonial locations), though institutions and their historical effects necessarily change as they take root in different cultural locations, as they act in relation.

Michel Foucault suggests that institutions shift our focus from relations to forms by obscuring the multiplicity of power at work. Historicising the growth of institutions such as the monarchy and the state in the Middle Ages, he acknowledges that they were established in relation to multiple, conflicting prior powers but gained acceptance 'because they presented themselves as agencies of regulation, arbitration, and demarcation, as a way of introducing order in the midst of these powers, of establishing a principle that would temper them and distribute them according to boundaries and a fixed hierarchy.'[100] Produced by power – which Foucault defines as 'the multiplicity of force relations' – institutions in turn produce power.[101] Importantly, such power is never limited to the boundaries and hierarchies established by institutions.

Because power operates relationally but creates forms, it constantly reproduces and integrates particular formal arrangements of power across, within and between institutions. *Novel Institutions* argues that the temporality of such reproduction and integration is important, for although the end result is that particular institutions become a 'network' – or even 'a general formula' as power extends beyond their bounded forms – the process of reproduction fosters discordance, contestation and the possibility for alternative futures.[102] For instance, Elizabeth Gaskell's *North and South* gestures to a model of liberal capitalism that will change Parliament, the university system and the education of the poor by integrating them into a 'general formula' that unites the disparate paces of the nation. Yet the novel defers this integration to the future. The present tense of *North and South* is startlingly heterogeneous precisely because each institution is connected to regional cultural practices that take time to root out. Although the future that the novel imagines upholds modern institutionalism, its present tense animates alternative political possibilities through the social relationships it represents.

By focusing on dynamic networks of power as a productive alternative to the narrow futurity of institutions, I question the recent return to liberalism in the field of Victorian studies.[103] We have yet to acknowledge liberalism's violence – in the Victorian past, in our present and as an imagined future.[104] Building on diverse work by Lisa Lowe, Sara Ahmed and Nathan Hensley, I suggest that Victorian liberalism lives on in our institutions not simply as a progressive ideal or pragmatic political philosophy but also as racialised, settler colonial violence.[105] Existing within what Lowe calls an 'economy of affirmation and forgetting', liberal institutions imagine a seemingly shared future which depends upon affirming an inherently violent understanding of the institutional subject (and human) while actively forgetting the colonial origins of these institutions.[106] Because the progressive, orderly history of liberalism that underwrites institutions cannot account for this continued violence, we must embrace the untimely temporalities of anachronism to expose social relationships that exceed institutions and imagine otherwise.

Seeking to unsettle the shared time of modern institutionalism, *Novel Institutions* is as much interested in the ends of realist narratives and the resolutions that consolidate institutional consensus as in the narrative middles that illuminate alternative paths, imagine alternative futures and thwart institutional expectations. Being in the midst of a narrative of modern institutionalism is similar to inhabiting an institution. Although the narrative, like an institution, locates authority in and directs attention towards a deferred future, it also fosters circuits of meaning that undermine this very future. Institutions that strive for homogeneity are profoundly heterogeneous – even 'plastic', as Sharon Marcus suggests.[107] Anachronistic characters who are excluded from a novel's narrative resolution, such as *Adam Bede's* Hetty Sorrel, demonstrate this plasticity: their exclusion consolidates modern institutionalism, but their untimely presence validates anachronistic pasts. In Hetty's case, her connection to contemporary readers even as she is increasingly erased from the novel's present tense encourages a transhistorical relationship between women that exceeds institutions.

Opposing the known future of modern institutionalism is a matter of small acts that unsettle institutional time. Although institutional time naturalises what Elizabeth Freeman calls 'chrononormativity' and what Pierre Bourdieu calls 'habitus', it also creates anachronisms that disrupt the regular, habituated rhythms of institutions. For Freeman, chrononormativity is 'a technique by which institutional forces come to seem like somatic facts'.[108] Habitus, in turn, refers to systems that structure, organise and regulate activities and behaviour in order to create 'a world of already realised ends'.[109] Both terms show

how modern institutionalism comes to be embodied – the institution creates rhythms that lead to 'realised ends', leaving little room for 'unrealised' possibilities or alternative 'ends'. But even within these regulated rhythms and established temporal patterns, untimeliness abounds. For Freeman, such untimeliness emerges from 'bodily potentiality';[110] for Bourdieu, from 'imaginary experience' – or literature.[111] I suggest that alternative temporalities also emerge from anachronisms themselves: anachronistic people and places draw attention to the untimely endurance of practices at odds with but embedded in institutions.

This book's three sections – 'Necessary and Unnecessary Anachronisms', 'Forgetting and Remembrance' and 'Untimely Improvement' – pair English and Irish realist novels to question modern institutionalism both in the Victorian period and in our political present. Arguing that the contradictory dynamics and temporal and political divisions in Irish realist novels offer a new understanding of realist form, I expect that my arguments extend beyond the specific novels that I read and can apply to a wide range of British and colonial texts that similarly move between institutional time and anachronisms.

My account of British realism begins in the eighteenth century, with Maria Edgeworth's *Castle Rackrent* (1800). The first chapter argues that establishing an origin for what we now call 'British realism' or 'the Irish novel' is both an institutional and an anachronistic endeavour: the stories that we tell about novels are actually stories about the cultural institutions that study novels. Thus, literary history is as much about the present as it is about the past. Considering *Castle Rackrent*'s formal and political divisions alongside its changing critical reception, I demonstrate how 'British realism' is an anachronistic formation and offer a new origin story where 'British realism' and 'the Irish novel' are not separate traditions or forms, but rather dynamically intertwined. *Castle Rackrent*, long thought to be an exemplary Irish novel precisely because it is not realist, develops realist contradictions that are taken up by later nineteenth-century Irish, Scottish and English novelists like Walter Scott, Jane Austen, Elizabeth Gaskell, Harriet Martineau and Anthony Trollope.

The next section, 'Forgetting and Remembrance', moves to provincial novels by William Carleton (1794–1869), Charles Kickham (1828–82) and George Eliot (1819–80), arguing that provincialism offers an alternative to institutionalised abstractions. Moving between being inside and outside of a culture and between being of a time and distanced from it through narrative metalepsis, these authors highlight the importance of local histories, embodied memory and anachronistic modes of reading in an era of institutional consolidation. Chapter 2 focuses on Carleton and Kickham, two native Irish writers who received critical and popular acclaim for their truthful portrayals of Irish life in the nineteenth century but are understood as ethnographic rather than realist writers in the twentieth and twenty-first centuries. Questioning this distinction between realism and ethnography by studying narrative metalepsis within their novels, I claim that both Carleton and Kickham demonstrate how institutions imagine a future that depends upon forgetting. Remembering what institutions work to forget, the politically conservative Carleton legitimates traditional practices that institutions seek to root out while Kickham, a Fenian who advocated revolution, cultivates an anti-institutional and anti-English political stance.

Chapter 3 focuses on narrative metalepsis in the novels of George Eliot, the most central figure in studies of Victorian realism and often the standard through which Irish novelists are deemed not realist enough. But Carleton's and Kickham's ethnographic realism allows us to understand Eliot's provincial realism in a new way: as divided rather than integrative. In novels that encourage institutional consolidation, Eliot uses narrative metalepsis to question modern institutionalism's drive toward futurity. *Adam Bede* (1859) and *The Mill on the Floss* (1860) produce a form of anachronistic literacy – a mode of reading and remembering that collapses historical distance as it celebrates the immediacy of the past – to question women's fraught relationship to modern institutionalism. Eliot's embrace of anachronism is surprising because her novels seem to produce a form of historicism grounded in path-dependency: in her novels, past choices tend to constrain present decisions. But, in novels that otherwise confirm the existing path, Eliot's anachronistic literacy creates radical ruptures that mobilise anachronisms to imagine otherwise.

The third section, 'Untimely Improvement', turns to novels by Charles Dickens (1812–70) – the most famous novelist of social reform – and George Moore (1852–1933) – an Irish writer who wrote 'new realist' novels at the end of the nineteenth century – to articulate forms of development that refuse institutional time, whether through Dickens's reactionary reform or Moore's untimely *bildung*. Although Dickens seeks to reform institutions and Moore desires to reject them, for both authors, anachronisms suggest modes of inhabiting institutions that resist integration into them. Chapter 4 demonstrates how Charles Dickens's novels embrace what I call 'reactionary reform', a vision of the future that is actually a return to an anachronistic past.

Reactionary reform restores origins that institutions erase in their drive towards futurity, whether those origins are Sissy Jupe's life with her father in *Hard Times*, Esther Summerson's parentage in *Bleak House* or the humble home that Pip mistakenly disavows in *Great Expectations*. Reactivating origins allows a different stance towards institutions: instead of settling down and accepting their established rhythms, characters inhabit institutions, dwelling temporarily in them without acceding to their terms. But Dickens's vision of reform does not extend to everyone. He reinforces settler colonialism by representing particular groups of people as outside of history and futurity altogether. Validating anachronisms and criticising them in turn, Dickens imagines progressive change that rejects modern institutionalism but, in the process, shores up the racialised abstractions upon which settler colonial institutions depend.

The final chapter argues that Moore's 'new realist' novels, which combine naturalist description with realist narration, imagine forms of untimely development that refuse institutional integration. Writing at the end of the nineteenth century, Moore's realist experiments both consolidated a realist movement in England and actively challenged institutions like circulating libraries that shaped the development of mid-century realism. But despite Moore's importance to the institutionalisation of realism in England and the flourishing of naturalism in Ireland, he remains woefully understudied in part because of his performative, often comic, refusal of institutions. This chapter takes this performance seriously as it focuses on his revisions to the realist *Bildungsroman* in the 'English' *Esther Waters* (1894) and the 'Irish' *A Drama in Muslin* (1886). In both of these novels of development, Moore claims that public institutions and private growth are at odds. *A Drama in Muslin* adopts an explicitly anachronistic narrative temporality that refuses to allow the protagonist's individual development to represent national development while *Esther Waters* validates the protagonist's stasis over time – her illiteracy despite education. Combining an anti-institutional impulse with an anachronistic narrative temporality, Moore questions the institutionalised assumptions of what constitutes proper growth.

Throughout, *Novel Institutions* argues that realism's divided temporalities offer strategies for inhabiting institutions without foreclosing political futures. Even as realism embraces modern institutionalism and what Jane Eyre calls institutions' 'foregone determinations', anachronisms restore historicity to the world of the realist novel and imagine otherwise. By animating an untimely historicism,

English and Irish realist novels encourage a politics grounded in the heterogeneous present that remains open to unknown futures.

Notes

1. Sedgwick, 'Queer and Now', p. 5.
2. Dickens, *Little Dorrit*, p. 303.
3. Ibid. p. 110.
4. Ibid.
5. Ibid. p. 706.
6. Ibid. p. 111.
7. As the Young Barnacle declares to Arthur at the end of the novel: 'Why, good Heaven, we are nothing but forms! Think *what* a lot of our forms you have gone through. And you have got nearer to an end?' Dickens, *Little Dorrit*, p. 705.
8. Ibid. p. 705.
9. Ibid. p. 113.
10. Explaining disciplinary power in *The Novel and the Police*, Miller argues that it 'extends from obviously disciplinary institutions (such as the prison) to institutions officially determined by "other" functions (such as the school) down to the tiniest practices of everyday social life' (17). In turn, Armstrong contends in *Desire and Domestic Fiction* that 'No history of an institution – whether that of prison, hospital, and schoolroom, as Foucault describes them, or of courts, houses of parliament, and marketplace, as more conventional historians prefer – can avoid the political behavior of the disciplinary model because these histories necessarily diminish the role of the subject in authorizing the forces that govern him' (22).
11. Said, *Culture and Imperialism*, p. 74.
12. Robbins, *Upward Mobility and the Common Good*, p. 6. Goodlad, *Victorian Literature and the Victorian State*; Anderson, *The Powers of Distance*.
13. Robbins, 'The Smell of Infrastructure', pp. 27–8.
14. *The Reorder of Things*, p. 18.
15. Valerie Rohy helpfully explains anachronism's complicated relationship with linear historical time: 'There is no simple opposition between a hegemonic calendar time and an apparently aberrant anachronism; instead chronology depends on anachronism. This double-time would suggest that no model of temporality bears a fixed political and ideological valence' (*Anachronism and its Others*, p. 34). Also see Srinivas Aravamudan's 'The Return of Anachronism', where he suggests that although anachronisms are often used to demonstrate the 'backwardness' of colonial subjects, they can also be used to question whether contemporaneity – or uniform, shared time – is desirable (pp. 343–4).

16. Dickens, *Little Dorrit*, p. 495.
17. Ibid. p. 192.
18. Ashon Crawley uses this phrase to describe the power of performativity within institutions, using Jenny Evans's performances at the Azusa Street Revival in Los Angeles as an example of such performativity in 'Otherwise, Instituting'. He asserts: 'What she played was an otherwise relation to organization, an otherwise possibility for movement that was grounded in the disruption of the logic of institutionalization, a disruption of the logic of law, practice, custom' (p. 86).
19. Here, I draw on Amy Martin's *Alter-nations,* which argues that the Act of Union both tried to absorb Ireland into the imperial nation and treat Irish people as a 'colonized and alien population, denied fundamental rights of citizenship and subjecthood, and constructed as culturally, religiously, and racially other' (p. 3).
20. Ashon Crawley further elaborates the concept of 'otherwise possibilities' in *Blackpentecostal Breath*, where he explains, 'Using otherwise, I seek to underscore the ways alternative modes, alternative strategies, alternative ways of life *already* exist, indeed are violently acted upon in order to produce the coherence of the state' (pp. 6–7).
21. Durkheim, 'The Field of Sociology', pp. 55–8. As Geoffrey Hodgson argues in 'What are Institutions?': institutions are 'systems of established and prevalent social rules that structure social interaction' (p. 2).
22. Spencer, *The Study of Sociology*, p. 8.
23. My definition of modern institutionalism draws on recent work by Christopher Castiglia which theorises institutionalism as 'orienting citizens from present negotiations to a perpetually receding horizon of futurity' in *Interior States*, p. 5. But while Castiglia holds that there can be no present tense within institutionalism – in his words, 'institutionalism left no present in which to associate' (p. 5) – in this book I argue that anachronisms can in fact open up space for politics in the present. I also build on work by Sara Ahmed and Caroline Levine, who draw on research in the interdisciplinary field of new institutionalism – a method in sociology, political science and organisational studies – to emphasise the temporal structure of institutions and institutionalism. See Ahmed, *On Being Included*, pp. 21–2, and Levine, *Forms*, pp. 57–8. My concept of modern institutionalism also builds on extensive work that understands modernity and modernization through institutions, or what Frederick Cooper calls modernity defined through 'a set of attributes'. See Cooper, *Colonialism in Question*, pp. 121–2. Robert Higney traces many of these arguments about institutionalism and modernization in '"Law, Good Faith, Order, Security": Joseph Conrad's Institutions', pp. 85–7. James Vernon offers another version of this argument, claiming that British modernity emerged from the 'increasingly abstract and bureaucratic forms' that 'were used to address the challenges of living around,

doing business with, and governing (often distant) strangers' (*Distant Strangers*, p. 7).

24. Recently, Caroline Levine has demonstrated how the concept of path dependency can help us understand the 'staying power' of historical periods in literary studies in *Forms*, 59.

25. George Levine begins his study of realism in *The Realistic Imagination* with an investigation of *Frankenstein*; Harry E. Shaw claims that *Waverley* is realist in *Narrating Reality*; Lauren Goodlad includes a chapter on Wilkie Collins's *Armadale* and *The Moonstone* in *The Victorian Geopolitical Aesthetic*; Nancy Armstrong's *Fiction in the Age of Photography* focuses on *Alice's Adventures in Wonderland*.

26. Joe Cleary is particularly good at showing how literary histories tend to equate 'the "novel"' with 'the realist novel' in *Outrageous Fortune*, p. 53.

27. Defining realism through contradictions, I build on George Levine's argument in *The Realistic Imagination* that realism is 'self-contradictory' – a literary method that mediates reality even as it seeks to present unmediated truth (p. 7). I suggest, however, that the reality that realist novels represent is doubly mediated: by institutions and by realist form. I also build on Ian Duncan's *Modern Romance and Transformations of the Novel*, which argues that debates about distinctions between romance and realism 'mark at the institutional level of genre a fruitful trouble and division' (p. 6).

28. In 'Signs of the Times', Thomas Carlyle questions what he sees as too great an emphasis on institutionalism – which he associates with 'mechanism' – and too little emphasis on human agency; he declares, 'Institutions are much; but they are not all' (p. 16). Herbert Spencer similarly worries about the increasing emphasis on institutions later in the century: 'In proportion as public agencies occupy a larger space in daily experience, leaving but a smaller space for other agencies, there comes a greater tendency to think of public control as everywhere needful, and a less ability to conceive of activities as otherwise controlled' ('Political Institutions', p. 199). John Stuart Mill's 'Considerations on Representative Government' embraces modern institutionalism; Mill links 'good institutions' to progress, suggesting that institutions work against the 'natural tendency' of men to degenerate (pp. 223–4). Harriet Martineau in *Life in the Sick-Room* similarly associates institutions with liberal progress and fixed futurity, declaring, 'It is scarcely now a question with any one what is the point towards which the vessel of the State is to be carried next, but how she is to be most safely steered amidst the perils which beset an ordained course' (p. 81). John Mitchel offers particularly powerful critiques of institutionality in Ireland in his *Jail Journal*, arguing, 'Property is an institution of Society – not a Divine endowment, whose title-deed is in heaven; the uses and trusts of it are the benefits of Society; the sanction of it is the authority of

Society; but when matters come to that utterly intolerable condition in which they have long been in Ireland, Society itself stands dissolved' (p. 69).

29. McClintock, *Imperial Leather*, p. 40.
30. Williams, *Marxism and Literature*, p. 122. Williams suggests that dominant culture works to absorb both the residual and emergent, but that their persistence shows that 'no mode of production and therefore no dominant social order and therefore no dominant culture ever in reality includes or exhausts all human practice, human energy, and human interaction' (p. 125).
31. Lukács, *The Historical Novel*, p. 63.
32. Ibid. p. 61.
33. 'St Clair of the Isles', p. 606.
34. Fabian, *Time and the Other*, p. 32.
35. Scott, *Waverley*, p. 193.
36. Dickens, *Our Mutual Friend*, p. 400.
37. Gissing, *The Odd Women*, p. 358.
38. Moore, *Esther Waters*, p. 22.
39. Recently, Bliss Cua Lim has extended Chakrabarty's temporal critique by articulating modes of temporality that do not collapse temporal heterogeneity into homogeneous time in *Translating Time*, p. 45. Jacques Rancière also notes how institutionalised methodologies constrain lived, historical relationships as he argues that the renunciation of anachronism in scholarship 'knots together the constraint of truth with a social constraint' ('The Concept of Anachronism and the Historian's Truth', p. 38).
40. *Provincializing Europe*, p. 243.
41. 'Theorizing Queer Temporalities: A Roundtable', p. 182. When referring to 'disqualified' knowledges, Halberstam builds on Michel Foucault's *Society Must Be Defended*. Foucault argues for the importance of 'subjugated knowledges', that is, 'a whole series of knowledges that have been disqualified as nonconceptual knowledges, as insufficiently elaborated knowledges: naïve knowledges, hierarchically inferior knowledges, knowledges that are below the required level of erudition or scientificity' (p. 7).
42. Sedgwick, 'Queer and Now', p. 8.
43. By distinguishing between futurity and institutional futurity, I build on Lee Edelman's work in *No Future*. Arguing that constructions of the social and political are rooted in the figure of the child, Edelman ultimately finds futurity so constraining that he rejects any depiction of the social in favour of a queer, anti-social embrace of the death drive. By contrast, I suggest that anachronisms offer a queer approach to history where the future is not guaranteed by institutions or institutional thinking.
44. As Kandice Chuh argues in *Imagine Otherwise*: 'To imagine otherwise is not simply a matter of seeing a common object from different

perspectives. Rather, it is about undoing the very notion of common objectivity itself and about recognizing the ethicopolitical implications of multiple epistemologies – theories about knowledge formation and the status and objects of knowledge – that underwrite alternative perspectives' (p. x). Ashon Crawley locates otherwise possibilities in performance and Blackpentecostalism in *Blackpentecostal Breath*, suggesting that Black social life performs 'otherwise possibilities in the service of enfleshing an abolitionist politic' (p. 6). Elizabeth Povinelli considers Foucault's own desire to think otherwise in 'The Will to Be Otherwise/The Effort of Endurance', suggesting that he sees 'thought as an experiment in and against power, a method of *trying things out* as a manner of capacitating thresholds' (p. 472).

45. Genette, *Narrative Discourse*, p. 40.

46. Eliot, *Adam Bede*, p. 179. Elaine Freedgood has recently considered how metalepsis is central to the realist novel's imperial politics in 'Fictional Settlements', p. 402. Arguing that metalepsis is the 'central trope of Victorian financial discourse', Anna Kornbluh also emphasizes the importance of metalepsis to realist form in *Realizing Capital*, p. 23.

47. Eliot, *Adam Bede*, 38.

48. Victorianists sometimes reinforce the assumption that nineteenth-century novels are novels of development. For instance, Nicholas Dames argues the novel remembers 'only what the self can employ in the present', as he suggests that the novel's narrative temporality moves towards futurity (*Amnesiac Selves*, p. 4).

49. Stockton, *The Queer Child*, p. 6. Feminist scholars have emphasised that the linear trajectory is only one version of development among many; they argue that gender unsettles linear development and draw attention to counter-narratives in realist novels. See Susan Fraiman, *Unbecoming Women*, p. xi, and Elizabeth Abel, Marianne Hirsch and Elizabeth Langland (eds), *The Voyage In: Fictions of Female Development*.

50. Esty, *Unseasonable Youth*, p. 7.

51. Townsend, 'The Drama of Peripheralized Bildung', p. 339.

52. Dickens, *Great Expectations*, p. 90.

53. Gissing, *New Grub Street*, p. 92.

54. Ward, 'Our Posthuman Past', p. 284.

55. Here, I weigh in ongoing debates about realism's relationship to history. While critics like Harry Shaw contend that realism is an inherently historicist form, Marxist and postcolonial critics object to nineteenth-century realism because it relegates history to the margins. Edward Said, for example, highlights the histories of oppression, empire and the uneven circulation of resources that make everyday life in England possible but are ultimately obscured by the form of realist novels. This critical disagreement in fact turns on whether history is defined as a disruptive force or a coherent institution. While Shaw suggests that realist novels convey how history works as a force by subjecting

characters to history, Terry Eagleton and Said critique the ways in which the realist novel functions as an institution. For Eagleton and Said, realism is an ahistorical form that creates social consensus only by excluding historical contradictions and social difference. Disagreeing over the politics of realist aesthetics, Shaw concludes that realism is open to history and thus open to change, while Eagleton and Said claim that it evacuates, even conceals history. See Shaw, *Narrating Reality*, p. 6, and Eagleton, *Criticism and Ideology*, pp. 120–1; Said, *Culture and Imperialism*, pp. xiv–xvii.

56. In *A Geography of Victorian Gothic Fiction*, Robert Mighall goes so far as to define the gothic mode through anachronism (pp. 6–7).

57. Braddon, *Lady Audley's Secret*, p. 240.

58. Morris, *News from Nowhere*, p. 79.

59. Haddon, 'The Aran Islands, County Galway', p. 308.

60. Edward Said famously focuses on realism in *Culture and Imperialism* where he argues that realism works to sustain 'the society's consent in overseas expansion' (p. 12). But while Said focuses on how realist space serves empire, I consider the politics of realist time.

61. Lloyd, 'Afterword: Hardress Cregan's dream', p. 230. Arguing that the novel is a distinctly modern form, Amanda Anderson suggests that the realist novel helps us understand 'literary liberalism' as she draws on, and revises, previous scholarship where 'the consolidation of liberal power and the development of the realist novel are coterminous' (*Bleak Liberalism*, pp. 48, 47).

62. Terry Eagleton most famously makes this argument in *Heathcliff and the Great Hunger*. Gordon Bigelow offers a more recent version of this argument in 'Form and Violence in Trollope's *The Macdermots of Ballycloran*', where he offers an exciting new approach to Trollope's early Irish fiction by focusing on its 'formal discontinuities' (p. 387).

63. O'Malley, *Liffey and Lethe*, p. 8. In addition to this reading of the vexed temporalities of *Castle Rackrent*, O'Malley's book offers a compelling account of how Protestant historiography in Ireland depends upon what he calls 'paramnesia', or an act of forgetting that allows people to imagine a liberal, peaceful future. Building on his work, I suggest that institutions and institutionalism encourage paramnesia: to assimilate into institutions and accept institutional time, people must forget the differences and violence that predate the institution.

64. Kickham, *Knocknagow*, p. 374.

65. Eagleton, *Heathcliff and the Great Hunger*, p. 20.

66. Bakhtin, 'Epic and Novel', p. 31.

67. Woloch, *The One vs. the Many*, p. 19.

68. Jameson, *The Antinomies of Realism*, p. 10.

69. W. B. Yeats, 'Irish National Literature', p. 140.

70. Sean Ryder argues, for instance, 'Not only did Yeats's views determine the literary canon; they also shaped the way literary critics

viewed the whole history of the nineteenth century' ('Literature in English', p. 119). Claire Connolly also notes that the Irish Literary Revival guides 'nationalist canon-making in the century to come' and still mediates Irish studies scholars' approach to nineteenth-century novels (*A Cultural History of the Irish Novel, 1790–1829*, p. 11).

71. James H. Murphy tracks the persistence of this search for an Irish *Middlemarch* in *Irish Novelists and the Victorian Age*. While he suggests that *Middlemarch* can ironically and thematically be understood *as* Irish and notes that some Irish writers wrote in the realist mode, he tends to highlight the historical and political circumstances that prevented realism from flourishing in Ireland (pp. 2–4).

72. Claire Connolly traces the transnational nature of these publication practices (pp. 6–7). William Carleton and Charles Kickham, the novelists that I focus on in Chapter 2, are important in the history of the Irish novel because they were published by Irish publishing houses.

73. Belanger, 'Introduction', p. 18.

74. Lloyd, *Anomalous States*, p. 128.

75. Lauren Goodlad seeks to 'prise open the category of realism to appreciate its suppleness, variety, and longevity', but focuses on British and French novels to argue for realism's transnationalism (*The Victorian Geopolitical Aesthetic*, p. 11). Defining cosmopolitan realism, Tanya Agathocleous focuses on the shifting scales of novels that represent London in *Urban Realism and the Cosmopolitan Imagination in the Nineteenth Century*, p. xvi. Nathan Hensley argues that one does not need to look beyond metropolitan novels to understand the violence of the British Empire because it is 'the general fact subtending the entirety of domestic life and therefore cultural production in the period' in *Forms of Empire*, p. 6.

76. Jed Esty and Colleen Lye, 'Peripheral Realisms Now', p. 277.

77. Here, I'm drawing on David Lloyd, who, in 'Afterword: Hardress Cregan's dream', warns against too easily assimilating nineteenth-century Irish novels into either a British canon or an Irish counter-canon (p. 236), and I also draw on Alison Hervey, who argues that Irish realist novels 'are less voluminous, less "major"' than their English counterparts ('Irish Aestheticism in Fin-de-Siècle Women's Writing', p. 808).

78. For a more complete version of this argument, see Mullen, 'In Search of Shared Time', pp. 107–19.

79. *Chartism*, p. 29.

80. Arnold, *The Study of Celtic Literature*, p. 10.

81. Brontë, *Jane Eyre*, p. 41.

82. Ibid.

83. Ibid.

84. Ibid.

85. Ibid.

86. Ibid. p. 270, p. 271.
87. Within these fields, 'new institutionalism' – or renewed attention to institutions as primary factors in social, historical and economic development – has thrived since the 1980s. New institutionalism includes a range of methodologies and disciplinary fields, but is united by an interest in institutions beyond the state; the field investigates how such institutions form and how they shape social, political and organisational life. For a useful overview, see André Lecours, 'New Institutionalism: Issues and Questions', pp. 3–26. Institutionalism is also a growing area of interest in literary study, with important work by Mark McGurl, *The Program Era* and Homer Obed Brown, *Institutions of the English Novel from Defoe to Scott.*
88. Vimalassery, Hu Pegues and Goldstein, 'Introduction: On Colonial Unknowing'. Edward Said makes a similar point when he reflects on British cultural institutions' lasting relationship with empire, lamenting: 'how little Britain's great humanistic ideas, institutions, and monuments, which we still celebrate as having power historically to command our approval, how little they stand in the way of the accelerating imperial process' (p. 82).
89. Vimalassery, Hu Pegues and Goldstein, 'Introduction: On Colonial Unknowing'.
90. Mill, 'England and Ireland', p. 511. Also see Maine, *Lectures on the Early History of Institutions*, pp. 185–6.
91. Edgeworth, *Castle Rackrent* and *Ennui*, p. 68.
92. As Elaine Hadley contends, the Irish were seen as 'singularly, palpably, and literally attached to Irish ground', unlike the English, who expressed their love for the country through institutions as well as the land (*Living Liberalism*, p. 242). Studying the 'unwritten law' in Ireland, Heather Laird tracks how the politics of the land wars were defined through 'sustained resistance to official law and its institutions' (*Subversive Law in Ireland, 1879–1920*, p. 16).
93. Uday Singh Mehta argues that this 'known future' is a characteristic of nineteenth-century British liberalism, writing 'the contemporaneity of these unfamiliar life forms cannot be spoken of in the register of historical time, for that register translates them into the linearity of backwardness and thus immediately conceives of them in terms of an already known future' (*Liberalism and Empire*, p. 108). Similarly, Dipesh Chakrabarty writes: 'Historicism thus posited historical time as a measure of the cultural distance (at least in institutional development) that was assumed to exist between the West and the non-West' (*Provincializing Europe*, p. 7).
94. Michael Rubenstein, *Public Works*, p. 19. See also Lloyd, *Irish Times*, p. 5, and Joe Cleary, 'Introduction: Ireland and Modernity', p. 9.
95. Mitchel, *The Last Conquest of Ireland (Perhaps)*, p. 139.

96. See Kiberd, *Inventing Ireland*, p. 23. As postcolonial theorists suggest, colonies functioned as 'laboratories of modernity'. Attributing that phrase to Gwendolyn Wright, Ann Laura Stoler provides examples of institutions that originated in colonies (*Race and the Education of Desire*, p. 15).

97. Maurer, *The Dispossessed State*, p. 7.

98. Kiberd, *Inventing Ireland*, p. 614.

99. Lloyd, *Irish Times*, p. 3.

100. Foucault, *The History of Sexuality*, pp. 86–7. In Stoler's words: 'Foucault locates how state institutions foster and draw on new independent disciplines of knowledge and in turn harness these microfields of power as they permeate the body politic at large' (*Race and the Education of Desire*, p. 28).

101. Foucault, *The History of Sexuality*, p. 92.

102. Foucault, *Discipline and Punish*, p. 209.

103. Most famously, Amanda Anderson seeks to reclaim liberalism throughout her work, especially in *Bleak Liberalism*. Also see Daniel S. Malachuk's *Perfection, the State and Victorian Liberalism*, which declares a paradigm shift in Victorian studies that allows people to 'read the Victorian liberal aspiration toward moral objectivity and perfectionism with genuine appreciation' (p. 4).

104. Amanda Anderson attempts to think through the relationship between liberalism and violence in *Bleak Liberalism,* where she argues that liberalism is not simply a progressive ideal, but also a mode of thought that grapples with bleak lived realities. However, her argument tellingly pushes imperialism and racialised violence to the margins as it questions Joe Cleary's literary history because it centres imperialism (p. 117) and reads Ralph Ellison's *Invisible Man* through white liberal writers like Lionel Trilling and Irving Howe without engaging with the many critical race theorists who critique liberalism.

105. Lisa Lowe argues that 'the intimacies of four continents requires a *past conditional temporality* in order to reckon with the violence of affirmation and forgetting, in order to recognize that this particular violence continues to be reproduced in liberal humanist institutions' (*The Intimacies of Four Continents,* p. 41). In turn, Sara Ahmed draws attention to how racism persists within institutions precisely because institutions believe themselves to be progressive and modern. Institutions thus view racism as 'being anachronistic, a sign of a time that is no longer' even when it is sanctioned by contemporary institutional practice (p. 48). Thus, Ahmed argues that 'any racism within an institution is explained as not really "going on", even when it is ongoing' (p. 48). Lastly, in his study of the violence of Victorian liberalism and empire, Nathan Hensley argues that 'we have yet to outlive the questions of legality and violence organizing this book' as he discusses 'the lure of progressive schemes' (p. 10).

106. Lowe, *The Intimacies of Four Continents*, p. 3.
107. Marcus, *Between Women*, pp. 193–4.
108. Freeman, *Time Binds*, p. 3.
109. Bourdieu, *The Logic of Practice*, p. 53.
110. Freeman, *Time Binds*, p. 19.
111. Bourdieu, *The Logic of Practice*, p. 64.

Part I

Necessary and Unnecessary Anachronisms

Chapter 1

Realism and the Institution of the Nineteenth-Century Novel

'It is curious to observe how good and bad are mingled in human institutions.'[1]

In the nineteenth century, the story goes, realism became an institution. Scholars tell different versions of this story. For some, realism functioned like an institution: seeking to represent everyday reality, it helped establish procedures and prescriptions that mediate social and political life.[2] For others, realism acquired institutional authority in the nineteenth century: it attracted critical attention and achieved canonical status.[3] For still others, realism participates in a larger process of institutional consolidation by shoring up the British imperial state and embracing the rule of law.[4]

This story about realism, in its various iterations, contributes to the marginalisation of nineteenth-century Irish realist novels by both Anglo-Irish and Irish writers.[5] Irish realist novels, like their English counterparts, work to represent a shared social reality through narratives that describe ordinary, everyday life. But, Irish settings more explicitly demonstrate how realism is a contradictory dynamic rather than a coherent social or literary form. Because representations of everyday life in Ireland often appear strange rather than familiar, extraordinary rather than ordinary, Irish realism did not acquire canonical authority, despite the early critical success of Irish writers like Maria Edgeworth. Instead, Irish novels belatedly enter the literary canon through modernist novels like James Joyce's *Ulysses*. Importantly, because of Ireland's colonial history, Irish realist novels also have a more uneasy relationship with the institutional power of the state and often represent forms of social organisation that actively undermine the rule of law.

Questioning the nation-based literary histories of British realism, this chapter traces an alternative genealogy of both 'British realism' and 'the Irish novel' through an attention to Maria Edgeworth's *Castle Rackrent* (1800). *Castle Rackrent*'s critical reception shows that realism is both an institutional and an anachronistic formation. Realism seems stable and coherent because institutions retrospectively produce what they study. But when realism became a coherent genre, belatedly constructed by fields of study and critical practices, peripheral realist novels like *Castle Rackrent* no longer seemed realist enough. As a result, although early nineteenth-century readers praised Edgeworth for her truthful tales and realistic accounts, later in the century her work seems too didactic, too Irish or not Irish enough to be realist. I turn to *Castle Rackrent*, then, to unsettle the stories we tell about realism, mobilising anachronism to view 'British realism' and 'the Irish novel' in relation rather than in opposition to one another.

In the twentieth and twenty-first century, scholars celebrate *Castle Rackrent* as an original text and an origin text, proclaiming it to be the first Irish novel, the first regional novel, the first historical novel and the first novel written in the voice of the colonised. Each of these 'firsts' show how *Castle Rackrent* institutes new forms: it creates narrative structures in which other writers and critics participate. But each of these 'firsts' also separates *Castle Rackrent* from what scholars now call realism, and *Castle Rackrent* becomes the foundation for an anti-realist Irish novel tradition or an Anglo-Irish novel tradition that suppresses native Irish forms. For example, Terry Eagleton understands *Castle Rackrent* in modernist terms, claiming that language in the novel *acts* but does not *represent*, while Seamus Deane approaches it as a document 'in the "civilizing mission" of the English to the Irish' that disciplines romantic Ireland.[6] These two lines of argument are sometimes starkly opposed to one another, but they both celebrate *Castle Rackrent*'s originality in order to find the Irish novel an institutional home other than that of realism – whether in modernist studies or in the history of Ireland's colonisation.

While I also emphasise *Castle Rackrent*'s originality, I argue that the novel's formal innovations not only establish an Irish novel tradition, they elucidate the formal and political contradictions at work, often more subtly, in more canonical English realist novels. *Castle Rackrent*'s narrative is starkly divided: Thady Quirk, the illiterate family steward, narrates the tale of the Rackrent family's decline while the fictional editor adds a preface, footnotes and glossary to his tale. While the events that Thady describes take place before 1782, the editor addresses the impending Act of Union that will take effect in January of 1801. These formal divisions lead to a mixed politics as readers choose between the editor's framing of the tale and Thady's story, between the narrator's work to consolidate the future union and Thady's anachronistic orientation. Moreover, the novel's contradictory efforts to integrate and exclude difference – to assimilate Irish settings into novelistic forms and integrate Ireland into the British state, on one hand, and to represent Irish peculiarities that cannot be assimilated into these literary and social forms, on the other – illuminates the more subtle ways in which British realist novels oscillate between incorporating social and historical difference and exposing it. Reading *Castle Rackrent* alongside novels by Walter Scott, Jane Austen, Elizabeth Gaskell, Margaret Oliphant and Anthony Trollope suggests that Irish realist novels differ from English realist novels only insofar as they expose realist conventions rather than seamlessly integrating them into the novel's narrative form.

While this chapter is not a conventional literary history – it does not track Edgeworth's influence on Victorian novelists or narrate the development of a single realist novel tradition – it does interrogate our literary histories. I ask why the novels of Walter Scott and Jane Austen are foundational to histories of 'British realism' while Edgeworth's novels are defined in opposition to it. I argue that rethinking the origins of 'British realism' allows us to understand realist form as a contradictory dynamic, while also demonstrating how institutions mediate our definitions of realism. Focusing on how *Castle Rackrent* engages with modern institutionalism through its narrative forms and temporal structures, as well as how disciplinary practices have shaped the novel's critical reception, this chapter offers a new origin story for Victorian realism by reading realism and Irish novels in relation. Reading realist novels does not need to confirm the literary histories that are already institutionalised; it can instead teach us how to inhabit institutions in ways that open up new political possibilities.

Literary History: Institutions and Anachronisms

The temporality that underlies modern institutionalism – which distinguishes between modern and non-modern in the present and establishes institutions as the horizon of futurity – shapes literary histories of the nineteenth-century realist novel. Contemporary disciplinary practices, fields of study, critical debates and understandings of the canon mediate the novels we read, the literary forms we study and the genres we identify. Thus, the stories we tell about novels are actually stories about the cultural institutions that study novels.[7] In fact, as Homer Obed Brown explains in his account of the origins of the English novel, many literary histories only confirm 'anew what is already institutionalised'.[8] We narrate the history of the novel as a path-dependent narrative, reinforcing contemporary institutional consensus and reassuring ourselves that the path that leads to the present is the legitimate path. Allowing the novel's end – its current institutional location in the university – to mediate its origin, these histories confuse 'the novel's institution with the institution's history of the novel'.[9]

Tracing how the novel's contemporary institutional location retrospectively shapes histories of the novel, Brown warns that institutions beget anachronisms. Brown suggests that anachronisms belatedly endow particular novels, as well as particular narratives about novels, with institutional authority, and thus construct a shared novelistic tradition out of fiction that was understood to be quite strange and singular in its own historical moment. Of course, literary history can also retrospectively undermine novels' claims to authority by deeming certain novels that use realist conventions, such as nineteenth-century Irish novels, to be anachronistic vestiges of other generic traditions. I am interested in the contradictory temporality of the practice of literary history. Insofar as literary history mediates how we read in order to affirm institutional consensus in the present, it closes down political possibilities from the past. But because literary history is always an untimely enterprise – shaped by the past as well as the present – it also draws connections between novels that for too long have been thought of as distinct.

Unlike Brown, who sees the anachronisms that institutions produce as a 'danger', or as historical errors, I think of these anachronisms as opportunities. In fact, I take up Brown's argument not to offer an approach to literary history that minimises anachronisms, but rather to insist that anachronisms are unavoidable in both realist novels and our own narratives about realist novels. Following postcolonial and queer theorists, I suggest that instead of trying to root out anachronisms in the name of historical accuracy, we can study these anachronisms to learn about our institutional practices and their limits.[10] As Valerie Rohy explains, 'Resistance to anachronism is resistance not to the other of historicism but to an abject aspect of its own methodology'.[11] Anachronisms do not simply confirm what is already institutionalised, as Brown claims; they push against institutional consensus by showing the mixed temporalities of our literary histories and the necessity of comparative practices that bring together traditions that have historically been interrelated but now appear to be separate.

Modernism retrospectively shapes our understanding of realism by separating nineteenth-century English novels from their Irish counterparts. In English literary studies, where realism is defined in opposition to modernism, English realism is understood to be national while modernism is cosmopolitan or international.[12] Irish studies scholars, however, understand realism as not only a national form, but also as an *English* one. They suggest that as nineteenth-century Irish writers sought to represent reality in Ireland, they produced the formal fragmentation and transnational discourse more commonly associated with modernism. For this reason, nineteenth-century Irish novels are seen, not as realist, but as proto-modernist precursors to canonical modernist Irish novels.

Questioning these nation-based literary histories, I suggest instead that nineteenth-century realism is a contradictory transnational formal dynamic. In the nineteenth century, Irish reality often looked different from English reality but the literary forms that Irish writers used to capture this reality not only were similar to but often shaped the forms that their English and Scottish counterparts employed. Nineteenth-century reviewers thus often foreground Irish difference – separating Trollope's 'Irish' novels from his clerical novels, for instance, or noting that novelists are drawn to Ireland because of the 'points which mainly distinguish it from other nations' – but nevertheless evaluate Irish novels in terms of how they represent reality.[13] The best Irish novels challenge the popular 'misrepresentations' of Irish national character[14] and are 'truer than any history'.[15] Tellingly, English realists who focused their attention on working-class people were understood to be building on an Irish novel tradition that represented strange, unknown cultural practices for a middle-class, metropolitan audience. As a reviewer of *North and South* claims, 'The Author of "Mary Barton" seems bent on doing for Lancashire and the Lancashire dialect what Miss Edgeworth did for Ireland.'[16]

Significantly, what has come to be known as Victorian realism is itself an anachronistic formation. We understand realism to be the dominant genre of nineteenth-century British writing, but the term realism emerged belatedly in the debates about realism and naturalism at the end of the century. As René Wellek reminds us, 'In England there was no realist movement of that name before George Moore and George Gissing, late in the eighties.'[17] Chapter 5 focuses on this moment in the history of realism as it shows how Moore's realist novels of development refuse modern institutionalism. In this present chapter, I suggest that although finding an origin for realism is always an anachronistic enterprise, the origins that we choose shape the stories that we tell. Thus, I tell a story of realism that begins with Maria Edgeworth's *Castle Rackrent* not to offer a more historically accurate origin for the realist novel but rather to mobilise an untimely text that challenges our assumptions about both realist form and literary history.

Today, many scholars note Edgeworth's influence on Scott and Austen, two novelists usually associated with the origins of Victorian realism, but they nevertheless distinguish her fiction from a realist novel tradition and understand her novels to be either didactic fiction or Irish fiction.[18] Didacticism was only retrospectively distinguished from realist writing.[19] Early reviews thus praise the realistic nature of Edgeworth's instructive fiction, writing, 'There is nothing here of romance, either in character or incident; every thing has been reduced within the compass of probability.'[20] But later critics suggest Edgeworth could not capture the contradictions of everyday life precisely because she was committed to imparting moral lessons. As one 1895 review suggests, 'The incidents, like the characters, are forced to serve the cause of morality at the expense of probability.'[21] Morality and probability, which were once aligned, become antithetical over time as realism and didacticism come to be thought of as distinct literary modes.

Similarly, when scholars and critics classify Edgeworth as an Irish writer in the twentieth and twenty-first centuries, they depict her fiction as a departure from realism, although Irish novels were understood in realist terms in the nineteenth century.[22] In the nineteenth century, like today, *Castle Rackrent* was commonly understood to be the first Irish novel, a subgenre of what was sometimes called 'the national novel'.[23] Understanding Edgeworth as an Irish writer highlights her humour, her engagement with history and her linguistic play rather than her didacticism. But noting the distinct style and setting of Edgeworth's fiction did not initially distinguish her novels from realism: Irish novels represented Ireland and Irish representative types, cultivated sympathy and engaged with history. Critics only began to make distinctions between Edgeworth's Irish novels and realism when they began to question whether Edgeworth, an Anglo-Irish writer, was Irish enough. As early as 1838, critics juxtaposed Edgeworth's writing with more 'authentic' – and more romantic – Irish writing by Lady Morgan to claim that Edgeworth's novels lacked 'national feeling'[24] and by the end of the century, when the Irish Revival brought new attention to Irish aesthetics, critics claimed that Edgeworth represented Ireland with 'the amused but unsympathetic deliberation of an Englishwoman'.[25] The rise of Irish studies in the 1980s paradoxically intensified both this reading of Edgeworth as too English and claims that her work exemplifies anti-realist Irish aesthetics.[26] Irish studies scholars thus tend to emphasise how Edgeworth's writing departs from realism – either because of its superficial, ideological representations of Ireland or because her Irishness emerges through its protomodernist experiments with fragmentation and non-referential language.

The slipperiness of Edgeworth's fiction over time – the fact that it is understood to be plausible and not plausible enough, Irish and not Irish enough, realist and not realist enough – shows that what Brown calls 'the institution's history of the novel' is too narrow and too neat a story. Novels do not easily fit on a single path or tell the story of a linear rise: their meaning changes in distinct historical and institutional contexts and their narrative forms participate in multiple genre traditions.

Necessary and Unnecessary Anachronisms: Scott and Edgeworth

Today, Edgeworth's importance to Victorian novelists that follow her is often understood to be thematic and political rather than formal or generic – realism rarely comes up.[27] When scholars do think about Edgeworth's formal contributions to realism, the contradictions in her novels are treated as problems to solve rather than as literary innovations.[28] For instance, Michael Gamer suggests that we should approach her novels as 'romances of real life', so that we can better understand their 'cohesiveness of construction'.[29] Gamer claims that thinking about Edgeworth's novels in relation to realism leads to too many contradictions.

But why do we assume that genre must be cohesive? How can the contradictions within Edgeworth's fiction, especially *Castle Rackrent*, help us tell a different story about realism? I contend that *Castle Rackrent* highlights the conflicting impulses within realism: to represent real life and capture history in its specificity and heterogeneity, on the one hand, and to naturalise modern institutionalism and establish institutions as the horizon of futurity, on the other. Realist novels work to transform the dynamism of history into the solidity of institutions. However, their anachronisms ensure that this never is realised: representing the world as it is shows how it could be otherwise. I suggest that scholars credit Scott with bringing a historicist dimension to literary realism in part because Scott's historicism is easily integrated into institutions: it encourages consensus. The historicism in Edgeworth's realist novels, however, better captures realism's contradictions because Edgeworth more clearly upholds and questions institutionalism within novels and society.

Scott's centrality to the history of British realism results in part from the way in which his novels transform the anachronisms of romance into the 'necessary anachronisms' that Lukács famously associates with the historical novel, and by extension, with realism.[30] For Lukács, Scott's anachronisms are necessary because they make the temporality of ordinary, everyday life historical – they convey a sense of history that exceeds what any one historical actor could actually know in order to 'elucidate the given historical relationship'.[31] Similarly, for Brown, Scott's novels use anachronisms to convey history – to express 'a present experience of the past's irrecuperable pastness'.[32] But as I argue in the introduction, the very idea of 'necessary' anachronism participates in the institutionalisation of a particular kind of history and a particular kind of novel by critics. For who decides which anachronisms are necessary and which are unnecessary errors? Are pasts only present as 'irrecuperable', or can they also invite us to imagine history and politics otherwise?

At stake in this distinction between necessary and unnecessary anachronisms is whether realism upholds or questions state institutions and the future they promise. In other words, focusing on the anachronisms *in* novels leads to assertions about the novel's relationship with institutional power – here, the British state and its corresponding legal institutions. *Waverley*'s anachronisms seem 'necessary' because they work to secure the path-dependent narrative of modern institutionalism: Fergus Mac-Ivor, the Highland chief who is sentenced to death for his participation in the rebellion, becomes an anachronism by the end of the novel as the British state and its courts of law define both the present and the future. His sister Flora lives but is also doomed to anachronism as she notes that 'it is vain to talk of the past . . . or even the future'.[33] At odds with the institutions of the British state, Flora appears at odds with historical time altogether and retreats to a convent. Scott relegates Fergus and Flora to an anachronistic past in order to consolidate modern institutionalism as the future.

But shifting the origins of realism from Scott to Edgeworth alters this story. Edgeworth's fiction, especially *Castle Rackrent*, highlights narrative and temporal divisions in realist forms that suggest a more contradictory politics. Although Edgeworth, like Scott, often promotes modern institutionalism and works to consolidate the rule of law, she also represents necessary and unnecessary anachronisms that refuse to allow institutions to delimit historical time and determine political futures.[34] I focus on Edgeworth's divided time and divided depiction of everyday life in the next two sections, but even a quick glance at the conclusion of *Castle Rackrent* highlights how anachronisms unsettle institutional futurity in this novel. Unlike *Waverley*, in which unruly, untimely subjects are denied futurity in the name of a consolidated British state, *Castle Rackrent* concludes ambivalently. After Thady's story, which revels in the out-of-date practices of the Rackrent family, the editor reflects on the impending Union, asking, 'Did the Warwickshire militia, who were chiefly artisans, teach the Irish to drink beer? or did they learn from the Irish to drink whiskey?' (*CR* 122). Such a question is temporally confusing, as the editor ponders the future effects of the Act of Union by asking a question about the past. It is also a question that encourages confusion, as the editor uses it to express the difficulty of establishing origins, tracing political effects and understanding historical causality. Indeed, as Daniel Hack argues, anxiety about historical influence and power are embedded in the very form of the question: it uses chiasmus to convey the 'metonymic reversibility of subject and object'.[35] Thus, the novel's ending destabilises modern institutionalism's faith in futurity by suggesting that the Union may lead to progress and improvement, but it also may lead to decline for both England and Ireland. Here, the future raises questions and prompts reflective returns to the past rather than pre-emptively deciding characters' fates.

Recognising Edgeworth's importance to realism does not simply mean extending histories of realism that currently begin with Scott or Austen back to Edgeworth. Rather, it means thinking about the limits of the institutions that shape our interpretations. For despite our preference for literary histories that follow a linear trajectory where genres are stable and self-contained, the realist novel does not have a single origin or a single trajectory; it is not a progressive story in which the 'necessary' anachronisms associated with realism and history replace the 'unnecessary' anachronisms of romance, or the institutions of the imperial state root out local customs and regional practices. As Scott Black argues, 'Novels are less sedimented forms than interactive fields'.[36] Novels are 'interactive fields', for Black, because of their anachronisms: they encourage the interplay of divergent timescales as they draw on enduring myths and local context, historical and transhistorical experience.[37] Realism can be distinguished from other novelistic forms, then, because of the particular ways in which it organises and orders this interactive field into two distinct temporalities: the shared time of institutions and the heterogeneous time of anachronisms.

Union and Futurity: Realism's Divided Temporalities

In 1829, Walter Scott famously asserted that Maria Edgeworth's fiction had done more 'towards completing the Union, than perhaps all the legislative enactments by which it has been followed up'.[38] Celebrating the political effects of literary representation, this statement shows how Edgeworth's novels mobilise public affect to support the Union as they work to transform a legislative act into an imagined community.[39] But this statement also demonstrates how, from the very beginning, the Union, as an institutional formation, mediates our approach to Edgeworth's novels. The Union created the United Kingdom of Great Britain and Ireland and established shared institutions like the Westminster parliament but did not fully integrate Ireland into these institutions. In literary histories, the Union becomes an overdetermined period designator, marking a shift from the eighteenth century to the nineteenth, as well as the beginning of 'modern' Irish writing in British forms like the novel.

For this reason, *Castle Rackrent* is understood to be the first Irish novel – although scholars have long noted the many Irish novels that preceded it – precisely because it coincides with the passage of the Union.[40] The editor notes the auspicious timing of the tale, closing his preface by including the date, 1800. He also alludes to the Union as he proleptically looks forward to the moment, 'When Ireland loses her identity by an union with Great Britain" and thus can look back with "good-humoured complacency' on the very past that the novel represents (*CR* 63). The publication date, coupled with this allusion, solidifies Edgeworth's place in Irish literary history, but sometimes at the cost of reflection on how *Castle Rackrent*'s significance extends beyond this specific historical context.

I suggest that Scott's statement about the Union works to conceptualise modern institutionalism writ large even as it points to the Union as a particular historical context for Edgeworth's fiction. In the quotation with which this section opens, Scott presents the Union as the instantiation of the protracted, future-oriented temporality of institutions rather than as a single historical event or political act.

Scott portrays the Union as a process that is moving 'towards' completion but not yet complete. The act is important because of the legislative changes it enacts as well as the future it works to secure: a completed Union that fully integrates Ireland into the United Kingdom in part by passing Catholic Emancipation.[41] Edgeworth works to 'complete' the Union in her novels, then, not simply by sympathetically portraying Ireland for an English audience but by adopting a future-oriented temporality where the Union becomes the horizon for futural imagining. In *Castle Rackrent*, the editor's proleptic jump to the time after the Union is one instance of this futural imagination. In an example of what Patrick Brantlinger calls 'proleptic elegy', the editor notes the loss of Irish identity, though it is not yet lost, in order to suggest that its loss is inevitable.[42] This prolepsis heightens the effects of the editor's frequent periodising gestures which create stark divisions between past and present. He insists that 'these are "tales of other times"' (63) and uses the past tense in the footnotes and glossary to describe Irish traditions. The subtitle, moreover, notes that the book is 'An Hibernian Tale taken from facts and from the manners of the Irish squires before the year 1782'. Working to express the distance between the past the story represents and the present of the reader, the editor's prolepsis implies that the Union will make the time before the year 1782 feel all the more distant as it works to secure modern institutionalism.

A narrative temporality that establishes institutions as the horizon of futurity is an important feature of Edgeworth's fiction beyond her direct engagement with the Union. In *Ennui* (1809), which is set before the Act of Union, Lord Glenthorn learns to think in terms of slow, future-oriented developments instead of immediate gratification as he transforms from a dissipated absentee landlord who suffers bouts of boredom into a dependable professional who thinks long-term.[43] The reward for his transformation is integration into institutions: first the law, where he works as an attorney, then marriage, then, finally, as a landlord associated with the institution of the Big House once again. *Patronage* (1814) similarly encourages an embrace of institutions – the law, professions, education, marriage – even as it dramatises how patronage warps these very institutions. Becoming a lawyer, Alfred Percy learns that moral justice and legal procedures are sometimes at odds. He admits that he 'had been so shocked at first by the apparent absurdity of the system, that he had almost abandoned the study' but, because of his continued legal study, 'he had at last discovered the utility of those rules'.[44] The novel thus encourages readers to look beyond 'the apparent absurdity' of institutions and accept their procedures as necessary even when they are fallible and fragile. The novel concludes by celebrating 'public virtue' as opposed to patronage.[45]

Castle Rackrent also works to consolidate modern institutionalism as the editor's preface, footnotes and glossary encourage the embrace of the rule of law in contradistinction to the 'honour' that Thady prefers (*CR* 68). The Glossary describes how Irish people mistakenly personalise abstract legal procedures, confusing 'justice' with 'partiality', while the story narrates how Thady's son uses these very procedures to acquire Castle Rackrent (*CR* 133). Unlike Thady, who remains attached to the past and organises his world through personal connections, his son, Jason, thinks in terms of the future and organises his world through impersonal procedures. Over the course of the story, Jason becomes an attorney and steadily acquires the Rackrent family lands. When Sir Condy Rackrent dies at the end of the story, he has nothing – he lives in the lodge on the estate that Jason owns. Thady marks Jason's transformation from a personal dependent of the Rackrent family into a professional who embraces modern institutionalism, noting: 'He had been studying the law, and had made himself attorney Quirk; so he brought down at once a heap of accounts upon my master's head' (*CR* 106). As 'attorney Quirk', Jason looks to the future, telling Sir Condy, 'We'll not be indulging ourselves in any unpleasant retrospects' (*CR* 117). Jason's professionalism and proceduralism expresses itself as a temporal orientation: unwilling to engage with a past that might question the legitimacy of his actions, Jason looks to the future guaranteed by the law.

But this future-oriented institutional time is constantly thwarted by the anachronisms that proliferate throughout Edgeworth's novel. Indeed, Thady is not only attached to an anachronistic past, but also functions as an anachronism in his own right. As Thady tells his story, the editor's footnotes remind readers that Thady's language represents how people '*formerly*' spoke in Ireland (*CR* 72). Against the grain of the editor's proleptic leaps to the time of the Union and periodising gestures that relegate the Irish manners that the novel chronicles to the past, Thady shows the continued efficacy of the past in the present, and, in the process, the possibility of imagining the future otherwise.[46] He expresses his attachment to the Rackrent family by celebrating their past, noting that they were 'one of the most ancient in the kingdom' and opening his story by telling of events that predate his service to the family (*CR* 66). Moreover, by filling Sir Condy's head with stories of his Rackrent ancestors, Thady encourages Sir Condy to imagine a future that reanimates the past. Sir Condy erects a monument to Sir Patrick and then dies as Sir Patrick did before him, of drink. Trying to recreate Sir Patrick's feat of drinking from his horn, Sir Condy 'swallows it down, and drops like one shot' (*CR* 120). Personal ties and irrational practices persist alongside the future-oriented institutional thinking that the editor embraces, showing that the future does not necessarily emerge from the past but often repeats it. Such moments, however humorous, suggest that traditional forms of sociality – hospitality and honour – endure even in a time otherwise defined by impersonal legal procedures.

Precisely because of the divided narrative structure of *Castle Rackrent*, scholars have long debated how this 'tale of other times' imagines the future, questioning whether the novel celebrates or laments Jason's successful channelling of institutional power and whether Thady actively contributes to the Rackrent family's demise or loyally supports them through their struggles. Indeed, although most histories of the Irish novel focus on *Castle Rackrent*, there is little consensus about how to understand either its politics or its form. While it is clear that the editor seeks to imagine a future that, as Mary Jean Corbett argues, consigns 'the unsettling differences of Irish culture to a vanished – albeit necessarily representable – past', the act of representing this past undermines the security of that future.[47] Thus, although Edgeworth clearly seeks to imagine the future guaranteed by modern institutionalism, the novel also actively undermines this future by returning to and reactivating the past.

I argue that this divided narrative structure, which encourages readers to choose between the editor's framework and Thady's tale, the editor's emphasis on institutional futurity and Thady's anachronisms, lays bare the formal contradictions of realism. Similar tensions and contradictions may be less pronounced in more canonical realist texts, but they are nevertheless there. Think of Elizabeth Gaskell's *Mary Barton* (1848), which describes the workers' misery 'in all its depths' in order to integrate masters and men into shared institutions.[48] As in *Castle Rackrent*, this institutional integration requires a proleptic leap. The narrator concludes by moving from the personal ties formed between masters and men in the wake of Henry Carson's murder within the time of the story to public improvements happening in the time of the discourse: 'Many of the improvements now in practice in the system of employment in Manchester, owe their origin to short earnest sentences spoken by Mr Carson.'[49] And yet, as in *Castle Rackrent*, the effort to establish institutions as the horizon of futurity is often undercut by anachronisms that survive in the present. The novel famously begins in pastoral fields with farm buildings that speak 'of other times and other occupations than those which now absorb the population of the neighbourhood' and ends in a Canadian settlement where one of the 'old primeval trees' remains, evoking the forest and Indigenous lives that predate colonial settlement while also noting their absence.[50] More than simply representing a natural landscape that marks industrial and imperial progress, Gaskell describes these fields, buildings and trees to show the disparate temporal scales and social formations that exceed the limits of institutional time.[51] The fields evoke a pastoral past that continues in an industrial era; the trees show how elements of the native landscape endure in an era of colonial settlement. Out of date but nevertheless enduring, these anachronisms point to other political possibilities as they suggest historical temporalities and trajectories that disrupt institutional time.

Later in the century, Margaret Oliphant's *Hester* (1883) expresses a similar tension between institutions and anachronisms as it chronicles the personal lives of the Vernon family in the provincial town of Redborough. Like *Castle Rackrent*, *Hester* merges familial and public institutions; the Vernon family is inseparable from Vernon's bank. But instead of modern institutionalism serving as an end of the narrative, it is the story's starting place. The young Hester arrives in Redborough and slowly integrates herself into the familial institutions, learning that 'the bank is everybody's first thought; that it must be kept up whatever fails'.[52] The conflict comes when Edward Vernon's wild financial speculations undermine institutional futurity. He dreams of escaping his role within the family, of 'Castles in the air more dazzling than ever rose in a fairy tale'.[53] Institutional futurity is restored at the end of the novel when Edward's speculations fail, he leaves the bank and family in disgrace, and Catherine Vernon, the matriarch, works with Hester to reassert the primacy of the bank and the family. To the chagrin of many readers, this novel about a strong, independent women doubles down on institutional futurity and concludes by looking forward to Hester's marriage. The narrator asserts, 'All that can be said for her is that there are two men whom she may choose between, and marry either if she please.'[54]

Although the bank and Vernon family remain the horizons for future imagining at the end of the novel, the novel's many anachronisms highlight the otherwise possibilities that persist. Throughout the novel, Catherine's power is both traditional and modern as she appears both monarchical ('she is more than the Queen') and ministerial.[55] In the moment of crisis, the narrator's analogies describing her calm demeanour reveal Catherine's dual role as a cultural throwback and a figure of modern institutionalism: 'She was like an Indian at the stake: or rather like a prime minister in his place in Parliament.'[56] The stereotypical image of the stoic Indian represents the people, practices and customs that modern institutions exclude (or, in this case, actively kill off) in order to imagine a future guaranteed through institutions. By representing Catherine simultaneously as an Indian doomed to die and a seasoned head of state who keeps the wheels of government moving, the novel demonstrates that every act to secure institutional futurity also highlights alternative temporalities and alternative political possibilities. Catherine, like Thady before her, reanimates otherwise possibilities from the past even as she works to consolidate modern institutionalism.

Ultimately, *Castle Rackrent*'s divided temporalities – its consolidation of institutional futurity that creates both unity and union, and its anachronisms that show the persistence of discordant times – draw attention to such temporal divisions within British realism more broadly. Scholars often emphasise what Jameson calls realism's 'solidity' – its representation of a social reality impervious to change.[57] But *Castle Rackrent* suggests that this solidity results from the realist novel's futural imagining rather than from its present tense. Realist novelists, like Edgeworth, work to 'complete' institutions by establishing institutions as the horizon of futurity. But against the grain of this futural 'solidity' that evacuates history are anachronisms that restore historicity to institutional time. Whether functioning as remnants of other historical moments or representing people who are excluded from modern institutions, anachronisms show the possibility of alternative political futures and social change. Realist novels do not achieve temporal consensus; they represent the discordant temporalities that comprise the historical present.

Integrating and Exposing Difference: Realism and Daily Life

Temporal and political contradictions also emerge in realist novels as they try, but fail, to integrate social, historical and geographical differences into stable narrative and institutional forms. As Roderick Ferguson suggests, institutions incorporate difference while minimising the 'ruptural possibilities' of that difference.[58] Realist novels function as institutions insofar as they work to integrate social difference into a shared understanding of ordinary, everyday life – a single, consensual time. But in Irish realist novels, such as Edgeworth's *Castle Rackrent*, the 'ruptural possibilities' of difference cannot always be minimised and everyday life continues to feel strange to English readers.[59] In these moments of rupture, social, temporal and geographical differences function like anachronisms, imagining the future otherwise precisely because they cannot be assimilated into the novel's shared time.[60] Focusing on how the strange features of everyday life are both integrated and exposed in English and Irish realist novels, I argue that realist novels set at a distance from England defamiliarise realist conventions.

Contrasting Jane Austen's enduring critical success with Maria Edgeworth's neglect, Mitzi Myers suggests that Edgeworth is *too* tied to local particulars. While Austen represents everyday life in ways that can be decontextualised, Edgeworth's fiction 'insists on its location, on a real world that it relates to and seeks to change'.[61] Myers's juxtaposition of Edgeworth's novels with Austen's implies that realism's historicity impedes its aesthetic portability: Austen's domestic realism receives transhistorical and transnational attention precisely because it can be detached from its particular context.[62] But is Edgeworth relatively neglected because she insists on a historically specific location, or because the historically specific location that she insists upon is Ireland? Can places like Ireland appear within the rubric of the ordinary, or does representing reality in Ireland always suggest the extraordinary?

I suggest that representing everyday life in Ireland demonstrates how realist novels integrate and expose difference. Local settings, distinct cultural practices and peculiar minor characters are made familiar as they are assimilated into shared institutional and novelistic forms, while forms of social and historical difference that cannot be assimilated remain strange. This contradictory dynamic explains both prevalent critiques of realism as naturalising a national, bourgeois reality and the recent impulse to see realism as a worldly form that, as Lauren Goodlad argues, represents both what 'everybody knows' – familiar spaces at the heart of the nation – and 'what everybody disavows: the imperial space subtending London's privileged place in the global network'.[63] Such claims about 'everybody' demonstrate how the nation shapes even transnational theories of realism: 'everybody' actually means English readers and thus the familiar means familiar English life. But the peculiarities that Irish novels represent suggest that as realism travels transnationally, it depicts an everyday reality that is both shared and very separate. Instead of affirming that different viewpoints and experiences 'converge upon the "same" world', as Elizabeth Deeds Ermarth argues, realist novels represent worlds within worlds.[64]

While many nineteenth-century critics and writers noted how Irish and English representations of reality differed, others bristled against these differences. David Masson's 1859 book, *British Novelists and Their Styles* – 'the first book-length monograph on fiction by a professor of English literature' and thus an important event in the institutionalisation of the novel – suggests that Irish difference makes Irish novels more successful.[65] Masson identifies thirteen distinct novelistic genres, distinguishing between 'The Novel of Scottish Life and Manners', 'The Novel of Irish Life and Manners' and 'The Novel of English Life and Manners'. While Masson claims that English novels have difficulty conveying 'that English system of life which was becoming the normal and conventional one for all', Irish and Scottish novels succeed because everyday life still contains elements of the 'barbaresque'.[66] In other words, these novels from the periphery work because everyday life in these nations deviates from the normal and conventional – it remains untimely. By contrast, Masson suggests that English novels either scale down to local regions or scale up to London, 'an epitome of the world', in order to capture heterogeneity and variety.[67] Masson thus implies that novels capture the differences and particularities of lived reality rather than creating an abstract structure of daily life. For him, novels do not represent what has already become conventional – or in the terms of my argument, what has already been institutionalised – but instead depict places where multiple modes of social organisation persist.

Despite Masson's critical celebration of Irish novels, writers like Anthony Trollope struggled with these genre distinctions because they devalued Irish novels. Trollope's first novels, set in Ireland, received so little attention that his publisher concluded, 'It is evident that readers do not like novels on Irish subjects as well as on others.'[68] After the success of his novels of English life, Trollope nevertheless turned his attention to Ireland again and wrote *Castle Richmond* (1860), a story of the Irish Famine. Again, his publisher (this time, George Smith) was suspicious: 'He wanted an English tale, on English life.'[69] In response, Trollope begins *Castle Richmond* by musing on its strange setting. The novel opens with the narrator writing, 'I wonder whether the novel-reading world – that part of it, at least, which may honour my pages – will be offended if I lay the plot of this story in Ireland,' challenging readers to disprove an 'eminent publisher' who believes that novels must represent 'daily English life' in order to sell.[70] For the narrator, Ireland does not significantly differ from other novelistic settings. He asserts: 'The readability of a story should depend, one would say, on its intrinsic merit rather than on the site of its adventures. No one will think that Hampshire is better for such a purpose than Cumberland, or Essex than Leicestershire. What abstract objection can there be to the county Cork?'[71] By questioning what 'abstract objection' there could be to Cork, the narrator implicitly makes Cork an abstraction – the very kind of abstract structure that, as Jameson suggests in 'The Realist Floor-Plan', allows realist narratives to construct daily life.[72] For Trollope, stories of 'daily life' and Irish settings are compatible, and thus generic distinctions between English and Irish novels mistakenly separate novels that share a form and a purpose.

It seems that readers remained unconvinced; *Castle Richmond*, like Trollope's earlier novels set in Ireland, was a failure. Together, Trollope's refusal of generic distinctions, his publisher's suspicion of Irish novels and Masson's celebration of novels of 'Irish Life and Manners' suggest a shared form that links English and Irish realist novels on one hand and points to Irish difference on the other. But the question remains – besides depicting a reality that differs from the conventional English one and being difficult to sell (in Trollope's case, at least) – what comprises this Irish difference? Elaine Freedgood's work on the Canadian adventure novel, *Canadian Crusoes*, is helpful here. Noting how the novel's Canadian setting reveals metaleptic movement between fact and fiction that metropolitan novels obscure, Freedgood suggests that such 'misplaced' novels make visible the formal characteristics and political effects of realism writ large.[73] Realist novels set at a distance from England are strange not because their representations of reality depart from realist conventions, but because they expose these very conventions. Thus, the opening of Trollope's *Castle Richmond*, which tries to distinguish a novel's 'intrinsic merit' from its setting, paradoxically demonstrates how setting actively shapes realist novels. Although the institutional aesthetics of realist novels try to make settings abstract – Hampshire, Cumberland and Cork should function in the same way – representing reality in Ireland is different because it defamiliarises everyday reality in England.

Castle Rackrent demonstrates how both narrative and institutional forms work to assimilate difference but, in the process, reveal social and historical relations that exceed these forms. Edgeworth manages *Castle Rackrent*'s distance from the reading public it addresses by framing the tale through a series of familiar forms: the editor presents the novel as an unmediated oral story, a historical narrative, a biography, a memoir, a tale, a novel.[74] In doing so, the editor reflects on what genre *does* as well as how it is written. Thady's unmediated account – his 'plain unvarnished tale' – does not look like the 'highly ornamental narrative[s]' from professional historians or biographers (*CR* 62). Without 'literary talents' to shape the story into a conventional biography or historical narrative, Thady simply relays the facts. But Thady's ignorance of rhetorical moves and professional expectations actually makes his story more historically accurate, according to the editor. Thady, like other biographers, helps 'collect the most minute facts relative to the domestic lives, not only of the great and good, but even of the worthless and insignificant' (*CR* 61). And precisely because he does not know narrative conventions, he can more accurately convey these facts. After celebrating Thady's historically accurate account, however, the editor quickly notes that story may not *feel* that way: 'the *ignorant* English reader' may find the events 'scarcely intelligible' or 'perfectly incredible' (*CR* 63). Nineteenth-century reviewers of Irish novels tended to agree with the editor, and praised Irish novels in which Irish characters appear 'natural, and *us* comparatively strange and foreign'.[75] By thinking about the differences between what a literary form does and how it appears, what it represents and how it feels, the editor of *Castle Rackrent* suggests that representing reality in Ireland is thus both dynamic and relational – Irish everyday life can be understood through shared genres, but it also unsettles these genres.

Every time the editor tries to frame Thady's tale through shared narrative and institutional forms, he also draws attention to Irish differences that exceed these forms. After presenting Thady's tale as history or biography, the editor shifts to suggesting that it is a novel. He indicates that the Rackrents simultaneously function as representative Irish types and novelistic characters: 'The race of the Rackrents has long since been extinct in Ireland; and the drunken Sir Patrick, the litigious Sir Murtagh, the fighting Sir Kit, and the slovenly Sir Condy, are characters which could no more be met with at present in Ireland, than Squire Western or Parson Trulliber in England' (*CR* 3). Although the editor individualises each Rackrent family member with a defining adjective, he also suggests that like *Tom Jones*'s Squire Western and *Joseph Andrews*'s Parson Trulliber before them, they are actually only characters in a novel. By shifting from history to fiction, the editor implies that Irish difference can be integrated into shared novelistic forms, even if Irish people cannot yet be fully integrated into Britain.

However, the editor's glossary works in the opposite direction, showing how peculiarities persist in novelistic forms that otherwise appear to be shared. Take, for instance, the seemingly commonplace beginning of Thady's story: 'Monday morning'.[76] It seems to be an innocuous temporal marker – the reader can assume that Thady narrates the story on 'Monday morning'. But the glossary suggests otherwise, and explains that Monday morning has cultural rather than temporal significance. The editor writes, 'Thady begins his memoirs of the Rackrent Family by dating *Monday morning*, because no great undertaking can be auspiciously commenced in Ireland on any morning but *Monday morning*. . . . All the intermediate days, between making such speeches and the ensuing Monday, are wasted' (*CR* 123). The familiar 'Monday' becomes strange as Edgeworth suggests that it represents a cultural practice rather than an actual day of the week.

Tellingly, the editor's glossary connects the strangeness of Thady's language to his anachronistic position within the narrative. When Thady describes how Lady Murtagh Rackrent expects 'duty fowls, and duty turkies, and duty geese' from her tenants, the editor explains in the glossary, 'In many leases in Ireland, tenants were *formerly* bound to supply an inordinate quantity of poultry to their landlords' (*CR* 69, *CR* 127, emphasis in the original). The editor repeats this phrase when he defines duty work, suggesting that 'It was formerly common in Ireland to insert clauses in leases, binding tenants to furnish their landlords with labourers' (*CR* 128). The editor's repeated emphasis on the term 'formerly' makes Thady's story doubly strange: it not only recounts cultural practices that are unfamiliar in England, but also references practices in Ireland that do not continue into the present. Thus, although the glossary's apparent purpose is to translate Thady's story and integrate it into English experience, the glossary's entries in fact expose the cultural and historical strangeness of that story by showing the importance of temporality. In Ireland, what is familiar is in flux and thus translation occurs across time as well as across cultural space.

While this dynamic of simultaneously integrating and exposing difference is explicit in Irish realist novels, it is not unique to Irish novels. The same dynamic, often in more implicit forms, also occurs in British realist novels of the period. My fourth chapter focuses on this dynamic in Charles Dickens's novels, as I argue that Dickens's novels reanimate anachronistic pasts to reform institutions but also suggest that minority and colonised subjects are too untimely and thus, for Dickens, remain outside of history and at odds with institutionalism altogether. Here, I focus on Trollope's *Phineas Finn* (1869), where Ireland appears both familiar and strange and Phineas's Irishness means both very much and very little over the course of the novel.[77] At times, Phineas's Irishness seems unimportant. Irish and English boroughs appear interchangeable: he begins his parliamentary career representing an Irish borough, Loughshane, but continues it by standing for an English borough, Loughton. He defies stereotypes of the lazy Irishman with the gift of gab, finding success amongst 'the working men of the party'.[78] Although Phineas may be Irish, his Irish difference can be easily assimilated. In fact, he is initially asked to stand because he is 'a safe man' rather than 'a cantankerous, red-hot semi-Fenian, running about to meetings at the Rotunda, and such-like, with views of his own about tenant-right and the Irish Church'.[79] Later in the novel, the narrator celebrates Phineas's social success by noting that few of his intimate friends even know of his origins.[80]

At other times in the novel, however, Phineas's Irishness matters very much and prevents him from finding a stable position in the government. Most notably, Phineas develops 'views of his own' and resigns his position over the question of tenant-right: 'His Irish birth and Irish connection had brought this misfortune of his country so closely home to him that he had found the task of extricating himself from it to be impossible.'[81] In his autobiography, Trollope laments the 'blunder' of making Phineas Irish, declaring: 'There was nothing to be gained by the peculiarity.'[82] Indeed, within the novel, being Irish often is a peculiarity that cannot be integrated into British institutions. Embodying realist division, Phineas thinks that 'he had two identities, – that he was, as it were, two separate persons'.[83] He is both a 'man of fashion and member of Parliament in England' and 'an Irishman of Killaloe' – he is integrated into institutions and fundamentally at odds with them.[84] Jane Elizabeth Dougherty captures this tension at the heart of the novel, understanding it as a *Bildungsroman* 'in which the young hero attempts to become assimilated into the domestic sphere of Britain through a career in "the House", an institution which also represents the apotheosis of the civil, and masculine, sphere into which post-Union Irishmen cannot quite be assimilated'.[85] As is the case in *Castle Rackrent*, the novel actively works to integrate Irish difference into familiar British forms – here 'the House' – while delimiting the peculiarities that cannot be assimilated – Finn's commitment to Ireland.

This dynamic is not limited to representing Ireland or Irishness, or even peripheral locations and minority identity positions, but also occurs whenever realist novels work to assimilate difference into the temporal rhythms and routines of everyday life and note that which cannot be assimilated. Often, this difference is historical. Take Elizabeth Gaskell's *Wives and Daughters* (1864). The subtitle declares this novel to be 'an every-day story' and the opening page indicates that the everyday, while slightly different for the disparate characters, is a shared, transhistorical structure. The church bells call 'every one to their daily work, as they had done for hundreds of years'.[86] But as the narrator establishes the scene, she also notes the institutions that have changed beyond recognition. Describing the Cumnors' school, the narrator writes:

> She and the ladies, her daughters, had set up a school; not a school after the manner of schools now-a-days, where far better intellectual teaching is given to the boys and girls of labourers and work-people than often falls to the lot of their betters in worldly estate; but a school of the kind we should call 'industrial', where girls are taught to sew beautifully, to be capital housemaids, and pretty fair cooks, and, above all, to dress neatly in a kind of charity uniform devised by the ladies of Cumnor Towers.[87]

The Cumnors' school shows how institutions structure everyday life in both the past and present. But the narrator also goes to great lengths to indicate that this school from the past has little in common with 'schools now-a-days' that readers encounter in their own lives. Thus, the Cumnors' school is both familiar and strange; it evokes a shared landscape while noting how the institutions that make up this landscape have changed.

Jane Austen excels at describing these small differences that disrupt otherwise shared structures. The novelist of 'small England', who, Myers claims, produces a decontextualised representation of everyday life, in fact constantly notes the limits and exclusions to the shared social forms she creates.[88] Focusing her narratives on English manor houses and country estates, Austen's plots often depend on places that are mentioned without being represented: in *Emma*, events are set in motion because Jane Fairfax does not accompany the newly married Dixons on their trip to Ireland, *Pride and Prejudice*'s resolution hinges on Elizabeth Bennett travelling to nearby Derbyshire rather than to the Lake District, and in *Mansfield Park*, Sir Thomas Bertram's absence in Antigua famously allows the plot to unfold.[89] The constant references to places on the margins of the novel – places at odds with everyday routines that are nevertheless necessary to understanding the material realities of everyday life – suggest that Austen's work to delimit the scope of her novel paradoxically points to historical and social relationships that the novel cannot entirely assimilate. In a telling exchange in *Emma*, Jane Fairfax and Mrs Elton discuss Jane's future as a governess. When Jane compares this employment to the selling of 'human flesh', Mrs Elton exclaims, 'You quite shock me; if you mean a fling at the slave-trade.' Jane quickly assures her, 'I did not mean, I was not thinking of the slave-trade . . . governess-trade, I assure you, was all that I had in view.'[90] The novel evokes the slave-trade in order to exclude it from the world of the novel. But such an explicit statement about what is 'in view' and what is not actually creates tension between the novel's centripetal and centrifugal forces. Mentioning locations and practices that cannot be assimilated into the novel's form fosters relationships between the novel's centre – 'small England' – and its peripheries – Ireland, Antigua, the transatlantic slave trade and even the romantic Lake District.

As realist novels represent everyday life in England and Ireland, they work to integrate diverse geographical and historical locations while noting the local particulars that cannot be integrated. These local particulars productively push against realism's drive towards consensus and institutional integration as they represent historical and social differences that exceed the novel's shared forms. When something as familiar as 'Monday morning' can be made strange, when a character's Irishness can matter both very much and very little, and when the idea of school can dramatically shift over the course of a generation, the very concept of everyday life becomes heterogeneous and discordant. This oscillation between the familiar and the strange, shared forms and that which exceeds them, suggests that realism's representation of everyday life cannot always minimise the 'ruptural possibilities' of difference. And, as I will show in the rest of this book, it is precisely through these moments of rupture that realist novels encourage readers to imagine politics and history otherwise.

Ultimately, beginning the story of realism with *Castle Rackrent* allows us rethink the relationship between realism and institutions through an attention to formal divisions in novels. For many Foucauldian critics, divisions within novels – both realist and non-realist – advance a coherent politics. As D. A. Miller famously suggests, novels seem to distinguish between everyday life and institutions only to extend the disciplinary power that undergirds both.[91] In turn, Nancy Armstrong argues that novels use stark gender divisions in order to centralise the domestic woman as a modern subject and, in the process, create a new mode of social control that applies to both women and men.[92] By contrast, I suggest that the realist novel's politics, as well as its forms, are divided. For this reason, scholars can approach *Castle Rackrent* as a feminist, anti-colonial text that critiques patriarchy, on one hand, and as a document 'in the "civilizing mission" of the English to the Irish', on the other. To use Michel de Certeau's language, the politics of the realist novel depend as much upon strategies that emerge from institutional locations and seek to convert time into space as they do on tactics, or fragmentary, temporal manoeuvres that never cohere into spatial sites.[93] Realist novels imagine a stable, solid reality while also depicting tactical ways to inhabit this reality.

Recognising these contradictory strategies and tactics in the realist novel not only allows us to see realism's divided politics, but also helps us reimagine the forms of our literary histories. *Castle Rackrent*'s critical reception and its divided form suggest that Irish novels' uneasy relationship with novelistic, critical and political institutions can actually transform the story that we tell about British realism. That story need not be simply a narrative of institutional consolidation or linear rise. Literary history might yet become comparative instead of continuous and transnational rather than national; it might move backwards and sideways as well as forward; and it might use anachronisms to question institutions rather than confirming 'anew what is already institutionalised'.

Notes

1. Edgeworth, *Castle Rackrent*, p. 137. Hereafter cited within the text, abbreviated as *CR*.
2. This approach is especially prevalent within Foucauldian criticism. Nancy Armstrong offers one version of this argument in *Desire and Domestic Fiction,* where she sees the novels as one of many modern institutions 'most responsible for domesticating culture' (p. 205). D. A. Miller offers another version in *The Novel and the Police*, in his reading of Balzac's omniscient narration, claiming, 'We are always situated inside the narrator's viewpoint, and even to speak of a "narrator" at all is to misunderstand a technique that, never identified with a *person*, institutes a faceless and multilateral regard' (p. 24).
3. Ina Ferris exemplifies this strand of argumentation in *The Achievement of Literary Authority*, where she argues that novels 'can achieve

"a place" in the canon only through recognition by the institutions granted the powers of inclusion and exclusion' (p. 15).

4. David Lloyd theorises the relationship between realism and the state, arguing that nineteenth-century Irish novels appear strange in relation to English realism because the violence they represent does not always serve the state. Thus, Irish novels challenge the systems of representation at work in 'the constitution of the political state as in that of the novel' (*Anomalous States*, p. 145).

5. Joe Cleary tracks how the form of our literary histories contributes to misunderstanding nineteenth-century Irish novels. He argues that Irish studies scholars employ 'the dominant models of English literary historiography' – namely, understanding the novel as a linear development and through a nationalist framework – in ways that encourage scholars to understand the nineteenth-century Irish novel as a failure ('The nineteenth-century Irish novel', p. 204). Also see W. P. Ryan who traces a tradition of Irish literature – including Irish realism – suggesting that Irish literary production does not follow a single path of development or even result from shared institutions. In his words, 'We have no straight record of growth, of influences, of development to follow. The chief workers are curiously independent of one another' ('The Best Irish Books', p. 90).

6. Deane, *Strange Country*, p. 31. In *Heathcliff and the Great Hunger*, Terry Eagleton argues that 'language is weapon, dissemblance, seduction, apologia – anything, in fact, but *representational*; it is in a perpetual condition of untruth, and truth can thus only be imported from the outside, by those disinterested enough to represent the people accurately both to others and to themselves' (p. 171). Sara Maurer aptly describes these contradictory approaches to Edgeworth in *The Dispossessed State*. Maurer explains that scholars approach Edgeworth both as 'the modestly dispossessed author' who does not own her own writing and the 'jealously possessive colonist' who encourages the Anglo-Irish monopoly on land (*The Dispossessed State*, p. 20).

7. Nancy Armstrong shows the gendered implications of institutions mediating the stories we tell in *Desire and Domestic Fiction* as she claims, 'Of late, it seems particularly apparent that such attempts to explain the history of the novel fail because – to a man – history is represented as the history of male institutions' (p. 7).

8. Brown, 'Why the Story of the Origin of the (English) Novel is an American Romance (If Not the Great American Novel)', p. 14.

9. Ibid. p. 14.

10. Here, I'm especially taking up Dipesh Chakrabarty's work in postcolonial theory in *Provincializing Europe*, p. 243.

11. Rohy, 'Ahistorical', p. 69.

12. Joe Cleary makes one version of this argument in 'Realism after Modernism and the Literary World-System', suggesting that modernism is

antithetical to realism and defining the former as 'the attempt to create a more radically cosmopolitan (whether of the right or of the left variety) idea of literature' (p. 261).

13. 'The Croppy, a Tale of 1798', p. 410. As a reviewer suggests in 'The Novels of Mr Anthony Trollope', 'Mr Trollope's novels may be divided into three classes, the clerical, the domestic, and the Irish' (p. 405).

14. For instance, G. Barnett Smith praises William Carleton for being 'one of the truest, the most powerful, and the tenderest delineators of Irish life' who challenged 'the constant misrepresentations of the character of his countrymen' ('A Brilliant Irish Novelist', p. 113).

15. 'Banim and the Irish Novelists', p. 270.

16. 'North and South', p. 403.

17. René Wellek, 'The Concept of Realism in Literary Scholarship', p. 229. Caroline Levine also traces realism's untimeliness as she argues that Victorians used the term realism to suggest a 'skeptical method' that put 'mimesis to the test' although later critics tend to associate realism with mimesis (*The Serious Pleasures of Suspense*, p. 12).

18. Scott himself indicates that he seeks 'to emulate the admirable Irish portraits drawn by Miss Edgeworth' (*Waverley*, p. 341). Jan Fergus argues that few scholars study Edgeworth's influence on Austen because of a lack of critical interest in Edgeworth's fiction and goes on to show that Edgeworth's early experiments with free indirect discourse influenced Austen's narrative techniques ('"Pictures of Domestic Life in Country Villages"', pp. 544–6).

19. As early as 1810, Anna Letitia Barbauld celebrated Edgeworth for her virtuous writing, claiming that her novels recommend 'order, neatness, industry, sobriety', in 'On the Origin and Progress of Novel Writing', p. 47. Classifying Edgeworth's novels as 'improvement fiction' – utilitarian writing that participated in a larger project of 'agricultural improvement, pedagogy, and estate management' – Helen O'Connell continues to encourage such an approach to Edgeworth's novels in *Ireland and the Fiction of Improvement*, p. 8.

20. 'Popular Tales by Maria Edgeworth', p. 461.

21. 'The Life and Letters of Maria Edgeworth', p. 322.

22. Katherine O'Donnell exemplifies this approach in 'Castle Stopgap', pp. 115–30. Margot Backus offers a different approach, and sees Edgeworth as producing a 'gothic realism' that ironises realist conventions in *The Gothic Family Romance*, p. 98. In *The Achievement of Literary Authority*, Ina Ferris also sees Edgeworth as a realist, arguing that 'Both *Castle Rackrent* and *Waverley* make the realist claim to nonfiction, more precisely to historical value, and each couches the claim in a narrative frame' (p. 108). Jacqueline Belanger considers Edgeworth's relationship with realism as well, suggesting that she questions whether readers can trust representations of Irish reality, even when they are grounded in experience. '"Le vrai n'et pas toujours vraisemblable,"' p. 115.

23. As a reviewer of Edgeworth's *Tales of Fashionable Life* indicates: 'the *national novel* – which, embodying, as it does, the characteristics of a people, their manners, their feelings, their faults, and their virtues, may be made the vehicle of conveying the most important truths, and of exciting a strong interest and sympathy in the minds of those to whom the nation in question would otherwise have been a name, and nothing more' ('*Tales of Fashionable Life*', p. 496).
24. '*Tales of Fashionable Life*', p. 498.
25. 'The Life and Letters of Maria Edgeworth', p. 317.
26. Seamus Deane's *Strange Country* was influential in encouraging approaches that emphasised Edgeworth's Anglo-Irish position and pro-English politics.
27. Following Sandra M. Gilbert and Susan Gubar's reading of Edgeworth as one of the many 'dutiful daughter-writers' in the nineteenth century, feminist scholars often celebrate Castle Rackrent precisely because Edgeworth wrote it without her father's guidance, displaying an originality that her father suppresses in her later fiction (*The Madwoman in the Attic*, p. 148). Clíona Ó Gallchoir traces this criticism and challenges it in *Maria Edgeworth: Women, Enlightenment and Nation*, pp. 60–1. Edgeworth's fiction is also taken up by scholars of the British empire; as Suvendrini Perera argues, Castle Rackrent provides a model 'for representing colonial relations elsewhere in the empire' (*Reaches of Empire*, pp. 32–3).
28. Yoon Sun Lee is a notable exception, recently arguing that Edgeworth's 'bad plots' 'represent a crucial step in the development of fictional realism' because they produce objectivity and facts within fictional space in 'Bad Plots and Objectivity', p. 36. Making this argument, Lee first wrestles with Edgeworth's neglect in genre studies and the fact that her novels have not entered the literary canon.
29. Gamer, 'Maria Edgeworth and the Romance of Real Life', p. 235.
30. Lukács, *The Historical Novel*, p. 63. Tellingly, when Anna Letitia Barbauld traces the history of the novel in 'On the Origin and Progress of Novel-Writing', she laments the anachronisms of romance, noting that 'it is full of the grossest anachronisms' (p. 9).
31. Lukács, p. 63.
32. Brown, *Institutions of the English Novel from Defoe to Scott*, p. 140.
33. Scott, *Waverley*, p. 322.
34. For this reason, in *Scott's Shadows*, Ian Duncan turns to *Castle Rackrent* to explain the strange temporalities at work in nineteenth-century Scottish fiction – even *Waverley*. Duncan goes so far as to name Edgeworth 'a modern founder of the Scottish school' (p. 72).
35. Hack, 'Inter-Nationalism', p. 150.
36. Black, 'Quixotic Realism and the Romance of the Novel', p. 241.
37. In Black's words, 'the claim of the novel to be an index of historicity rests on the genre's ability to register the irresolvable interplay of

divergent scales of history (the long time of myth and the local time of
realism), or – same thing – the genre's ability to model and provoke the
anachronisms necessarily entailed in reading' ('Quixotic Realism and
the Romance of the Novel', p. 243).
38. Scott, 'General Preface [1829]', p. 352.
39. See, for instance, Ferris, *The Romantic National Tale and the Question
of Ireland*, pp. 12–13.
40. Mullen, 'Anachronistic Aesthetics', pp. 238–9. Derek Hand also makes
this argument, suggesting that critics return to the novel because of
'the fortunate timing of its publication in 1800' (*A History of the Irish
Novel*, p. 60).
41. Ina Ferris and Claire Connolly both note how the Union was understood to be incomplete and thus inspired literary and discursive production. See Ferris, *The Romantic National Tale and the Question of
Ireland*, p. 6, and Connolly, *A Cultural History of the Irish Novel,
1790*, pp. 32–3. In 'The other within', Kevin Whelan argues that the
Union was the beginning of a larger process of imperial rationalisation
(pp. 15–16).
42. Brantlinger, *Dark Vanishings*, p. 4.
43. Lord Glenthorn's personal transformation suggests a broader historical
transformation from violence to law and order. As Patrick O'Malley
argues, '*Ennui* invokes historical violence precisely in order to defang
it, to transform it into the raw material for a future-oriented liberalism that can safely forget it' ('"The length, breadth, and depth, of the
wound"', p. 151).
44. Edgeworth, *Patronage*, p. 278.
45. Ibid. p. 623.
46. Mullen, 'Anachronsitic Aesthetics', p. 259.
47. Corbett, *Allegories of the Union in Irish and English Writing*, p. 50.
Of course, because the editor so heavily relies on prolepsis to secure
modern institutionalism, there is not even scholarly consensus about
the editor's drive towards futurity. As Marilyn Butler argues, 'There
is no sense of the impending future in it – no clash between the Rackrents' values and those of the people replacing them' (p. 357). Butler usefully traces contradictory readings of *Castle Rackrent* as both
the most nationalist of Edgeworth's tales and not nationalist enough
(pp. 391–3). Recently, Patrick O'Malley suggests in *Liffey and Lethe*
that the constant movement between past and future complicates the
present of the novel, suggesting that there seems to be 'a temporality
both evacuated of fantasies of past and future and filled with them' as
he argues that the novel moves between 'historical remembrance' and
'strategic forgetting in the interest of an ameliorative move into the
future' (p. 8).
48. Gaskell, *Mary Barton*, p. 83.
49. Ibid. p. 374.

50. *Mary Barton*, p. 5, p. 378.

51. Thus, the novel does not simply have difficulty achieving narrative simultaneity, as Helena Michie argues, but instead actively represents history occurring through different temporal paces and scales in ways that undermine the forms of temporal consensus that the narrative imagines ('Hard Times, Global Times', pp. 605–26).

52. Oliphant, *Hester*, p. 49.

53. Ibid. p. 131.

54. Ibid. p. 456.

55. Ibid. p. 42.

56. Ibid. p. 424.

57. Jameson, *The Antinomies of Realism*, p. 5.

58. Ferguson, *The Reorder of Things*, p. 18.

59. Here, I am building on David Lloyd's argument in *Anomalous States* that realism works to integrate the individual and the local community 'into the larger frame of national society', which he suggests ultimately requires 'the negation or exclusion of what cannot be drawn into identity' (p. 152). But unlike Lloyd, I suggest that this dynamic is present in English as well as Irish realism and that the novel's resolution does not close down the political possibilities that the unassimilable elements within the novel suggest.

60. In *Novels of Everyday Life*, Laurie Langbauer suggests that women novelists used domestic realism's emphasis on everyday life to play with this dynamic. She argues that women use novelistic conventions to critique the novel's gendered ideology and to render everyday life a site of contradiction and contestation. In her words, 'An emphasis on the everyday may provide instead a way of inhabiting those confines [of the everyday], working with them, without simply overlooking them or accepting them as natural' (p. 58).

61. Mitzi Myers, 'Shot from Canons', p. 197. Joseph Rezek has made a similar argument more recently, in *London and the Making of Provincial Literature*, suggesting that Austen's realism imagines a small England that Edgeworth and other Irish writers were distanced from (p. 63). Also see John Plotz, who considers how Austen's novels create a 'known place' in 'The Semi-Detached Provincial Novel', p. 408.

62. Many Irish studies scholars similarly claim that the historicity of Irish novels makes them less portable and less successful. Sean Ryder claims that 'Unlike F. R. Leavis's "great traditions" of nineteenth-century fiction and poetry, which were canons ostensibly constructed on moral and aesthetic grounds, Irish literary historians have usually based their claims for the value of nineteenth-century texts on their historical or political importance' in 'Literature in English', p. 122. James Murphy makes a similar argument in 'Canonicity', pp. 45–54.

63. Goodlad, *The Victorian Geopolitical Aesthetic*, p. 33.

64. Ermarth, *Realism and Consensus in the English Novel*, p. x.

65. Farina, 'On David Masson's *British Novelists and their Styles* (1859) and the Establishment of Novels as an Object of Academic Study'. Nicholas Dames suggests that Masson's work differs from most literary theory in the Victorian period, which tends to be amateurish and was still in the process of institutionalisation, in 'Realism and Theories of the Novel', p. 290.

66. Masson, *British Novelists and Their Styles*, p. 219.

67. Ibid. p. 328.

68. Trollope, *An Autobiography*, p. 78. Of course, it is also important to note that despite the failure of these Irish novels, 'Ireland did indeed "make" Trollope,' as Mary Jean Corbett argues (*Allegories of the Union in Irish and English Writing*, p. 115). Trollope worked for the Post Office in Ireland, and as his autobiography suggests, living in Ireland allowed him to make and save more money than he would have in England.

69. Trollope, *An Autobiography*, p. 142.

70. Trollope, *Castle Richmond*, p. 1, p. 2.

71. Ibid. p. 2.

72. In this essay, Jameson argues that realist novels produce a new 'spatial and temporal configuration itself: what will come to be called "daily life"' ('The Realist Floor-Plan', p. 375). Jameson suggests that this configuration works as a form of programming, creating an abstract structure through which we apprehend specific details.

73. Freedgood, 'Fictional Settlements', p. 394.

74. As Patrick O'Malley argues in his reading of the novel as simultaneously 'history, memoir, novel', each of these forms understand the past differently (*Liffey and Lethe*, p. 7).

75. 'The Croppy, a Tale of 1798', p. 411.

76. I discuss how this defamiliarisation of 'Monday morning' depends upon metalepsis in Mullen, 'Anachronistic Aesthetics', p. 252.

77. As Jane Elizabeth Dougherty argues in 'An Angel in the House', Phineas's Irishness 'is both crucial and incidental to his characterization' (p. 133).

78. Trollope, *Phineas Finn*, vol. II, p. 241.

79. Trollope, *Phineas Finn*, vol. I, p. 6.

80. Ibid. p. 200.

81. Trollope, *Phineas Finn*, vol. II, p. 340.

82. Trollope, *An Autobiography*, p. 318.

83. Trollope, *Phineas Finn*, vol. I, p. 330.

84. Ibid. p. 330.

85. Dougherty, 'An Angel in the House', p. 136.

86. Gaskell, *Wives and Daughters*, p. 3.

87. Ibid. p. 7.

88. Moretti, *Atlas of the European Novel*, p. 19.

89. Edward Said famously argues that 'Thomas Bertram's slave planta-
    tion in Antigua is mysteriously necessary to the poise and beauty
    of Mansfield Park', *Culture and Imperialism*, p. 59. Joseph Rezek
    reflects on the fact that Elizabeth Bennett goes to Derbyshire instead
    of the Lake District (*London and the Making of Provincial Litera-
    ture*, pp. 62–3).
90. Austen, *Emma*, p. 279.
91. Miller, *The Novel and the Police*, pp. 97–101.
92. Armstrong, *Desire and Domestic Fiction*, pp. 8–11.
93. Certeau, *The Practice of Everyday Life*, p. xix.

Part II

Forgetting and Remembrance

Chapter 2

William Carleton's and Charles Kickham's Ethnographic Realism

'The "living Present?" and the "dead Past?" We hold that the Past is the more living of the two, sometimes.'[1]

'Beauty, whether mental or physical, is ignored by Parliament.'[2]

Studying nineteenth-century Irish realism raises questions about the relationship between realism and ethnography. As James Buzard suggests, all realism is ethnographic insofar as it offers thick descriptions of everyday cultural life.[3] Realism and ethnography share an epistemological interest in lived experience as opposed to abstract theory. They also share a primary formal tension between sociological details – descriptions of individual acts, cultural practices, local events – and a sense of a unified whole – the idea of culture that unites and thereby explains these disparate acts, practices and events.

But if all realism is ethnographic, not all ethnographic writing qualifies as realist. Indeed, literary critics have used 'ethnography' to separate realistic nineteenth-century Irish writing with a cultural focus from the literary genre of realism.[4] In this criticism, realism is a modern, metropolitan genre that produces shared time, while ethnography represents peripheral, premodern cultures through anachronisms.[5] For instance, critics celebrate William Carleton (1794–1869) and Charles Joseph Kickham (1828–82), the two authors on whom I focus in this chapter, for their authentic portrayals of Irish life without understanding them as realist writers. Unlike Maria Edgeworth, whose authenticity is often questioned because she writes from an Anglo-Irish position, Carleton and Kickham are both native Irish, Catholic writers.[6] Nineteenth-century critics praise Carleton as a 'peasant novelist' and note Kickham's thorough knowledge of and sympathy for the Irish middle and lower classes.[7] Their novels capture everyday life in rural Irish communities, representing Irish dialect, gossip, music, sport and religious practices.

Scholars today suggest that Carleton's and Kickham's novels are not realist precisely because they are ethnographic. Their writing is understood as an authentic expression of a peripheral culture rather than realist representation, extra-literary experience rather than literary form.[8] Reading Carleton's fiction, for instance, Terry Eagleton claims that ethnography caters to 'the anthropological curiosity of the outsider', while realism integrates fact and fiction, anthropology and literature, politics and plot.[9] Marjorie Howes similarly notes the 'formal fragmentation' of Carleton's fiction.[10] In turn, David Lloyd suggests that while Charles Kickham's political work as a Fenian is important, his novels are too sentimental to be considered realist.[11] Such accounts define the nineteenth-century Irish novel through its failure to reproduce English literary realism, which tends to be associated with unity, formal integration and temporal consensus.

In contrast, I argue that Carleton's and Kickham's 'formal fragmentation' demonstrates how ethnography and realism in fact share a divided narrative temporality that moves between modern institutions and anachronisms. By focusing on ethnographic realism's formal divisions, I build on Buzard's argument that metropolitan British novels are 'self-interrupting forms' where narrators dynamically move between the position of a cultural insider and an outsider.[12] These novels depict an *'insider's outsideness* – "outside enough" to apprehend the shape of the culture (and its possibilities of reform)' but 'inside enough' to participate in this very culture.[13] But while Buzard argues that these narrative interruptions ultimately lead to formal and cultural unity – the idea of a self-contained national cultural unit – Carleton's and Kickham's novels instead suggest that narrative interruptions can also reveal unresolved divisions and important political differences both within a national culture and across nations. Narrative interruptions unsettle the apparent coherence of the political and social order and imagine politics otherwise.

For Carleton and Kickham, spatial movement between an insider's immersion in a culture and an outsider's perspective also produces temporal movement between Irish traditions that seem to be remnants of a premodern time and the supposed modernity of the reading audience. Insofar as this movement confirms institutions as the horizon of futurity, it upholds modern institutionalism. Carleton's *The Black Prophet* (1847), for instance, transfers authority from cultural practices like prophecy to abstract institutions – the rule of law, the legislature – and concludes with the execution of Donnel Dhu, the corrupt prophecy man, after he is found guilty by a court of law. But the movement between traditional practices and modern institutions does not travel in only one direction: it also produces anachronisms that imagine alternative political futures. While Kickham's novels foster an anti-institutional, and anti-English, political stance, Carleton's fiction suggests that institutions themselves should be subject to ethnographic observation – that is, understood through their everyday practices rather than their abstract principles.

I claim that the very formal features that critics consider characteristically Irish – ethnographic intrusions, self-interrupting narrative forms – also make Carleton's and Kickham's novels realist. In fact, Carleton's 'formal unevenness' and Kickham's discordant plots exemplify the productive tensions and self-interruptions that realist representation requires.[14] I pair these novels with my reading of George Eliot's provincial fiction in the next chapter, where I argue that Eliot also moves between past and present in order to interrupt a historical narrative of institutional consolidation. The self-interruptions in Carleton's and Kickham's ethnographic realism, like the self-interruptions in Eliot's provincial realism, are not exceptional, but show how realism works. Realism is not a coherent form that integrates social and historical difference, but instead a dynamic that moves between the shared temporality of institutions and the heterogeneous historical time of anachronisms.

Although both Carleton and Kickham produce ethnographic realist writing that moves between institutions and anachronisms, reading these two authors together is in many ways counter-intuitive.[15] Carleton was a liberal conservative who favoured the Union between England and Ireland; his troubled relationship with institutions resulted from his careerist approach to writing and contentious personality. By contrast, Kickham more self-consciously rejected English institutions – and modern institutionalism – as he embraced the revolutionary Fenian cause.[16] Stylistically, their writing also differs: Carleton is famous for his peasant characters and authentic dialogue but criticised for his inability to merge plot with politics, while Kickham made his name by recycling conventional realist plots in his sentimental representations of pastoral communities. Yeats emphasised these stylistic differences, claiming that while Carleton's writing remained that of a true Irish peasant, Kickham made the mistake of reading – and, worse, liking – Dickens.[17] Despite their distinct political positions and literary approaches, Carleton's and Kickham's novels are formally similar insofar as their representations of traditional Irish life highlight politicised temporal divisions between its premodern elements and English modernity.

Reading Carleton's *Valentine M'Clutchy, the Irish Agent* (1845) and *The Black Prophet: A Tale of Irish Famine* (1847) alongside Kickham's *Knocknagow; or the Homes of Tipperary* (1873), I show how Carleton and Kickham insist on the importance of personal experience, local context and heterogeneous time in the face of institutional abstractions, or formal procedures as opposed to embodied practices.[18] Reducing the unsettling effects of local differences and particularities, institutional abstractions depend upon a process of forgetting. Carleton suggests that British governmental institutions actively forget just how prevalent and pervasive famine is in Ireland, while Kickham claims that British statesmen forget the violence that the Irish people remember. Both novelists imply that, through a process of forgetting, modern institutionalism – the discourse that locates modernity and futurity in institutions – tries to convert the 'living Present' into the 'dead Past'. Anachronisms in these novels, however, remind readers of what institutions forget. In the process, they view social organisation otherwise by imagining political futures that emerge from lived experience rather than abstract principles.

Ultimately, Carleton's and Kickham's ethnographic realism offers a new way to think about ethnographic time on the one hand and realist novels on the other, precisely because their novels do not result in formal integration. Ethnography famously produces a temporal division between ethnographers and the cultures they study, thereby constructing an imperial narrative of the vanishing primitive. Although ethnographers interact with the people whose cultures they study in a shared present, ethnographic representation emphasises the spatial and historical distance that separates the two cultural positions.[19] As a result, the practice of ethnography converts a heterogeneous historical time in which diverse cultural traditions and institutions coexist into a homogeneous, linear developmental trajectory through which particular cultural traditions disappear as modern institutions are consolidated. Realism is one such modern institution insofar as it participates in the ethnographic project that narrates distinct cultural practices in ways that minimise their disruptive potential. As I argued in the previous chapter, the realist novel's narrative procedures and prescriptions – its formalisms – work to assimilate cultural difference.

However, Carleton and Kickham do not use ethnography to consolidate modern institutions as an inevitable future for seemingly backward Irish people. Instead, they show that modern institutionalism is one narrative and cultural form among many. In their hands, the temporal divisions upon which ethnography and realism both depend do not simply establish institutions as the horizon of futurity, but also ask what has been forgotten in the standardisation of social practices, social spaces and historical time. Carleton and Kickham chronicle everyday cultural life in ways that highlight dynamic movement across disparate cultural scales – the local, the national and the transnational – that are not easily fused into a shared and stable narrative form. Their formal unevenness emphasises lived experiences that exceed a single cultural framework and do not resolve into a sense of shared time. Their ethnographic realism is thus able to imagine political futures at odds with modern institutionalism.

Modern Institutionalism and Irish Literature

In the nineteenth century, Irish culture was understood as antithetical to modern institutionalism. English authorities and the English public perceived Irish culture as backward, oral and violent; Ireland supposedly needed large-scale institutional interventions in order to become modern.[20] For Helen O'Connell, nineteenth-century Irish writing both spreads these views and seeks to modernise Irish people through 'improvement fiction' that relegates 'backward' Irish practices to the past where they properly belong. 'Improvement fiction' is a realist genre that consolidates institutional futures secured through schools, laws, regulations and desires in order to render 'the fraught tensions of post-Union Ireland an anachronism'.[21] In contrast, according to David Lloyd, nineteenth-century Irish novels refuse modern institutionalism and instead represent 'forms of social organisation and resistance inassimilable to either the legality of the British state or the political desire of nationalism which is for the state'.[22] He implies that nineteenth-century Irish writers celebrate rather than subdue the unruly politics of anachronism.

Critics have thus identified two responses to modern institutionalism in Ireland: imagining institutional futures in order to root out Irish backwardness and embracing anachronism in order to refuse assimilation into the British state. I argue that these are not mutually exclusive positions, but rather dynamically overlap in nineteenth-century Irish realist novels. On the one hand, representations of everyday life in Ireland provide readers with cultural knowledge so that Irish people can be better incorporated into British institutions. Employing a familiar trope in Irish fiction, Kickham has a character assert that the leases would be more fair if the landlord could only 'see personally how his estate is managed' (*K* 118). Insofar as realist novels offer one way for readers to do just this – to *see* everyday life in Ireland – they assimilate seemingly backward Ireland into modern institutions. However, Irish novels not only change how readers see Ireland, but also change how they see institutions and understand the broader theory of modern institutionalism. Representing the temporal disjunction between traditional Irish culture and modern institutions, Carleton and Kickham show that institutional assimilation is not the only path to modernity. They insist that local differences and personal memories do not signify Irish 'backwardness'; instead they productively resist the homogenising forces that define modernity entirely through institutions.

Carleton, for instance, presents the development of Irish literature alongside 'the progress of science' and 'improvements in steam and machinery', suggesting that literature, like these technological developments, fosters 'mutual intercourse' and thus 'mutual respect' between England and Ireland.[23] He also argues that national literature is important insofar as it establishes cultural institutions. After chronicling the genius of Irish writers such as Maria Edgeworth, Lady Morgan, Anna Maria Hall, Gerald Griffin and John Banim, Carleton comes to a surprising conclusion: that Ireland is 'utterly destitute of a national literature' (*TS* v). He contends that although these authors successfully represent Ireland to an English reading public, they fail to contribute to Irish culture because their success hinges on English publishing houses, audiences and literary markets. Employing a provocative metaphor, Carleton declares: 'Our men and women of genius uniformly carried their talents to the English market, whilst we laboured at home under all the dark privations of a literary famine' (*TS* v). Instead of nourishing Irish readers, Irish literature is exported to England. Shifting from the question of literary 'genius' to literary institutions, Carleton defines national literature in terms of its effects: the extent to which it creates '*in her* [Ireland] a taste for literature or science' (*TS* v). Implying that the Irish people do not yet have a taste for literature or science, Carleton looks forward to a future improved through the strengthening of cultural institutions.

And yet, despite this explicit plea to use literature to develop national institutions, Carleton derives authority from his authentic experience rather than an institutional position. Many critics suggest that Carleton was able to produce original, lively portraits of Irish life precisely because he lacked education and knowledge of novelistic conventions. Yeats, for instance, celebrates Carleton as a 'true peasant' who surpassed Maria Edgeworth's literary accomplishments 'with no conscious art at all'.[24] Yeats was not alone in his assessment. One critic goes so far as to trace Carleton's literary success to his evolutionary backwardness: 'In his genius there is much of clay and the earth – of the animal'.[25]

Carleton savvily moves between these two positions – the voice of modern institutionalism and that of the true peasant untouched by modern institutions – as he reflects on his literary career. In the 'Auto-biographical Introduction' added to an 1843 edition of his most popular work, *Traits and Stories of the Irish Peasantry* (1830), Carleton suggests that while his native origins establish his cultural authenticity, his willingness to locate such origins in the past establishes his authority as a writer. For example, he notes the decline of the Irish language: 'In my own native place, for instance, there is not by any means so much Irish spoken now, as there was about twenty or five-and-twenty years ago' (*TS* ii). Carleton implies that although the village lives on unchanged in his fiction, its authentic culture no longer exists in reality. Similarly, when explaining his literary success, Carleton points to his 'uninterrupted intercourse with the people as one of themselves, until I . . . left the dark mountains and green vales of my native Tyrone, and began to examine human life and manners as a citizen of the world' (*TS* viii). The 'until' registers the move from unmediated experience to novelistic authority: English readers can trust Carleton's stories of the Irish peasantry not simply because of his 'uninterrupted intercourse' with them, but also because he has left them behind to live in Dublin as 'a citizen of the world'.

In this autobiographical narrative, Carleton highlights the temporal gap between the culture he represents (his 'native Tyrone', where the Irish language and other traditional practices are disappearing) and the position he represents it from (the ever-present position of 'a citizen of the world'). But, tellingly, because Carleton's cultural authority results from moving between two positions in Ireland – Tyrone and Dublin – he emphasises differences within the nation rather than representing it as a bounded whole.[26] Indeed, even as Carleton discusses the importance of developing a national literature, he reveals the local differences that make it difficult to describe 'the general character of our people' (*TS* xxi). He repeatedly distinguishes between the provincial locations where peasants live and 'the metropolis', Dublin, where he writes (*TS* vi). He notes how hedge schools – rural, community schools that resulted from the penal code's suppression of education in Ireland – brought diverse students together, 'rich and poor', but then quickly qualifies this claim by adding the parenthetical aside, '(I speak of the peasantry)' (*TS* xi). This aside suggests that the peasantry both does and does not represent the Irish nation. While representations of the peasantry can provide insight into traditional Irish practices, distinct forms of communal life and the effects of unjust British laws, they alone cannot capture national character. For Carleton, the 'general character' of Irish people must account for both the peasantry and the people living in the metropolis, Protestants and Catholics, landlords and tenants, counties like Tipperary where agrarian outrages are prevalent and counties that peacefully accept the existing land system. Although he wants to represent the 'general' character of Irish people, Carleton suggests that it is not yet possible – and that such generalisation, in Ireland, will be more possible in the future as modern institutions take hold.

As Carleton's attention to local differences shows, although he believes that literature should participate in a process of modernisation and institution building, his writing resists the abstractions upon which modern institutionalism depends. Instead of unifying Irish culture as an abstract whole, he complicates the very idea of a 'general' national character as he moves between locations and across cultural scales. Carleton is simultaneously a provincial novelist who represents his native Tyrone in relation to metropolitan Dublin, a national novelist who distinguishes between Irish and English cultural institutions, a British novelist who seeks to further the union between England and Ireland by fostering 'mutual respect' and 'mutual intercourse' (*TS* iv). By shifting between these distinct but overlapping cultural frameworks, his writing not only establishes his cultural authority as a novelist, but also, crucially, resists easy assimilation into institutions by refusing to align the particular with the general or to move from the concrete to the abstract.

Carleton's movement between cultural frameworks emphasises a plural historical time where modernisation is not simply a process of institutional integration. For although Carleton points to the different cultural institutions that might allow us to better generalise about Irish national character in the future – local schools, a more robust national education system, a more enlightened and equal Union between England and Ireland – his depiction of local differences in the present also refuses that neat linear narrative. In the present, Ireland and Irish national character emerges through shifting social relationships among starkly divided cultural positions – Catholic and Protestant, tenants and landlords, rich and poor, law-abiding citizens and violent agitators – as well as among distinct cultural locations – Tyrone and Dublin, Ireland and England, Ireland and Britain. These relationships do not cohere into an abstract cultural space and cannot be consolidated into a single institutional form.[27] Insofar as Carleton legitimates these overlapping, often unstable social relationships, his work contemplates the political possibilities of being untimely – of stubbornly refusing to be assimilated into either shared institutional time or abstract cultural space. In these moments, Ireland's supposed backwardness does not need to be corrected by institutions: it productively unsettles the belief that institutions are the only form of modern sociality or the only path to modernity.

Kickham similarly moves between embracing and refusing modern institutionalism in his novels. For Kickham, politics preceded writerly ambitions. Starting out as a repealer eager to catch a glimpse of Daniel O'Connell at a monster meeting, Kickham radicalised to become a Fenian who rejected parliamentary politics and favoured revolution over reform. He published poetry, ballads and articles in various newspapers before working for the Fenian newspaper *Irish People*. Claiming that parliamentary politics are a 'demoralising sham', Kickham insisted that even if laws were reformed and policies changed, Parliament would preserve the same structure of authority that did not – and, to his mind, could never – represent the Irish people.[28] Having learned from the failure of the Young Ireland rebellion in 1848, the Fenians actively worked to improve their tactics and organisation so they could challenge the British state.[29] Unlike the Repeal movement, they broke with Catholic authorities who feared, and preached against, revolution and violence. Mobilising what Amy Martin calls 'a radical critique of institutionality in the form of both Church and state', Fenians challenged the narrow boundaries of 'legitimate' political action.[30] When the paper was suppressed, Kickham's public trial (and more public release from prison) increased his fame and encouraged him to publish the two novels for which he is now best known, *Sally Cavanagh; or Untenanted Graves* (1869) and the Irish classic, *Knocknagow; or, the Homes of Tipperary* (1873).

Given Kickham's firm political convictions, his novels' sentimental, elegiac and nostalgic tone sometimes surprises contemporary critics. As Emer Nolan suggests, *Knocknagow* seems to be more interested in cultivating an Irish pastoral ideal than encouraging Fenian politics.[31] Kickham recounts the evils of the land system, questions British military presence and police practices in Ireland, criticises the workhouse, and remembers the communal politics of the 1798 rebellion that the English brutally and violently suppressed – but when a victim of the land system, Mick Brien, contemplates murder, the novel celebrates the fact that he does not go through with it.

Because politics are present in *Knocknagow* but often seem to be less important than the novel's representation of traditional Irish life, the novel was easily institutionalised by the Irish Free State and subsequent Republic. While *Knocknagow* stages a conflict between official state history and native Irish remembering, it tends to be taken up in ways that allow native Irish remembering to achieve the aesthetic authority of official history.[32] Well into the twentieth century, Irish people turned to *Knocknagow* because it taught moral lessons, offered an Irish counterpart to Dickens's 'English Christmas' and was appropriate for nationally focused English classes in Ireland.[33] In 1953, the post office considered issuing a 'special "Knocknagow" stamp', and in 1939, official state receptions closed with performances of *Knocknagow*.[34] Although the novel is now out of print, Kickham continues to be mentioned in newspaper reports of particularly exciting hurling games and featured in documentaries of the history of Irish national sport because of his lively description of a hurling match in the middle of the novel.

Yet *Knocknagow*, like Carleton's fiction, questions whether modernisation consists solely of institutional integration or institution building. Although Wat Murphy asserts that an independent parliament would lead to a more just land system – as this character puts it, 'An Irish Parliament wouldn't thrate 'em that way' – the novel spends most of its energy critiquing institutions rather than trying to build new ones (*K* 617). The problem with modern institutionalism, for Kickham, is that the State and other institutional forms pre-emptively render the past 'dead'. Thus, the novel's nostalgia – its seeming retreat into the past – is not a retreat into idealised traditions but rather a way to illustrate the futurity that modern institutionalism has foreclosed.

Tellingly, the novel is most oriented towards the past in moments when the law is most violent. Take, for instance, when Mat Donovan is wrongfully imprisoned. Outside the prison, the villagers think back to previous Christmas mornings, lamenting the strange silence without Mat there to play the Knocknagow drum. Inside the prison, Mat nourishes hope for the 'dead past' as he longs for news of his love, Bessy Morris. In moments like this, indulging memory is not simply nostalgic or elegiac: it has counterfactual force. In *Knocknagow*, holding onto the past is a mode of imagining institutions otherwise, a way of asserting that existing institutions – here, the prison and the legal system that land agents easily manipulate to foreclose the futures of people like Mat – do not represent the Irish people and cannot be the only possible path to modernity. Kickham's ethnographic authority thus ultimately challenges liberal authority. Instead of looking forward to an improved future, he retreats into the past. Instead of affirming the importance of existing democratic institutions, he depicts characters who refuse the seeming coherence of present political arrangements.[35]

For both Carleton and Kickham, moving between embracing modern institutionalism and questioning it leads to formal unevenness rather than formal integration. Carleton's work moves ethnographically between positions inside and outside of a culture that does not resolve into a coherent or stable cultural form precisely because there are always more local details to account for and more social relationships between distinct places and positions to consider. Kickham's work, in turn, refuses to adopt liberalism's progressive trajectory, which pre-emptively renders the past 'dead', and instead represents the past to make it live once more.

Institutional Ethnography: The Orange Order in *Valentine M'Clutchy*

William Carleton's *Valentine M'Clutchy, the Irish Agent; or, Chronicles of the Castle Cumber Property* (1845) combines its ethnography of traditional Irish life with an ethnography of the institutions that govern Ireland. Originally written for the Young Ireland newspaper, *The Nation*, this novel marks a departure for Carleton in that he self-consciously courted the nationalist readers whom he had previously angered with his early anti-Catholic writing. The narrative follows the slow rise and speedy decline of a corrupt land agent, Valentine M'Clutchy – or 'Val the Vulture', as the people call him. Using the laws to his own ends, the newspapers to justify his actions and the Orange Order to muster critical support, Val terrorises tenants in order to support his landlord's political ambitions and to further his own personal vendettas. The narration of events is thus often doubled: what actually happened on the one hand, and on the other, what Val claims to have happened in newspapers, letters to the landlord and conversations. This doubleness emphasises the fact that in order to learn how a particular institution functions, one must experience it first-hand rather than believe its abstract principles or formal procedures. In other words, to 'know' an institution and understand how it shapes behaviour, one must inhabit it. I argue that ethnography, in this novel, does not simply represent traditional Irish culture in opposition to modern institutions, but also chronicles lived experiences of unjust institutions to question whether institutions do in fact lead to modernisation.

The novel represents institutions in need of modernisation rather than remote locations that need to be integrated into institutions. The Castle Cumber property is brimming with conflicting social organisations that either support or oppose Val's villainy: churches, political parties, foundling hospitals, yeomanry corps and secret societies dominate the landscape. The sheer number of these groups suggests what David Lloyd calls the 'as yet unreduced multiplicity of forms of socialization' – or institutions that have yet to cohere into a shared discourse of modern institutionalism.[36] For Lloyd, modernisation and state formation are one and the same: the state is the ultimate end of both cultural representation and institution building. But Carleton represents institutions that have complicated relationships with the state as well as complicated, and often antagonistic, relationships with liberalism itself. While liberal institutions depend upon abstraction – formal rather than personal procedures – the system that Carleton describes is saturated with personal and sectarian politics. As he represents the gap between these institutions' stated liberal principles and their illiberal practices, Carleton validates learning about institutions through lived experience.

To see how the institutions that Carleton represents undermine liberalism's emphasis on abstraction, we need only compare the role of the law in this novel with its role in Edgeworth's *Castle Rackrent*. The editor in *Castle Rackrent* intervenes in the story to highlight the Irish servants' surprising legal knowledge, telling a humorous anecdote about how the Irish waste the magistrate's time with long-winded tales. The moral of the story is simple: the Irish may know legal phrases, but they fail to understand the principles that underlie legal procedures – one such principle notably being that 'time is money'.[37] In *Valentine M'Clutchy*, however, the protagonists do not have recourse to a magistrate, for the villains of the novel become magistrates to further corruption and carry out acts of personal vengeance. Illustrating how the legal system oppresses the poor Irish Catholic population, the novel claims, 'There was then no law *against* an Orangeman, and no law *for* a Papist.'[38] The law underwrites the land agent's villainy and Carleton reminds the reader that '[e]very step he took was strictly and perfectly legal'.[39] Thus, for Carleton, the Irish do not need to learn what Elaine Hadley calls 'liberal cognition' to better understand the principles of the law – they need better institutions.[40]

In many ways, the Ireland represented in this novel is familiar to theories of liberalism: it is a premodern political landscape in need of rationalisation. Carleton's sentimental depiction of the misguided desire for violence among the victims of the worst institutional abuses shares much with John Stuart Mill's lamentation of 'states of feeling' in 'savage life':

> These deplorable states of feeling, in any people who have emerged from savage life, are, no doubt, usually the consequence of previous bad government, which has taught them to regard the law as made for other ends than their good, and its administrators as worse enemies than those who openly violate it.[41]

Like Mill, Carleton's narrator distances himself from Val's victims, who begin to 'look upon murder as an act of justice' (*VM* 371). In overtly sentimental language, he laments their 'desperation' without legitimating it (*VM* 371). Father Roche, the parish's only uncorrupt priest, intervenes in the secret society to prevent violence by reminding them that even if the law is unjust, they still need to follow God's law. But the plot of the novel subtly undermines the narrator's distance from such violence, for the novel's resolution is achieved through Val's murder at the hands of the son of one of his victims. Importantly, such punishment occurs in opposition to, rather than through, the law.

In this way, *Valentine M'Clutchy* betrays a distrust of abstract institutions even as it consolidates them. Carleton implies that more established liberal institutions – such as elections in which individuals vote according to their opinions, juries that judge impartially and land leases that follow abstract procedures – would thwart Val's rise to power. However, he also carefully documents how institutions are never impersonal and never thoroughly liberal because their actions always depart from their abstract principles. The Orange Order, in particular, represents the failure of institutions to enact their abstract principles. This organisation becomes the focus of an extended interruption of the story, when the novel moves from describing Val's actions to the institutions that enable his actions. The narrative perspective shifts from that of an omniscient narrator to that of a stranger visiting the property. As is the case in many Irish novels, this stranger, Richard Topertoe, is actually related to the landlord and thus can right the estate. In letters, Richard Topertoe recounts how the Orange Order's principles and practices are at odds after attending a meeting at the Orange Lodge.[42] His ethnography of the order suggests that the institution actually embodies the lessons of Val's hypocrisy: that 'fiction is as good and better than the truth' (*VM* 132). Through fiction, the institution demonstrates a commitment to general principles that the actions of the institution constantly betray. Topertoe's ethnography of the Order, by contrast, gathers 'some faint conception of what it generally is' precisely because he focuses on concrete behaviour as opposed to general principles (*VM* 290).

Topertoe begins his study of the Orange Order by citing its founding principles as stated in 'a short but significant report' of a meeting of the Grand Orange Lodge of Ireland in 1798 (*VM* 281). The report acknowledges how the order appears from the outside, highlighting its 'fairness, and liberality, and moderation' (*VM* 285). But Topertoe's experience suggests that the order looks different from the inside: 'These obligations, however, admirable as they are and ably drawn up, possess neither power nor influence in the system' (*VM* 285). Instead of fairness, the local lodge preaches corruption; instead of liberality, it advocates sectarianism; and instead of moderation, it fosters zealousness and drunkenness. Violating both the established agenda and the code of the order, the meeting involves a series of toasts and the singing of inflammatory loyalist songs like 'Boyne Water' and 'Croppies Lie Down'.[43] As Solomon M'Slime, the hypocritical religious attorney who works alongside Val the Vulture, informs Topertoe, members join the institution to seek personal gain rather than to endorse liberal principles. In his words, 'There are few here who are not moved by some personal hope or expectation from something or from someone . . . insolent, fierce, furious men, with bad passions and no principles, whose chief delight is to get drunk' (*VM* 295). M'Slime could be describing himself: he preys on innocent women and gets publicly drunk while hypocritically presenting himself as a 'religious' attorney dedicated to Christianity above all else.

In 1835, ten years before Carleton's novel, an inquiry into the Orange Order's practices initiated by the House of Commons reached similar conclusions: despite its stated principles, the Orange Order undermined rather than supported the government. In this period after Catholic Emancipation, the Orange Order's mobilisation of Protestantism to maintain power became more troubling for the Tory politicians who had previously supported it. Articles that reported on this inquiry adopt the same ethnographic logic as Carleton's novel – they praised the institution's written principles only to provide anecdotes showing its pernicious practices. Noting how Orangemen parade after their processions have been deemed illegal and take secret oaths at a time when secret societies were outlawed, one article contrasts 'the professions of Orangemen of their solicitude to maintain the law, and this palpable evasion of it'.[44] Another concludes: 'according to the printed rules of a society, the society may be perfectly legal; yet in practice the rules may not be adhered to, and, the society be illegal'.[45] Of course, not everyone agreed with the conclusions of the inquiry. The *Dublin University Magazine* continued to support the Orange Institution and challenged 'those who employ so questionable and perilous machinery' to make Orangeism appear illegal.[46] Thus the magazine's editors responded to the exposure of the Orange Order's institutional fictions by accusing the inquiry itself of fictionalising – of claiming a spurious 'constitutional authority' for the sole purpose of undermining the Orange Order.[47]

I highlight the tension between institutional realities (lived experiences of institutions) and institutional fictions (principles that are not followed, 'machinery' used to other ends) in both criticism and defenses of the Orange Order because it says as much about institutionalism writ large as it does about this particular institution. Sara Ahmed's suggestion that institutions rely on 'nonperformative' speech acts is helpful here.[48] Unlike performative speech acts, such as marriage vows, that do what they say they are doing, nonperformative speech acts '"work" precisely by not bringing about the effects that they name'.[49] For this reason, textual production within institutions – mission statements, diversity statements, even official procedures – become a way of masking how the institution actually functions. Just as the Orange Order's most 'admirable code' allows it to encourage sectarian violence without defining itself through that violence, contemporary institutions declare themselves to be liberal so that their implicit racism, imperialism and sexism seems aberrant rather than engrained in institutional practices.

In the particular case of the Orange Order, one of the institution's greatest fictions is its claim to operate outside of history. Their contemporary parades commemorate 'the violent origins of Protestant supremacy' and, in their desire to follow old routes, seem to neglect the shifting political landscapes of cities, often with violent results.[50] As Northern Ireland changes, the Orange Order gives the deliberate impression of 'an unchanging political opposition'.[51] The Orange Order self-consciously uses institutional time's evasion of history – its vision of a future that only extends the past – in order to mask how it violently intervenes in and shapes the historical present.

In the novel, Carleton historicises the Orange Order by claiming that it is already anachronistic in 1803, a mere eight years after its founding. Betraying his suspicion of Irish nationalist movements, he writes that the order 'rendered most important services to the state, at a time when such services were, no doubt, both necessary and acceptable' (*VM* 288). Carleton means that the Orange Order helped suppress the 1798 rebellion and put down the United Irishmen. But he implies that the state is now strong enough to control citizens on its own. By taking on the role of the state after it has achieved stability, the Orange Order acts 'against men who were no longer either in a disposition or capacity to resist' (*VM* 289). Such a statement implies that once the state achieves authority – namely, a monopoly of legitimate violence – it renders 'self-constituted' institutions like the Orange Order obsolete (*VM* 290). In this way, by identifying the obsolescence of one institution, Carleton legitimates the ahistoricism of another institution – the state.

But despite thus justifying the centrality of the state, Carleton ultimately does not understand the state to be different from other institutions. In fact, he implies that the state may also be critiqued through ethnographic descriptions of the gap between its stated principles and its everyday actions. The state, like the Orange Order, engages in fictions. Tellingly, Topertoe – the man who uncovers the reality of the Orange Institution and rights the estate – initially fled Ireland because of his frustration with the 'fraud and profligacy' that led to the Act of the Union (*VM* 13). In his opposition to the Union, however, Topertoe is the anachronism – his father was a man 'peculiar to his times, or, rather who aided in shaping them' (*VM* 16) and his brother embraced 'all the fashionable prejudices of the day' (*VM* 17). Here anachronism suggests critical distance. Because he is not a man of his times, nor a typical landlord, nor a follower of fashion, Topertoe is able to understand Irish reality – namely that the British state fosters rather than prevents unjust practices. The fact that Carleton both trusts the state and questions it indicates the ways in which his criticism of the Orange Order actually extends to other institutions.

Carleton's ethnographic study of the Orange Order challenges the logic of institutional abstraction in favour of what Elaine Hadley calls 'embodied localisms'.[52] Hadley's account of Victorian liberalism, like Carleton's ethnography, treats liberalism as a lived practice rather than merely a set of principles. According to Hadley, Ireland shapes and also challenges liberalism's cosmopolitan orientation because Ireland reflects a 'transpolitical philosophy of locational attachment'.[53] Such attachment is rooted in the Irish love of the land; for example, many Irish nationalist organisations of the period take up the stereotypical portrayal of the Irish as 'of the soil'.[54] This attachment is troubling for liberal institutions precisely because it shifts from liberal abstractions to material sites, from concepts of property to literal dirt.

Published before the Liberal Party began to take the questions of Ireland and Irish land seriously, Carleton's novel reflects on liberal abstraction not in terms of the individual liberal subject – which is Hadley's focus – but in terms of institutions. At the level of the subject, liberalism's emphasis on abstraction violently restricts who participates in institutions by distinguishing between subjects who can be abstracted from their historical, social positions and those who remain defined through these embodied positions.[55] At the level of the institution, liberalism's emphasis on abstraction masks how institutions actually operate. Daily institutional practices do not bear out the abstract principles that legitimate these social organisations. Local rather than straightforwardly national and material as well as abstract, Irish institutions underscore the importance of institutional inhabitation: in order to understand an institution, one must actually experience its practices from the inside. Thus, Carleton's ethnography of the Orange Order of Castle Cumber is important not because it shows how peculiar social organisations shape everyday Irish life, but rather because it reveals the fundamental gap between what institutions say and what they do – the abstractions that authorise them and the everyday practices that define them. By legitimating how Irish people experience institutions, the liberal conservative Carleton actually undermines abstract institutional authority.

Prophecy, Providence and Institutional Knowledge in *The Black Prophet*

Serialised in the *Dublin University Magazine* in 1846, *The Black Prophet* represents a famine that took place in 1817, even as it self-consciously engages with the events of the still-unfolding Irish Famine. In 1846, the potato crop had already failed, but the extent of the devastation, hunger and death that would occur was still unknown. Peel's government in 1845–6 attempted to address the needs of the Irish population – the worst was still to come.[56] The collision of the novel's two contexts – the famine of 1817, and the famine that had just begun in 1846 – is somewhat dizzying, for the novel seems to suggest two contradictory approaches to famine in Irish life: first, that famine is 'perennial' in Ireland and, second, that the novel's representation of famine will render it a thing of the past.[57]

Part of the confusion emerges from Carleton's use of what James Clifford calls the 'ethnographic pastoral' – a 'structure of retrospection' in ethnographic writing that, in the act of representing a culture, relegates it to the past.[58] When such a structure is applied to Irish peasants, it confirms the imperial narrative of 'the vanishing primitive'.[59] The Irish peasants that Carleton represents are teetering on the brink of survival as they try to maintain traditional community life in the face of famine on the one hand and modernisation on the other. Naturalising hunger as a reality of traditional Irish life, Carleton upholds modern institutionalism as that which will eliminate hunger and transform Irish people from primitives to modern subjects. But, importantly, Carleton also shows that governmental institutions have caused famines in Ireland; therefore, merely integrating Irish people into institutions will not solve this ongoing problem. Carleton's novel implicitly questions how governmental institutions can consign famine to the past if they thwart rather than usher in modernity and cause rather than prevent famine. Examining these contradictions, I argue that *The Black Prophet* accepts the future that modern institutionalism imagines while working to change how institutions engage with the past.

The Black Prophet tells the story of a mysterious murder that haunts the inhabitants of the Black Glen. The unsolved murder prevents love matches (the niece of the victim, Mave Sullivan, cannot marry the son of the presumed murderer, Condy Dalton, because their families oppose the match), leads to supernatural events, and explains the effects of the famine (the decline of the Dalton family seems to occur because 'shadow of crime was upon them') (*BP* 140). As community members slowly gather more clues about the murder, the famine intensifies. The novel ends when the true murderer is found and prosecuted – Donnel Dhu, the prophecy man, is put to death for murdering his brother-in-law.

The two plots – the story of the murder and the story of the famine – focus on different approaches to futurity: Providence and prophecy. While Providence is a distinctly Christian structure of belief represented in the novel by the assumption that murder will out, prophecy is a more flexible – and more Irish – practice that allows the prophecy man, Donnel Dhu, to predict and shape the future. For most of the novel, Providence is an open question: the murder took place twenty years ago and the murderer has yet to be punished. For this reason, characters threaten one another with providential justice, but there is no answer when Sarah, Donnel Dhu's wild daughter, asks, "But isn't there a Providence?' (*BP* 61).

Only at the very end of the novel – when Donnel Dhu is hung for the murder, and the corrupt middleman, Dick O'Grange, dies of typhoid fever – is the force of Providence confirmed. The novel concludes moralistically: 'Providence never, so to speak, loses sight of the man who deliberately sheds his fellow-creature's blood' (*BP* 426). Thus, the law ultimately functions as a vehicle for Providence, merging the Christian belief in moral justice with modern institutionalism's emphasis on a political future secured through institutions.

By contrast, prophecy is a traditional practice that characters actively legitimate even as the novel's narrative interventions relegate it to the past. Suspicious of Donnel Dhu because of his individual failings, the community nevertheless trusts his prophecy because he represents an established practice and known type – he is 'like every prophecy-man of his kind' (*BP* 21). He draws on cultural currency to establish himself as a prophet, for, as the narrator explains, his 'reputation as a prophecy-man arose, in the first instance, as much on account of his mysterious pretensions to a knowledge of the quack prophecies of his day – Pastorini, Kolumbkille, &c. &c. and such stuff – as from any pretensions he claimed to foretell the future himself' (*BP* 221).[60] The narrator's statement is typical insofar as it explains an established cultural practice (Pastorini's and Kolumb-kille's popular prophecies circulated amongst the Irish peasantry in the late eighteenth century and early nineteenth century) only to delegitimise it. While Donnel Dhu uses prophecy to further his own plots, he seems to have more control over it as a cultural discourse than as an actual act. His knowledge is a mere 'pretension'.

Representing prophecy as a cultural practice ultimately renders it an anachronism. In a typical ethnographic interruption, the narrator instructs the reader that the prophecy man, once a familiar type, is 'a character in Ireland, by the way, that has nearly, if not altogether, disappeared' (*BP* 21). He is not the only traditional type who disappears in the novel. Donnel Dhu's daughter, Sarah, a 'wild Irish girl' who was 'like some beautiful and luxuriant flower . . . permitted to run into wildness and disorder', dies at the end of the story while the more cultivated characters live on (*BP* 452). This disappearance of cultural types has double significance. On the one hand, it shows the violence of the Famine.[61] As people died, Irish cultural practices changed. On the other hand, it shows how the temporal structure of ethnographic representation implicitly supplants a living culture with a textual representation of that culture. Writing about prophecy, Carleton relegates it to the past.

Carleton's own narrative position is implicated in this ethnographic structure: his narrator moves between legitimating prophecy (in the story) and relegating it to the past (in the discourse) in sites of narrative metalepsis – or places where the story and discourse collide. Tellingly, when introducing Donnel Dhu, Carleton shifts from the particular to the general and from the present to the past tense:

> the very nature of his subject rendered a figurative style and suitable language necessary, a circumstance which, aided by a natural flow of words, and a felicitous illustration of imagery – for which, indeed, all prophecy-men were remarkable – had something peculiarly fascinating and persuasive to the class of persons he was in the habit of addressing. The gifts of these men, besides, were exercised with such singular delight, that the constant repetition of their oracular exhibitions by degrees created an involuntary impression on themselves, that ultimately rose to a wild and turbid enthusiasm, partaking at once of imposture and fanaticism. Many of them were, therefore, nearly as much the dupes of the delusions that proceeded from their own heated imaginations as the ignorant people who looked upon them as oracles. (*BP* 21)

Acknowledging that the existence of the prophecy man depends upon a willing audience, Carleton recounts the cultural practices that give rise to such men only to refuse them legitimacy: they are the practices of 'ignorant people' who foster 'delusions', rather than of rational people. Such strong language is slightly confusing because, in the story itself, the 'ignorant people' who listen to and legitimate Donnel Dhu's prophecy are the very characters who comprise the novel's sentimental focus. For instance, Mave Sullivan, an 'ingenuous and kind-hearted girl' whom the entire community loves and respects, overcomes her initial distrust of the prophet and is reassured by his prophecy (*BP* 42). Moreover, one of his most repeated prophecies – that the weather and unhealthy crops foretell 'famine, pestilence, an' death' – certainly turns out to be true (*BP* 20). If the narrator ultimately relegates prophecy to the past, he nevertheless shows that the characters' belief in prophecy is not delusional – it is a way of affirming their own reading of the landscape and predictions for their lives.

In *The Black Prophet*, this auto-ethnographic movement validates institutionalism by suggesting that modern institutions, which are tied to Providence in the novel, will inevitably replace traditional prophecy. Trust in institutions that guarantee an improved future replaces individuals who foretell the future. Donnel Dhu's providential death – in which he follows his daughter's dying wish that he die like a man – consolidates the rule of law. His death makes him subject to the very laws he despises: he died 'firmly, but sullenly, and as if he despised and defied the world and its laws' (*BP* 455). Because prophecy is not a legitimate epistemology in the eyes of the court, witnesses in the case produce damning evidence, but do not always tell how they acquired it. Charley Hanlon, for instance, begins tracking Donnel Dhu after a dream tells him to go to the site of the murder, 'but his dream was not permitted to go to the jury' (*BP* 425). In this final death scene, modern institutionalism and Providence, or the sense that murder will out and moral justice will prevail, work together to root out prophecy, here, Charley's faith in his dream. The effect of such a scene transfers authority from cultural practices and individual people to abstract institutions – the rule of law, legal procedures.

By having Providence work through the law, Carleton subtly echoes and questions British responses, both in the press and by the government, that treated the Irish Famine as a divine act. Charles Trevelyan, who was Assistant Secretary to the Treasury during the Famine and is often blamed for the government's failed relief efforts, famously declared the Famine to be an act of God that punished the Irish for their bad habits and helped establish better, more industrious habits in their place.[62] He was not alone – when Carleton was writing *The Black Prophet*, before the still-unfolding famine became the Great Irish Famine, the British press was already treating the failure of the potato as a God-sent opportunity for improvement in Ireland. In 1845, for example, Lord Devon wrote a letter to the editor of *The Times* that urged support for relief efforts but concluded: 'This visitation of Providence may teach us all some useful lessons; if we profit by them rightly, good may arise out of the present evil.'[63] The word 'profit' here is telling, for in Famine discourse, Providence often means submitting to the inevitable logic of free market capitalism as much as accepting God's will.

Unlike these accounts, Carleton quite vigorously argues that famine in Ireland results from failures in government rather than acts of God, and yet he also sees the famine as an opportunity for institutional consolidation and reform. As Melissa Fegan suggests, characters like Darby Skinadre – the meal-monger who represents 'the very Genius of Famine' – are the villains of the story because they try to explain Irish famine through Providence (*BP* 70).[64] The famine itself is not providential but rather political, a result of 'principles of Government' (dedication page). But, like Lord Devon, Carleton wants to make use of the Famine. Dedicating the 1847 edition of the novel to the Prime Minister, Lord John Russell, Carleton writes:

> the man who, in his Ministerial capacity, must be looked upon as a public exponent of those principles of Government which have brought our country to her present calamitous condition, by a long course of illiberal legislation and unjustifiable neglect, ought to have his name placed before a story which details with truth the sufferings which such legislation and neglect have entailed upon our people. This, my Lord, is not done from any want of respect to your Lordship, but because the writer trusts that, as it is the first Tale of Irish Famine that ever was dedicated to an English Prime Minister, your Lordship's enlarged and enlightened policy will put it out of the power of any succeeding author ever to write another. (dedication page)

Narrative interventions into the story also insist that the problem of famine is a problem of legislation as they question 'draconian enactments' that contribute to the suffering of the poor. In fact, one of the narrator's repeated refrains conveys disbelief that people die of neglect in a Christian country. This has two implications: first, that Christians should do more for one another, and second, that Ireland's Christianity prevents any providential explanation for the famine (*BP* 368).

For Carleton, representing how governmental institutions have caused famine in Ireland paradoxically projects these very institutions into the future. Such future-oriented projection depends upon the ethnographic structures of representation that relegate prophecy to the past. The dedication suggests that the act of representing famine and its institutional origins will eradicate it: 'it is the first Tale of Irish Famine that ever was dedicated to an English Prime Minister, your Lordship's enlarged and enlightened policy will put it out of the power of any succeeding author ever to write another'. Although nothing in the novel suggests an 'enlarged and enlightened policy' as it represents Ireland under previous prime ministers, here Carleton expresses faith in governmental policies. Such faith is providential: Carleton believes, despite extensive evidence to the contrary, that 'the day has come when education, progress, improvement, and reward, will shed their mild and peaceful lustre upon our statute-books' (*BP* 368). Adopting ethnography's narrative of modernisation, Carleton represents famine in part to usher in the rationalised future associated with modern institutionalism.

Terry Eagleton suggests that including such direct social commentary in the novel – addresses to prime ministers, discussions of statute-books – undermines Carleton's realism. Unlike English novelists who seamlessly merge the fictional frame with their ideological approach, Carleton, like other Irish writers, must 'drop the fictional pretence and speak poignantly or angrily from the heart'.[65] Elucidating the larger political significance of the suffering of his characters, Carleton both explicitly questions the British government and demonstrates faith in it in turn.

However, I argue, contra Eagleton, that this is exactly what realism does: realist novels interrupt themselves to demonstrate the political and social importance of their representation of everyday life as realist narrators move from being immersed in a culture to viewing that culture from a more distanced perspective. In other words, realism's 'fictional pretence' depends upon the constant disruption of formal integration. In fact, we can think of ethnographic realism as the movement between 'fictional pretence' and that which disrupts this pretence, or, in other words, between the realist novel as an institutional form and the moments when the novel refuses the generalising impulse of institutions. The Irish setting dramatises such movement precisely because, in pre-Famine Ireland, cultural practices seem to have more authority than modern institutions. Thus, by directly addressing British governmental institutions, Carleton highlights how they are responsible for many of the miseries that the Irish people face, despite the perceived absence of modern institutions in the landscape.

Carleton's ethnographic realism both consolidates and unsettles institutional time. Although he implies that institutions are central to Ireland's future, he questions the ways in which they conceal historical time and forget historical events. Interrupting his own address to the Prime Minister, Carleton asks why the legislature forgets famine. Acknowledging that 'ignorance prevails' on the subject of famine because 'it is not generally known, that since the introduction of the potato into this country, no year has ever passed which, in some remote locality or other, has not been such [a year of famine] to the unfortunate inhabitants' (*BP* 248).[66] Though famine is 'almost perennial', Carleton implies that its existence is still unknown because it occurs in 'remote' localities (*BP* vi). In other words, government institutions 'forget' about famine because it happens in places that they know little about. As the novel's preface says, 'the memory of our Legislature is as faithless on such a subject as that of the most heartless individual among us' (*BP* vi).

Thus, ethnography helps people remember the things that institutions forget: not only remote localities, but also varied, local experiences caused by institutional policies themselves. Although Carleton looks to modern institutions as that which will replace traditional Irish life, his ethnography also challenges the imperial narrative of the 'vanishing primitive'. Rather than suggesting that the Irish people will enter history through institutions, he implies that they will restore historicity to institutions that actively erase it through a process of 'forgetting'.[67] The temporality of Carleton's ethnographic representation works in two directions: it not only relegates traditional Irish life to the past as it extends institutions into the future, but also challenges these very institutions' understanding of the past. Carleton represents the peculiarities of Irish experience not to 'salvage' them from an encroaching modernity that will render them obsolete, but rather to show that local Irish experience – forgotten by Parliament and the Prime Minister alike – is a form of knowledge that modern institutions both need and neglect.

Adopting a familiar liberal approach, Carleton seems to believe optimistically that merely representing the reality of famine in Ireland will help English institutions remember. For this reason, he suggests extending the reach of institutions by incorporating these remote localities into the 'sanatory statistics of the country' (*BP* 248). In other words, after showing how everyday Irish life teaches us things that institutions forget, Carleton nevertheless embraces modern institutionalism and 'forgets' about alternative epistemologies, such as prophecy, that offer other approaches to famine. Statistics will counter the Legislature's failure to remember famine, Carleton implies, because they will incorporate famine into institutional knowledge. The way to make 'remote localities' less remote, then, is to transform them into abstractions that the institution understands. In fact, ethnographic realism itself does the same thing without the statistics: it takes the 'real' experience of remote localities and transforms it into a representation that the leaders of institutions can apprehend. In *The Black Prophet*, descriptions of suffering and local knowledge of famine expose failures in government: populations excluded from statistical surveys, ignored by the law. Allowing peasant life to cohere as a culture, then, becomes a method of extending governmentality to a new population.

Ultimately, although Carleton demonstrates how anachronisms productively unsettle institutional time in *The Black Prophet*, he prevents these anachronisms from imagining alternative political futures. While he intervenes in institutional time to change the way the government remembers remote localities and their pasts, he accepts modern institutionalism's narrow future.

Charles Kickham's Future-Oriented Nostalgia

Unlike Carleton, whose politics vary with his shifting self-interest, Charles Kickham actively challenges modern institutionalism by questioning the legitimacy of imperial institutions. But although Kickham's politics are far more radical than Carleton's, his reading taste is more conventional. John O'Leary, a Fenian who worked alongside Kickham and influenced W. B. Yeats, remembers Kickham reading canonical English authors, noting that 'among the authors whom I remember as familiar to him were Shakespeare, Tennyson and Dickens, and, among later writers, I know he greatly admired George Eliot'.[68] Kickham happily acknowledged his debt to and admiration for Dickens, which is readily apparent in *Knocknagow*.[69] The Christmas setting of the story echoes Dickens's *A Christmas Carol*, and the idealised character of Norah Lahy, who infuses morality throughout the community as she slowly dies, shares much with *The Old Curiosity Shop*'s Little Nell, including readers' desire that she live.[70] Kickham's biographer, R. V. Comerford, suggests that *Knocknagow* also owes much to *Adam Bede* and that Mat the Thrasher, one of its protagonists, is an Adam Bede figure – a manly peasant shy about love but not afraid of hard work.[71]

Such self-conscious debts to English realist writers fit Irish studies' institutionalised narrative of Irish literature: that Irish writers try but fail to adapt English plots to an Irish setting. But, as is the case with Carleton's novels, this understanding of Irish realism misses what Kickham's novel actually *does*. Like Carleton's novels, *Knocknagow* uses ethnography to represent lived experiences that challenge the abstractions upon which modern institutionalism depends. But while Carleton mobilises anachronisms to reform modern institutions, Kickham more radically argues that British institutions will always fail to represent Irish people. He uses realism's institutional authority to refuse institutional time, suggesting instead that the heterogeneous temporalities of everyday Irish life do not need to be rationalised or improved. *Knocknagow*'s multiple temporalities, which emerge through the novel's unwieldy plots, show that realism's emphasis on lived experience can help us imagine political futures that refuse modern institutionalism and its abstractions.

Kickham's novel insists on the co-existence of multiple temporalities by moving among distinct novelistic plots. As Con Houlihan claims in his celebration of the novel in a newspaper article, '*Knocknagow* is like a great basket in to which Kickham threw observations and ideas . . . *Knocknagow* doesn't tell a story.'[72] Certainly the novel does not tell *one* story. Merging, and sometimes shifting between, the conventions of the national tale, the marriage plot novel, the novel of suspense and ethnographic realism, the novel does not simply go forward in time. It jumps between plots as it moves between characters, making it difficult to identify a single narrative trajectory or protagonist. The novel employs what Emer Nolan calls 'flash images' that show characters and settings immersed in the rhythms of everyday life: 'the vision of Norah saying her prayers, the light at Mat the Thrasher's window every night, and the three poplar trees on Phil Morris's deserted farm'.[73] As narrative time moves on, the narrative trajectory often abruptly shifts. Although the novel integrates the characters into a shared community, it does not always integrate them into a unified plot or even into a sense of shared, continuous time.

Throughout its various plots, *Knocknagow* narrates a struggle between the pull of two times: 'the "dead past" and 'the "living present"' (*K* 374). 'The "dead past"' encompasses both history and personal memory. This past varies for different characters – for Bessy Morris, it is the time of childhood; for Mary Kearney, it is the early moments of her first romance; and for Mick Brien, it is the time of relative financial stability when his family could joyfully gather around the fireside. But for all of these characters, the powerful force of the past belies its characterisation as dead. As the narrator asserts, 'The "living Present?" and the "dead Past?" We hold that the Past is the more living of the two, sometimes' (*K* 374).

For readers unfamiliar with *Knocknagow*, this description of a 'dead Past' that is, in fact, living might suggest gothic fiction rather than realism. Mobilising the uncanny power of the past, gothic fiction famously shows how seemingly 'anachronistic vestiges' live on in a supposedly modern age.[74] As Siobhan Kilfeather suggests, Irish gothic writing questions the legitimacy of modern institutions insofar as 'the originating violence of the narrative is the violence of the state and its militia'.[75] In these gothic tales, state violence reverberates outwards. *Knocknagow* describes state violence – evictions, military campaigns, police brutality – but it is not a gothic tale. Its frequent reflections on the disjunction between past and present do not create terror or suggest the supernatural, but rather redefine the daily rhythms of life. In this realist register, state violence is ordinary rather than spectacular, embodied rather than imagined: it is a feature of everyday life.

As Kickham moves among distinct plots, he also moves back and forth between ethnography and auto-ethnography – that is, between the study of a culture by outsiders and the study of it by insiders. Opening like a national tale, *Knocknagow* begins with a familiar journey – an Englishman venturing from the 'metropolis' to the heart of Ireland (*K* 1). The details of the journey emphasise geographic distance and cultural difference: after arriving in Dublin, Henry Lowe travels 'some eighty miles' by mail coach and then a 'dozen miles in his host's gig', and readers find out that 'the young gentleman knows little of Ireland from personal experience, having spent most of his life in what is sometimes oddly enough called "the sister country"' (*K* 1). Misinformed letters from his mother in England serve to dramatise the difference between his ethnographic perspective and her prejudicial assumptions: while Henry learns about Irish culture by experiencing it as a participant observer, she repeats the agent's misrepresentation of the community as violent and threatening. Thus, though she laments the 'dreadful occurrences' that 'take place in the middle of the noon-day' (*K* 116), Henry Lowe learns that there have been no agrarian outrages, but instead 'an unusually large number of ejectments served this year' (*K* 118). His first-hand experience of Ireland allows him to challenge English stereotypes about Irish people and conclude that Irish tenants are the victims rather than the perpetrators of violence.

However, even as the novel presents Henry Lowe as a participant observer who challenges misrepresentations of Irish culture that circulate abroad, it does not stabilise him as the only ethnographic authority. The omniscient narrator functions as an auto-ethnographic figure who translates local knowledge for readers. In a domestic scene at the Donovan family home, when one character declares, 'Look at them', the narrator interrupts him:

> here a difficulty presents itself: we are not sure whether it be possible to convey by means of the English alphabet the only name ever given to potatoes in Knocknagow. 'Praties' would be laughed at as a vulgarism only worthy of a spalpeen from Kerry, while 'potatoes' was considered too genteel except for ladies and gentlemen and schoolmaster. The nearest approach we can make to the word we were about writing is 'puetas' or 'p'yehtes.' (*K* 143)

This narrative interruption draws attention to the difficulty of capturing oral speech in writing. But, just as importantly, it works to navigate between cultural insiders and outsiders as it shows the narrator's familiarity with the nuances of Knocknagow idiom. Such narrative interruptions, which occur throughout the novel, draw attention to the narrator's mediating work. Readers do not have unmediated access to Irish culture, but rather an ethnographic representation of it.

Henry Lowe is central to the novel's opening scenes, but he becomes more marginal to the story as it progresses – he even leaves for India partway through the novel. His departure thwarts the future-oriented romantic plot of the national tale, in which the English stranger marries a native Irish woman and thus symbolically unifies England and Ireland. Although Henry Lowe falls in love with a local Irish woman, Mary Kearney, Mary is in love with Arthur O'Connor – a man that she met years ago in Tramore. Readers learn of Mary's love for Arthur through an abrupt narrative interruption that flashes back to the years before Henry Lowe's arrival. In the middle of a hurling match, the narrator declares that he must 'interrupt the regular course of our chronicle, in order to throw light upon certain circumstances of which the reader may have caught fitful glimpses in the foregoing chapters' (*K* 391). This extended narrative interruption solves the mystery of the tracks in the snow leading to Mary's window – an event that has long puzzled the characters – and, in the process, diminishes Henry Lowe's authority in the narrative. When the narrator returns to the present tense, he declares, 'And now the reader knows more of the tracks in the snow than Mr Henry Lowe; to whom we will return, just to see him safe out of Tipperary' (*K* 419). Returning to the past thus not only unsettles the future-oriented conventions of the national tale but also represents a shift from ethnography to auto-ethnography. The novel turns away from Henry Lowe's spatial movement from England to Ireland and eventually to India, and toward the narrator's temporal movement between past and present.

As is the case in Carleton's *The Black Prophet*, such temporal movement between past and present both enacts the ethnographic pastoral and undermines it. On the one hand, the entire structure of the novel depicts the slow destruction of Knocknagow. As the plot moves forward in time, Knocknagow retreats further into the past. Characters leave Ireland for America and Australia, tenants are evicted and houses are levelled. As the narrator declares near the end of the novel, 'Half of Knocknagow is swept from the face of the earth' (*K* 515). The novel seems to preserve what the culture cannot. On the other hand, though, the novel relentlessly refuses to see the past as 'dead' and suggests that the past continues to be an active force and viable source of possibilities in the present. However, unlike Carleton, who aims to reform institutions by incorporating forgotten places and histories into them, Kickham validates such anachronistic pasts in order to imagine politics otherwise.

Thus, the slow erasure of Knocknagow as a material site does not banish it from historical time. Instead, the novel's retreat into the past allows the villagers and readers alike to imagine a future at odds with present social and political arrangements. The end of the novel juxtaposes past and present in ways that acknowledge the extent of the villagers' loss. Jemmy Hogan returns to his father's land, rolling a stone to mark 'the exact spot where the ould house stood' (*K* 615). Mat the Thrasher remembers a past hurling match only to note, 'The hurlers are gone' (*K* 616). But instead of suggesting that such loss is inevitable, this juxtaposition of past and present allows characters to imagine new futures. While the narrator acknowledges the 'deadly system at work now', the novel implies that the country's losses do not mean 'death' (*K* 617). The novel concludes with Mary Kearney thinking of how her 'bright future' – her marriage to Arthur O'Connor – resulted from a 'dream of the Past' (*K* 619). The implication is that Ireland, too, can reanimate dreams of the past as the future. Thus, the novel's nostalgia is in fact future-oriented: it keeps dreams and possibilities alive by detaching Knocknagow from British institutions that pre-emptively render the past dead.[76]

Throughout the novel, remembering the past becomes a mode of imagining futurity otherwise. Take, for instance, Mrs Donovan's 'sad face' (*K* 368). Reflecting trauma but also endurance, the narrator suggests that she got the sad face in '98 when 'her only brother, a bright-eyed boy of seventeen was torn from the arms of his mother, and shot dead outside the door' (*K* 368). When her son, Mat the Thrasher, independently pursues an education, her face becomes 'a shade sadder' because she fears that education will only result in him joining the police (*K* 368). Her face shows how she has embodied and internalised her experience and thus legitimates her perspective in the face of a more abstract understanding of education as good. Her fear for her son shows that experiencing the injustice of one institution (the violence of the soldiers and yeoman who killed her brother) extends to distrust of other institutions (education). This brief passage ends with an interruption from the narrator: 'It strikes us that statesmen might learn something from the sad look in Mrs Donovan's face' (*K* 369). Importantly, the 'something' that the statesmen might learn is not explicitly articulated, in part because the implied lesson is the failure and violence of the colonial state. Mrs Donovan's sad face thus operates as a form of knowledge that can only be silent in the face of continued state power but that, nevertheless, offers its own disciplinary lessons to 'statesmen'.

Such narrative shifts between past and present continually validate the power of the past. In another important scene, Mick Brien, a 'poor maddened victim of tyranny', contemplates but ultimately decides against murder (*K* 387). His desire for revenge emerges from the disjunction between past and present. In the past, he was a comfortable and respectable small farmer with a happy domestic life; in the present, he has no land, no home and no food. Ashamed of his ragged appearance, he no longer socialises with his neighbours or attends Mass. Tellingly, when Mick Brien contemplates the past, it becomes present. The narrator writes in the present tense: 'His hand rests on the shoulder of a blushing girl; and he tells her that the field is his, and points out how thickly it is studded with stooks, and what a rich harvest it will prove' (*K* 376). But, in the actual present, Mick is 'like a spectre' because, although he lives on, he has no hope for the future (*K* 378). He continues on only by remembering the past.

Mick Brien's foreclosed futurity ultimately shows how oppositional power lies in reanimating the supposedly dead past. Contemplating the insurmountable distance between his pleasant memories of the past and his present misery, Mick Brien is able to reactivate the past:

> He looked down into the square bog-hole, and touched the smooth black surface of the water with his hand. The action reminded him of the holy water with which he used to sprinkle himself on entering and leaving the chapel before his clothes had become too ragged to allow him to appear with decency among the congregation; and involuntarily he sprinkled his forehead, and made the sign of the Cross. (*K* 377–8)

The act unifies past and present as it distinguishes between religion as an institution and religion as an embodied practice. While the state of his clothes now bars his entrance at Mass, making the sign of the Cross at the 'bog-hole' encourages Mick to abandon his plans for murder. Inspired by this action, once so familiar to him, Mick Brien is emboldened to repeat other familiar habits from his past life. Although he is embarrassed by 'his tattered habiliments', he ventures to the 'light in Mat's window' to spend time with his neighbours as he used to do (*K* 378). I argue that Mick Brien's involuntary act of making the sign of the Cross is a silent refusal of institutional time. It not only insists that Mick Brien's Catholicism continues long after he stops attending Mass, but also suggests that the past continues to have power in the present.[77] His newfound strength emerges from legitimating the continued force of the past in spite of his present misery.

Kickham's ethnography of pasts that remain silent but neverthe-less powerful insists on heterogeneous historical time and refuses the state's ahistorical institutional time. Converting time into space, states consolidate power by appearing to be outside of time and mak-ing other times unimaginable. As Ian Baucom argues, the state 'has seemed to succeed in putting the question of time outside itself or, at most, in producing a simple binary code of before and after'.[78] *Knock-nagow* unsettles this easy binary by validating pasts that the colonial state constantly works to render dead. For example, the dragoon who courts Bessy Morris represents the atemporality of the state. Arriving in Knocknagow to visit Bessy, whom he met in Dublin, the dragoon reminds the villagers of previous moments of state violence: Bessy's grandfather tells stories of the 1798 rebellion, and Mick Brien scowls as he remembers 'when a troop of these formidable-looking warriors rattled through his little farmyard the day the old house was pulled down' (*K* 254). But the dragoon, unaware of past violence, does not understand why the villagers hate 'the sight of a red-coat' (*K* 253). A representative of the state, he remains unaware of the state's violence in Knocknagow. Instead, 'the dragoon, in all probability, would never have heard of the existence of Knocknagow' unless he had met Bessy (*K* 273). The villagers of Knocknagow, who know so much about how the state contributes to a system of colonial oppression, do not exist in the eyes of the state.

Ultimately, *Knocknagow*'s insistence that the dead past lives on encourages readers to trust themselves and their memories rather than the dictates of institutional time. The novel's didactic closing – when Knocknagow is no more – implies that the landlords, complicit in the unjust land system that has forced many of the villagers to emi-grate, finally begin to see that the very people they have oppressed understand the state better than they do. At the very end of the novel, Dr O'Connor notes that the landlords who evicted their tenants are now learning how little England cares for them, saying: 'The Irish landlords were encouraged to exterminate the people . . . and when the work was done, many of themselves were exterminated. England cares just as little for them as for the people' (*K* 613). Alluding to the fact that many landlords were forced to sell their land for low prices in the Incumbered Estates Court after the Famine, Dr O'Connor shows how the landlords began to learn what the people already knew. The people's memories of state violence help explain the Brit-ish state's unwillingness to help even their loyal Irish and Anglo-Irish supporters. The close of the novel thus retreats to the past in order to imagine an anti-institutional future that 'will yet cause another

English monarch to exclaim, "Cursed be the laws that deprived me of such subjects"' (*K* 600).[79] Identifying the root problem as 'the laws' that perpetuate violence rather than protecting the people, the novel's solution involves trusting the people's knowledge rather than institutional authority.

Taken together, Carleton's and Kickham's novels suggest that modern institutionalism in Ireland leads to contradictions and conflict – between centralised laws and local knowledge, abstract principles and personal experiences, presentist policies and memories of the past. Carleton and Kickham confront these contradictions in different ways: Carleton validates personal experiences of institutional failures but still believes in modern institutionalism and the future it promises, while Kickham insists that English institutions will always fail to represent Irish people. Nevertheless, their novels share an approach to ethnographic representation in which anachronism does not simply confirm the imperial narrative of the 'vanishing primitive'. Instead, anachronisms suggest that provincialism, and even 'primitives', can challenge the future that institutions assume by showing how these institutions need to better confront, acknowledge and remember the past.

Notes

1. Kickham, *Knocknagow*, p. 374. Cited in the text hereafter, abbreviated as *K*.
2. Kickham, *For the Old Land*, p. 184.
3. Buzard, *Disorienting Fiction*, p. 8. Buzard is ultimately interested in a more limited understanding of ethnographic fiction in his study, as he focuses on the participant observer.
4. Christopher Herbert emphasises the differences between ethnography and novels: while novels are invested in individuals and narrate plotted events, ethnography emphasises the primacy of culture and describes static systems (*Culture and Anomie*, pp. 259–60).
5. Here, I am building on Nancy Bentley's work, which argues that the novel of manners establishes cultural authority in the same ways that ethnographies do despite their seemingly different geographic valences. In her words, 'These two genres, though assigned in this period to utterly different zones of "civilised" and "savage" life, were linked through an indeterminate exchange of images, narrative energies, and structures of feeling' (*The Ethnography of Manners*, p. 19).
6. In fact, Maria Edgeworth reportedly said, 'I have read all the works that Carleton has yet written, and I must confess that I never knew Irish life until I had read them' (quoted in Fegan, *Literature and the Irish Famine*, p. 136).

7. As John O'Leary put it, Kickham 'knew the Irish people thoroughly, but especially the middle and so-called lower classes, and from thoroughness of knowledge came thoroughness of sympathy' (*Recollections of Fenians and Fenianism*, p. 265).

8. Studying the reception of African novelists, Eleni Coundouriotis notes how pernicious the idea of an 'authentic' writer can be: 'To attribute authenticity is to mask a particular history by an act of violent repression.' She suggests that understanding a colonial or postcolonial author's works as ethnographic not only cuts them off from history, but also views them as representing a static cultural present rather than engaging with history in their novels (*Claiming History*, p. 3).

9. Eagleton, *Heathcliff and the Great Hunger*, p. 207. Tellingly, when Eagleton argues that Carleton's anthropological focus departs from realism, he compares Carleton's fiction to Kickham's *Knocknagow*. Noting Carleton's fame as the 'peasant novelist', James Murphy suggests that 'Carleton seemed to be the fulfilment of the anthropological trend in Irish fiction in the 1820s' and indicates that for many critics, Carleton's success seems tied to his personal experience and biography rather than his literary accomplishments (*Irish Novelists and the Victorian Age*, p. 46). Derek Hand points out that Carleton 'is unable to fully disregard an English readership and he is constantly at pains to give the autobiographical source for many of his stories, providing an air of the authentic beyond the dreaded footnote' (*A History of the Irish Novel*, p. 90). Helen O'Connell notes that Carleton, himself, was suspicious of 'literary indulgence' and instead 'strives to validate his stories as truth' (*Ireland and the Fiction of Improvement*, p. 88).

10. Howes, 'William Carleton's literary religion', p. 110.

11. Lloyd, 'Afterword: Hardress Cregan's dream', p. 233.

12. Buzard, *Disorienting Fiction*, p. 7.

13. Ibid. p. 12.

14. Howes, *Colonial Crossings*, p. 24.

15. R. V. Comerford notes Carleton and Kickham's shared interest in representing the peasantry but asserts, 'Intellectually they had little in common, and they did not inhabit the same moral universe' (*Charles J. Kickham*, p. 198).

16. Of course, Fenianism is itself a complicated political movement. As Amy Martin argues in *Alter-nations,* 'Fenianism combined various, seemingly opposed, forms of anticolonial strategy; for example, the revolutionary advocation of "physical force" and preparation for militarized resistance, nonviolent forms of activism, republican gestures such as the creation of an Irish currency, forms of cultural nationalism such the publication of nationalist writing, and serious engagement with other forms of radicalism including the First International and anticolonial insurgency in other areas of the British Empire' (p. 63).

17. R. F. Foster cites a letter where W. B. Yeats says that Kickham is 'marred by having read Dickens' in *Irish Story*, p. 114.

18. Elaine Hadley associates such abstractions with formalism; she argues that 'Mid-Victorian political liberalism outlines *how* one ought to think but not precisely *what* to think. Through this formalized cognition, however, the liberal subject's ideation is itself prone to formalist predilections that continually seek to harmonize the disagreements, dissensions, and general disarray that otherwise upset the liberal mind, the liberal individual, the liberal political sphere, and society more generally' (*Living Liberalism*, p. 10).

19. Johannes Fabian calls this the 'denial of coevalness' in *Time and the Other*, p. 32. Through his concept of the 'ethnographic pastoral' – a 'structure of retrospection' that relegates a culture to the past through the very the act of representing it – James Clifford also notes how ethnographic representation renders traditional cultures anachronistic ('On Ethnographic Allegory', p. 110). Scholars in the field of Native studies, in turn, have noted that 'salvage ethnography' – a form of ethnography that seeks to represent traditional cultures that are thought to be disappearing – is particularly pernicious because it not only denies Native culture's coevalness, but also denies Native people futurity ('Tradition', p. 234).

20. In her chapter 'The Irishness of Liberal Opinion' from *Living Liberalism*, Elaine Hadley both articulates this problem and suggests that trying to reconcile Irishness and mid-century liberalism led to a new form of liberalism grounded in occupation (labour, habitation) rather than land ownership; see especially pp. 229–36. Lloyd's *Irish Culture and Colonial Modernity 1800–2000* also traces this ideology; see pp. 4–13.

21. O'Connell, *Ireland and the Fiction of Improvement*, p. 19.

22. Lloyd, *Anomalous States*, p. 6.

23. Carleton, *Traits and Stories of the Irish Peasantry*, p. iii, p. iv. Cited in the text hereafter, abbreviated as *TS*.

24. W. B. Yeats, 'Introduction', p. 28. Reviews also celebrated the fact that he remained untouched by 'metropolitan influences' ('Mr William Carleton', p. 126). In *Irish Novelists and the Victorian Age*, James Murphy suggests that Carleton himself claimed this 'extra-literary' authority (pp. 46–7).

25. K. T., 'A Literary Causerie', p. 353.

26. For Buzard, the Irish novel is important to the development of British ethnographic fiction precisely because it portrays a unified national culture. He argues that Irish novelists like Maria Edgeworth and Lady Morgan move between the Irish culture they represent and an English reading audience in ways that produce a national cultural unit. In Buzard's words, 'the idea that an autoethnographer's own culture was an abstraction visible only from the outside set a premium upon those Irish or Scottish figures most advantageously situated in relation to an English audience and able to look "back" at their own lands through English eyes' (*Disorienting Fiction*, p. 41).

27. In other words, I argue that Carleton legitimates what David Lloyd calls 'oral spaces' that 'furnish what we can call counter-modern spaces and practices, captured and determined by institutions of modernity, yet preserving and refunctioning elements of the non-modern that remain recalcitrant or antagonistic to the disciplines of capitalist labour or state formation' (*Irish Culture and Colonial Modernity 1800–2000*, p. 9).
28. 'A Retrospect', p. 89.
29. Jenkins, *The Fenian Problem*, p. 24.
30. Martin, *Alter-Nations*, p. 202.
31. Nolan, *Catholic Emancipations*, p. 111.
32. For a longer version of this argument, see Mullen, 'Empire and Unfielding'.
33. See respectively: 'Charles Kickham's Career', p. 5; 'Leader Page Parade', p. 4; 'English Books for Irish Children', p. 12.
34. See respectively: Maher, 'Tale of a Stamp', p. 4; 'Garden Party and Reception', p. 10.
35. For Amanda Anderson, realism highlights liberalism's tension between 'skepticism and hope', between understanding existential political challenges and 'the commitment to a reformist politics that engages and affirms existing democratic institutions and structures' (*Bleak Liberalism*, p. 34). Kickham also alternates between 'skepticism and hope', but he locates hope in his characters' willingness to think beyond existing institutions and remains sceptical about the possibilities of liberal reform.
36. Lloyd, *Anomalous States*, p. 149.
37. Edgeworth, *Castle Rackrent*, p. 133.
38. William Carleton makes this claim when he reflects on the novel in his autobiography, which was ultimately completed by David J. O'Donoghue (*The Life of William Carleton*, p. 29).
39. Carleton, *Valentine M'Clutchy, The Irish Agent*, p. 92. Cited in the text hereafter, abbreviated as *VM*.
40. Hadley, *Living Liberalism*, p. 7.
41. Mill, 'Considerations on Representative Government', pp. 209–10.
42. I refer to Topertoe as Richard throughout this chapter, but Carleton changes the character's name over the course of the novel. At the beginning, he is called Alexander; by the end, he is called Richard.
43. *The Freeman's Journal* published the Orange Order's resolution not to sing this song as early as 1798, declaring the singing of this song 'directly contrary to our Principles' ('The Grand Orange Lodge of Ireland', p. 1).
44. 'Article XIV. Reports from the Select Committees appointed to inquire . . .', p. 352.
45. 'Art. XI. Orange Societies in Great Britain – Their Illegality and Criminality', p. 502.
46. 'The Orange Institution', p. 406.

47. Ibid.
48. Ahmed, 'The Nonperformativity of Antiracism', p. 105.
49. Ibid.
50. Cleary, *Literature, Partition and the Nation State*, p. 68. Of course, in practice, they follow old routes in part to incite violence.
51. Bryan, *Orange Parades*, p. 7.
52. Hadley, *Living Liberalism*, p. 288.
53. Ibid. p. 231.
54. Ibid. pp. 241–2. The nationalist newspaper *The Nation*, for instance, stated its mission as 'to create and foster public opinion in Ireland, and make it racy of the soil' (Duffy, *Young Ireland*, p. 23).
55. See Hadley, *Living Liberalism*, p. 13. Also see Lisa Lowe, who argues that 'as liberalism defined the "human" and universalized its attributes to European man, it simultaneously differentiated populations in the colonies as less than human' (*The Intimacies of Four Continents*, p. 6).
56. Kinealy, *This Great Calamity*, p. 37.
57. Carleton, *The Black Prophet*, p. vi. Cited in the text hereafter, abbreviated as *BP*.
58. Clifford, 'On Ethnographic Allegory', p. 110.
59. Ibid. p. 112.
60. Melissa Fegan discusses Carleton's complicated relationship to peasant prophecy, noting that while he disliked the prophecies of the downfall of the Protestant church made by people like Pastorini and Colmkille, Carleton often made decisions based on prophecy and tends to be prophetic in his writing (*Literature and the Irish Famine*, pp. 143–4).
61. Melissa Fegan holds that the practice of Irish prophecy dwindled away before the Famine, in part because Irish prophets foretold the end of the Protestant church in 1825, but 1825 came and went without event (*Literature and the Irish Famine*, p. 156).
62. Trevelyan, *The Irish Crisis*, p. 148.
63. Devon, 'The Apprehended Irish Famine', p. 5.
64. Fegan, *Literature and the Irish Famine*, p. 158.
65. Eagleton, *Heathcliff and the Great Hunger*, p. 152.
66. By connecting the advent of famine to the introduction of the potato, Carleton echoes English suspicions about Irish diets. As Catherine Gallagher argues, the potato was 'an icon of the autochthonous body for certain late-eighteenth- and early-nineteenth-century writers' ('The Potato in the Materialist Imagination', p. 111). The English populace favoured bread as opposed to the potato because they associated bread with a higher state of civilisation. Bread required more labour and was more distanced from the land. By claiming that famine originates with the potato instead of showing how the potato allowed Irish people to subsist on very little, Carleton perhaps betrays his interest in agricultural improvement and capitalist rationalisation.

67. Michael Elliot argues that ethnography in the nineteenth-century novel can challenge as well as reinforce Fabian's argument about the 'denial of coevalness' because ethnography had not yet been institutionalised. In his words, 'thinking about time within the domain of ethnography returns us to the conditions upon which this discursive form was founded, not as a disciplinary mode of inquiry but as an undisciplined form of writing that could circulate through a wide variety of texts' ('Other Times', p. 491).

68. O'Leary, *Recollections of Fenians and Fenianism*, p. 264.

69. *The Nation* apparently suggested that Kickham was 'Dickens without his exaggeration, and Thackeray without his bitterness' (M. R., 'A Few More Relics of Charles Kickham', p. 131). In response, Kickham said, 'But Dickens with his exaggeration is exactly what I would strive to be, the ideal at which I would aim, but could never hope to get within leagues of' (M. R., 'A Few More Relics of Charles Kickham', p. 132).

70. Comerford, *Charles J. Kickham*, pp. 200–1.

71. Ibid. p. 201.

72. Houlihan, 'Kickham's work up there with the great Irish novels', p. 20.

73. Nolan, *Catholic Emancipations*, p. 118.

74. Mighall, *A Geography of Victorian Gothic Fiction*, p. 18.

75. Kilfeather, 'Terrific Register', p. 54.

76. Kilfeather also suggests that Irish gothic tropes sometimes 'suggest that nostalgia may be a future, rather than a past, mode of being in the world' ('Terrific Register', p. 67).

77. This validation of Catholic practice outside the bounds of the Catholic Church was especially important to Kickham because he remained a devout Catholic despite his frequent opposition to the Church and clergy. Near the end of his life, he visited Archbishop Croke to see if he could be admitted to the sacraments without renouncing his Fenianism (Comerford, *Charles J. Kickham*, p. 160).

78. Baucom, 'Afterword: States of Time', p. 713.

79. George II reportedly made this statement in 1745 after the Irish Brigade was instrumental in securing a French victory over the British.

Chapter 3

George Eliot's Anachronistic Literacies

'The more deeply we penetrate into the knowledge of society in its details, the more thoroughly we shall be convinced that *a universal social policy has no validity except on paper*.'[1]

'Here and there is born a Saint Theresa, foundress of nothing.'[2]

Like William Carleton and Charles Kickham, George Eliot wrote novels set in provincial locations in the near-distant past. But most scholars suggest that Eliot's provincialism works differently. While Carleton's and Kickham's provincialism remains minor – they represent peripheral Irish settings related to but distinct from metropolitan centres – Eliot's provincial settings function as what Ian Duncan calls the 'authentic site of an imperial England able to select and absorb the forces of change, renewing rather than surrendering its traditional properties'.[3] Thus, while critics believe Carleton and Kickham produce ethnographic realism that records an anachronistic culture slowly disappearing, they suggest that Eliot's novels 'absorb the forces of change' by creating an ever-expanding, ahistorical web of imperial consensus. Indeed, Eliot's importance to the institutionalisation of realism within the Victorian period and within scholarly criticism about realism today is tied to her ability to create integrative novelistic forms. Associated with 'settlement and stability', *Middlemarch* (1871) dominates discussions of Irish realism because it so clearly seems to represent the unified, integrative narrative form that Irish realism fails to reproduce.[4] Victorianist scholars have more varied interpretations of Eliot's fiction, but they also tend to see it as exemplifying realist form.[5]

Instead of using *Middlemarch* as a standard through which to measure Irish realism's failure, however, I claim that Irish realist novels allow us to understand the narrative form and political effects of

Eliot's novels in new ways. Like Carleton and Kickham, Eliot moves between being inside and outside of a culture as well as between past and present. James Buzard even goes so far as to suggest that in *Middlemarch*, 'narrative self-interruption . . . becomes almost embarrassingly overt'.[6] And, as is the case in Carleton's and Kickham's novels, this self-interruption both consolidates and questions a larger narrative of institutional consolidation. Eliot represents how modern institutionalism absorbs the forces of change, as Duncan suggests, but also, like Carleton and Kickham, represents the political possibilities of anachronism that unsettle social consensus.

In Eliot's fiction, gender and literacy demonstrate Eliot's contradictory approach to modern institutionalism. Adopting the distanced narrative structure of Walter Scott's novels – *Adam Bede* (1859) takes place sixty years before the narrative, while *The Mill on the Floss* (1860) takes place forty years before the narrative – Eliot's narrators use historical distance to reflect on 'the explosion of reading' in the Romantic period.[7] She represents early evening schools in *Adam Bede*, Tom Tulliver's antiquated education in *The Mill on the Floss*, and women's exclusion from formal schooling in order to distinguish between the past that she represents – a moment of limited literacy and ineffective schools – and the present in which she writes – a more educated time when novel reading and standardised meaning is widespread. Literacy functions as an index of modernisation in her novels that relegates illiterate characters, such as Hetty Sorrel, to an anachronistic past. These characters with limited literacy are necessary anachronisms insofar as they define who counts as a political agent and a historical subject in terms of institutions and suggest that modernisation occurs through increased literacy and education.

But although increased literacy and education create historical distance in Eliot's novels, she also represents reading practices that collapse this distance. In *The Mill on the Floss*, Eliot celebrates what I call anachronistic literacy – a mode of reading that mobilises unnecessary anachronisms, or anachronisms that do not elucidate development, by collapsing the distance between past and present. Although all reading has the potential to mobilise anachronisms insofar as the time of reading differs from the time of the text's production, often institutionalised reading practices minimise the untimely nature of the text by situating literary works in their historical moment or in a broader intellectual tradition. In fact, institutions often mediate literary texts from the past so that they stay in their proper historical moment and reinforce a narrative of development. By contrast, anachronistic literacy actively explodes historical distance by making the past speak in the present. In the revenge plot, Mr Tulliver uses writing to ensure stasis, and Maggie Tulliver's reading of Thomas à Kempis activates old beliefs within modernity. More than simply a dangerous form of literacy that increased education must root out, anachronistic literacy is a practice that fosters lived relationships to the past that work against modern institutionalism's emphasis on futurity and distance.

The fact that literacy, as an index of modernisation, creates historical distance, and literacy, as a practice, collapses this very distance leads to contradictions within Eliot's novels. Reading, for Eliot, alternates between being an institutional and an anachronistic practice; it supports and questions modern institutionalism in turn. Eliot welcomes the future that educational institutions promise – increased literacy – but remains suspicious of the codified, rationalised and regulated practices that these very institutions teach. Moreover, she questions women's relationship to these educational institutions, noting how, even in modernity, women are often excluded from formal education. Eliot uses historical distance and necessary anachronisms to produce a narrative of modernisation through institutions, but also represents how establishing lived relationships with the past through unnecessary anachronisms allows people to imagine new social arrangements.

Thinking about Eliot in terms of institutions is in many ways counterintuitive. Scholars tend to understand her realism as evacuating history and politics in favour of ethics. Her choice of provincial settings located in the past allows her to represent a 'knowable community': a community defined through custom and face-to-face interactions rather than modern institutions.[8] Her narrators consistently describe the realist project in experiential and individual terms, insisting that they narrate personal experience rather than more systematised and abstract, 'correct views'.[9] When her novels do allude to institutions, they tend to express scepticism. *Adam Bede* values education but questions college education – 'life has been a better school' for Adam than college has been for Arthur Donnithorne; *The Mill on the Floss* suggests that Maggie learns more from her patchwork reading than Tom does from his systemised education; and *Middlemarch* favours Dorothea Brooke's thirst for knowledge over her husband Edward Casaubon's established – but very dry – scholarship (*AB* 167). At first glance, educational institutions function in very similar ways as the police in D. A. Miller's famous account – they are minimised in the novel because their practices are so thoroughly dispersed throughout society. If everyday experience – and representations of everyday experience in novels – is educational, then we hardly need college or formal schooling.[10]

Although Eliot is sceptical of the institutions that she refers to in her novels, I suggest that she nevertheless embraces modern institutionalism – the social theory underlying institutions – through the narrative structure of her plots. Her novels adopt a form of historicism that contemporary social scientists would call 'path dependency'. Path dependency is a historicist method that explains why institutions endure over time.[11] Suggesting that organisations make decisions at 'critical junctures' and that subsequent developments reinforce these decisions, social scientists use path dependency to suggest why it becomes more difficult to change or reject institutions after they have been established.[12] Path dependency explains why institutions feel inevitable by showing how institutions reduce historical possibilities over time. George Eliot's plots show path dependency in action. In *Daniel Deronda* (1876), for instance, Gwendolen Harleth agonises over whether she should marry Grandcourt. But as soon as she decides to marry him, she recognises that she must follow a new path. She thinks to herself on her wedding day, 'She could not go backward now.'[13] As a historicist model, path dependency demonstrates how institutions – in this case, marriage – acquire force over time by restricting actors' choices.

Against the grain of these path-dependent narratives, however, Eliot imagines alternative paths through anachronisms that restore the full range of historical possibilities and imagine history otherwise. These anachronisms suggest that characters and readers alike can 'go backward' as they unsettle path dependency's sense of historical inevitability. In Eliot's fiction, these anachronisms are gendered insofar as they emerge in relation to a divided social landscape that distinguishes between men and women, economic and social reproduction, present and past. Showing how the idea of 'separate spheres' is as much a temporal structure as a spatial one, Eliot indicates that women are associated with tradition, even timelessness, rather than modernisation.[14] But in Eliot's novels, representations of women's untimeliness not only uphold this divided social structure, they suggest that characters and readers alike can imagine the future otherwise. I argue that anachronistic literacy – a mode of reading that collapses the distance between past and present – is a method that uses women's uneasy relationship to modern institutionalism to imagine alternative social arrangements. While path dependency assumes that the existing institutional path is inevitable, anachronistic literacy shows that history does not necessarily follow a single path. Representing 'forces of change' which cannot be 'absorbed', as well as historical temporalities that resist institutionalisation, anachronistic literacy fosters lived relationships to the past that reveal multiple historical possibilities rather than confirming the existing institutional path.

'Tis Sixty Years Since; or, Gender and Institutions

Reviewing a new edition of Margaret Fuller's *Woman in the Nineteenth Century* (1843) in 1855, George Eliot turns to Mary Wollstonecraft's *Rights of Woman* (1792) – a text that, in the nineteenth century, 'is now rather scarce'.[15] Eliot suggests that despite their 'difference of date', these two texts betray strikingly similar thoughts. The 'difference of date' is fifty-one years (in the review, Eliot adds another temporal layer by noting that Wollstonecraft wrote 'between sixty and seventy years' ago).[16] However, unlike Walter Scott's ''tis sixty years since', where sixty years is just enough historical distance to measure progress while maintaining important affective connections to the past, these two texts show very little change. Eliot even indicates that they share 'every important idea'.[17] Both question social anxieties about educating women, suggesting that women are capable of doing and learning more than society allows. By bringing the texts together, Eliot collapses historical distance to show Wollstonecraft's continued relevance in the Victorian period, but, just as importantly, to suggest that 'sixty years' is not as stable a measure of historical distance as Scott indicates. For if sixty years is long enough to change the Scottish nation dramatically, it is hardly enough time to produce substantial changes to the institution of marriage or women's access to education.

I suggest that this review is an act of anachronistic literacy: a mode of reading that collapses the distance between past and present. By choosing to read Margaret Fuller in relation to Mary Wollstonecraft in 1855, Eliot does more than reclaim two authors that have 'been unduly thrust into the background'.[18] She suggests that books, especially books that are relatively forgotten, allow us to rethink the relationship between past and present. After all, the review conveys Eliot's uncanny sense that these two books have received less lasting critical attention precisely because they are so politically important – they are ignored in favour of 'less comprehensive and candid productions on the same subject'.[19] Emphasising the importance of reading texts rather than simply repeating received wisdom, Eliot indicates that these books can reanimate the past in ways that challenge the social assumptions of the present. As Elizabeth Freeman argues, close reading in itself can be a queer act: a way of challenging the belief that history moves uniformly in one direction.[20] Thus, even as Eliot argues for gradual change and reform within the review, her practice of reading mobilises untimeliness to question social norms and historical assumptions.

Eliot pairs these texts to show stasis and argue for institutional change. She indicates that while some people think that women need to improve in order to change their position, others suggest that women cannot improve until institutions change. Her conclusion merges these two positions as it promotes slow reform: 'There is perpetual action and reaction between individuals and institutions; we must try and mend both by little and little – the only way in which human things can be mended.'[21] This statement of 'perpetual action and reaction' suggests that although institutions are not all-powerful, women still need to route individual reform through institutions. It is a relatively conservative position, but one that nevertheless allows for institutional critique. Eliot concludes that if women could be easily improved – or if they were already 'perfected' – 'then there would be a case in which slavery and ignorance nourished virtue, and so far we should have an argument for the continuance of bondage'.[22] The best way to change institutions, for Eliot, is to show that individuals *cannot* change without institutional reform because institutions shape, constrain and, in many cases, harm individuals.

Of course, women's lives and institutions governing women's lives *did* change throughout the nineteenth century. As Eve Kosofsky Sedgwick suggests, Eliot chronicles many of these changes in *Adam Bede* as the novel narrates how women's and men's economic roles, once overlapping, become distinct.[23] And women's relationships to modern institutionalism are not entirely coherent – some nineteenth-century women effected change outside of public institutions, while others participated in and shaped them.[24] Yet Eliot's rhetorical move to make these two disparate historical texts contemporaries, to adopt a form of anachronistic literacy, demonstrates how feminist and proto-feminist theory depends upon untimeliness as a mode of critique. As Sara Ahmed suggests, feminism confronts 'what has not ended'.[25] While path dependency promises both continuity and development as it suggests that people progress by following an established institutional path, feminism suggests that this institutional path does not bring progress for everyone. Progress for some people is stasis for others. Thus, although early activists in the women's movement 'aspired to gain a place in linear time',[26] such desire for timeliness gave way to the more radical assertion that feminist theory 'should be about what is *untimely*, what is out of time'.[27] Despite Eliot's conservatism that delimits the possibilities of social change by defining the future as an extension of the present, her novels also use anachronism, untimely irruptions of the past, to imagine history and politics otherwise.

To suggest that Eliot's novels imagine alternative historical paths by thinking through the radical potential of untimeliness, of course, works against the dominant form of path-dependent historicism in her novels. Focusing on the contingent moments of critical juncture and the resulting stability over time, path dependency helpfully shows that the early history of the institution matters. But path dependency also highlights the problem of modern institutionalism: that the future of the institution is determined early on by the chosen 'path' and thus seems to be inevitable. Narratives of path dependency are thus deterministic narratives insofar as they naturalise the existing path as the only possible path. Except in moments of untimely irruption that briefly open up alternative possibilities, Eliot's novels embrace this conservative narrative structure.

Examining how the consequences of individual actions live on, Eliot narrates the contingency of critical junctures and the inevitable consequences that emerge from actions at these very junctures. In *Adam Bede*, Arthur Donnithorne has an affair with Hetty because of 'a disastrous combination of circumstances' that the novel painstakingly documents: his horse is lame so he cannot get away, Hetty begins to cry, he does not know that Adam loves Hetty, he is unable to confess to Mr Irwine (*AB* 126). But attention to such contingencies ultimately underscores just how important his decision to pursue Hetty is: '*it can never be undone*' (*AB* 422). In *The Mill on the Floss*, Maggie refuses to marry Stephen after they venture too far on a boat and must stay overnight, saying, 'I will not begin any future . . . with a deliberate consent to what ought not to have been.'[28] But her refusal of this new path is not enough – because of her decision (or avoidance of a decision) during her transgressive adventure with Stephen, society still speaks badly of her. Maggie's subsequent actions cannot change the narrative about her or the consequences she faces.

At first glance, these path-dependent narratives seem to be about individuals rather than institutions, character rather than culture. They highlight what Stefanie Markovits calls George Eliot's 'problem with action': because Eliot is concerned about the consequences of actions at critical junctures, she advocates for good habits that ensure that individuals make the right decision.[29] Or, to put it slightly differently, when it comes to individual character, Eliot doubles down on path dependency, suggesting that individuals should choose a path long before they confront any critical junctures to guarantee that they stay on the straight and narrow in the face of any contingencies. For this reason, her novels often present characters in dichotomous pairs to distinguish between good and bad habits, characters who struggle at moments of crisis and characters who can handle crisis – Hetty and Dinah, Maggie and Lucy (as well as, more ambiguously, Maggie and Tom) – to elucidate how action is, and should be, habitual.

But although Eliot's narratives focus on individual actions, they aestheticise institutionalism through their path-dependent historicism – or change that emerges from constraining choices, blending the past and the present, and affirming rather than altering the established path. Such institutional aesthetics of blending are explicitly apparent in *Felix Holt: The Radical* (1866), where Eliot argues for social change but questions whether the nation should too quickly abandon the path it is following. In this novel, Harold Transome's decision to stand as a radical is troubling because it represents rupture rather than continuity with traditional expectations. Questioning how far his nephew's radicalism extends, Mr Lingon asks, 'But you'll not be attacking the Church and the institutions of the country – you'll not be going those lengths; you'll keep up the bulwarks, and so on, eh?'[30] Having no desire to protect these bulwarks, Harold evades the question by suggesting he'll only 'remove the rotten timbers' – addressing abuses rather than the institutions themselves.[31] By contrast, Felix Holt's radicalism celebrates 'the wonderful slow-growing system of things', unequivocally suggesting that despite the prevalence of institutional abuses, society must maintain these very institutions and change them from within.[32] In this political novel, path dependency means maintaining the old institutions but imagining a new future from these very institutions.

Despite the predominance of path-dependent historicism, Eliot's novels, like her review, play with historical distance. Adopting Scott's distanced narrator, Eliot nevertheless indicates that such distance is unstable because of how both literacy and gender shape one's relationship to the past.[33] In her review, reading Mary Wollstonecraft's relatively forgotten text disrupts the linear sequence of history and validates anachronisms that unsettle modern institutionalism's emphasis on futurity. In her novels, the act of memory has a similar effect. When Romola's godfather, Bernado del Nero, is sentenced to death for treason, Romola feels 'the full force of that sympathy with the individual lot that is continually opposing itself to the formulae by which actions and parties are judged'.[34] Bernado laments that in death he cannot help her, but she asserts: 'you *will* help me – always

– because I shall remember you' (*R* 498). Remembering him means recalling his guidance and support, and, just as importantly, how his death inspires opposition to 'formulae by which actions and parties and judged'. Thus, like Kickham's future-oriented nostalgia, memory and reading in Eliot's novels keep pasts alive that have no future in existing institutions.

Through her depictions of women characters and narrative addresses to women readers, Eliot's novels show that historical distance becomes unstable precisely when there are questions about whether education is possible or desirable. The numerous debates about women's education in the nineteenth century – debates that Wollstonecraft, Fuller, but also Eliot participated in – questioned whether women should or could be educated, and discussed the proper mode of educating women. Kate Flint identifies the contradictions at work in such debates, suggesting that there was a great deal of ambivalence about whether reading and education would improve women or would lead to their downfall.[35] Because of such ambivalence, there were concerted efforts to control what women read, when they read and where they read. Participating in these debates, George Eliot's famous 1856 essay, 'Silly Novels by Lady Novelists', warns against 'feminine silliness' within novels precisely because 'it tends to confirm the popular prejudice against the more solid education of women'.[36] Arguing that women novelists mistakenly celebrate their individual intellect rather than merging their knowledge with culture, Eliot suggests that properly 'serious' women novelists blend individual intellect with the community: they integrate individual talent into cultural institutions. Debating women's education introduces questions of utility – would more education and reading help women or only distract them from their domestic responsibilities?; questions of ability – are women capable of learning the same things that men are?; and questions of representativeness – how do individual women need to act differently in order to represent women's ability to learn?

These Victorian discussions about women's education seek to manage women's relationship to modernity. John Ruskin's *Sesame and Lilies* not only famously articulates the separate spheres that men and women inhabit, but their differing relationships to modernity. While men can (and should) read ancient as well as modern texts, Ruskin advises: 'Keep the modern magazine and novel out of your girl's way: turn her loose into the old library every wet day, and let her alone.'[37] Safe in the 'old library', girls should follow established paths rather than forge new ones. Reading 'old' texts detaches women from present debates, prevents them from reading literature of unknown merit. Ruskin's guidelines for women readers indicate that separate spheres designate 'not social spaces per se but temporal *structures* – linear (public) or extralinear (private) time', as Dana Luciano contends.[38] Eliot takes up these temporal structures to both track the ways in which women are excluded from modern institutionalism and to insist that the seemingly static time of private life and the domestic sphere can encourage transhistorical relationships that disrupt the logic of path dependency. Reading old texts as if they were present and making them speak within modernity becomes a way of challenging the assumption that the present is inevitable. The past, as Eliot shows, does not always confirm the inevitability of the present; it can also disrupt existing social arrangements.

Working to extend existing institutional arrangements into the future, modern institutionalism, as a discourse, believes that institutions can integrate social difference without fundamentally changing social expectations. But anxiety about whether educated women will be good or bad institutional subjects, whether they will continue to preserve existing social arrangements or actively disrupt them, whether women should read modern texts or be restricted to the 'old library', suggests that the path that educational institutions map out is not the only path. The practice of reading, while actively shaped by institutions, can also be anachronistic.

Adam Bede and Institutional Blending

Hetty Sorrel, the character in *Adam Bede* that has received the most scholarly attention, reveals the complicated intersection of institutions and anachronisms in this 'paradigmatic' realist novel.[39] The novel excludes this 'distractingly pretty' milkmaid from the future of the community by transforming her from an active community member who disrupts the harmony of Hayslope to a memory that unifies it (*AB* 83).[40] Hetty's exclusion consolidates a future for the community that upholds the institutions of class, education and marriage. Eliot suggests that although the villagers mourn Hetty's death, they have nevertheless fashioned a more stable future from this very death, and ends the novel with Adam Bede and Dinah Morris's children. Hetty's character is a site of contradictions within the novel: a bad institutional subject that the narrative relegates to the past, Hetty both functions as a warning that establishes institutions as a horizon for futurity and shows the need for alternative paths.

The love affair between Hetty Sorrel and Arthur Donnithorne, which destroys the harmony of pastoral Hayslope, can be seen as the product of too little institutional thinking on the one hand, and too much faith in institutions on the other. Hetty is tempted by Arthur because she remains unaware of how institutions determine futures. Imagining a future with Arthur detached from existing social realities – namely, class and marriage – Hetty misunderstands what their love affair means. By contrast, Arthur pursues the affair despite his better judgement because he believes too strongly in institutions and the abstract agency they create. Believing that institutions, themselves, have agency makes him misunderstand his own actions as he defers his responsibility to his future position as landlord to the estate.

Imagining a future with Arthur, Hetty is able to break from both the present and the past. She imagines 'days that were not to be as the other days of her life had been' (*AB* 136). Arthur's appeal is thus not only his high position and the relative luxury he can provide her, but the fact that he can transport her to an alternative social reality. The narrator questions, 'Does any sweet or sad memory mingle with this dream of the future – any loving thought of her second parents – of the children she had helped to tend – of any youthful companion, any pet animal, any relic of her childhood even? Not one' (*AB* 154). Suggesting that Hetty's imagined future is a problem because it does not 'mingle' with the past, the narrator implies that 'proper' futures emerge from the past. When she reads Arthur's letter breaking off the affair it hurts all the more because 'reasons why he could not marry her had no existence for her mind' (*AB* 333). These 'reasons' are, of course, institutional: that marriage, as an institution, is supposed to unite people of the same class, not be a mode of transcending class distinctions. As Arthur puts it, their marriage would offend 'against my duty' (*AB* 332). Not willing to think in terms of duty, Hetty is thrust into 'dark unknown water' because she must face 'the uncertainty of the future' (*AB* 319). This 'uncertainty' results from the fact that she has already strayed from the proper path – she is pregnant but unmarried. Although Hetty attempts to navigate this uncertainty on her own terms, institutional certainty violently reasserts itself. Leaving the Poyser family with little money and then leaving her newborn baby to die, Hetty must confront institutional realities that she cannot ignore: the threat of '"the parish!"' and, later, prison and the law (*AB* 378).

Arthur, by contrast, is fully aware of the myriad reasons why he will never marry Hetty but pursues the affair nonetheless because he mistakenly trusts how institutions – especially his future institutional position as landlord to his grandfather's estate – have agency. Believing that he will be an improving landlord both popular with and useful to his tenants, he neglects his responsibility for his actions in the present. In fact, the deferred futurity associated with institutions becomes a model for his own decision-making as he convinces himself that 'good comes out of evil' (*AB* 312). Arthur seeks out Mr Irwine to confess his flirtation with Hetty only to keep his attraction a secret and question whether he is actually responsible for his actions. Commenting on Arthur's failure to confess, the narrator writes: 'Our mental business is carried on much in the same way as the business of the State: a great deal of hard work is done by agents who are not acknowledged' (*AB* 173). Like 'the business of the State' which fails to acknowledge individual agents at work, Arthur trusts the security of his future position without acknowledging how his relationship with Hetty might prevent this future. Assuming that he will be a good landlord in the future, Arthur fails to understand how the 'unrecognised agent' – his individual desire – shapes his present actions (*AB* 173). He actively forgets how he has already harmed his tenants because he believes he has successfully integrated his desire with institutional expectations.

Unlike Hetty and Arthur, Adam Bede embodies the proper relationship to institutions – a man of habit, devoted to work, he blends his desires with institutional realities that constrain these desires. He does not scheme to separate himself from his drunken father, but instead, upholding family as an institution, merges his 'conception of the future' with 'the painful image of his father' (*AB* 50). Similarly, although he loves Hetty, he does not fill his time at church with idle thoughts of her, these thoughts 'rather blended with all the other deep feelings for which the church service was a channel to him' (*AB* 199). When Hetty's act of infanticide dissolves his one hope for the future – to marry Hetty – he embraces the present: 'he conceived no picture of the future but one made up of hard-working days such as he lived through, with growing contentment and intensity of interest' (*AB* 488). Never diminishing his own agency, Adam nonetheless submits to the constraints of family and class – blending his desires with institutional expectations, his past with his future.

The contrast between Hetty and Arthur and Adam offers a thick description of how institutions shape and constrain the lives of members of this 'knowable community'. For if the village of Hayslope seems to be a rural ideal anchored to the past because of the predominance of social relations ungoverned by modern institutions – there

are no 'separate spheres' on the Poyser's farm and Dinah's Methodism is 'not indeed of that modern type' – the novel nevertheless shows
how institutions shape habits and, in turn, futures (*AB* 38).[41] Specifically, the novel highlights the differences between what John Stuart
Mill calls institutions 'interwoven with the daily habits of life' and
'weak' institutions that have not yet been incorporated into everyday
behaviour.[42] Class, marriage and family have blended with the habits
and social expectations of the community, while modern education,
legal institutions and 'the parish' that Hetty fears are relatively weak.
Because of the strength of family within the community, Arthur has
to give up his institutional position – joining the army rather than acting as landlord – in order to try to restore the social relations within
the village (*AB* 466). And yet, the social relations of the village are
not enough to change the law: despite Arthur's political influence,
Hetty does not receive a full pardon for killing her and Arthur's baby
and she is transported. In the face of the inflexibility of 'weak' institutions that are not intertwined with daily life, the novel encourages
further blending of individual desire and institutional expectations
so that these modern institutions never have to be encountered. By
encouraging this integration of individuals and institutions, the past
and present, Eliot embraces modern institutionalism even when she
spends little time representing modern institutions.

Metalepsis and Managing Historical Distance

Formally, *Adam Bede* blends individuals and institutions, past and
present in sites of metalepsis – places where the story (the plot) and
the discourse (the narration of the plot) collide. In postmodern fiction, such collisions tend to be transgressive, deliberately confusing
the plot with the narration of the plot in order to highlight the constructed nature of knowledge. In Carleton's and Kickham's novels,
metalepsis establishes the narrator's ethnographic authority as it distinguishes between the narrator's cultural knowledge and readers'
relative ignorance, traditional Irish culture and the modern moment
of writing. But in *Adam Bede*, metalepsis integrates disparate historical moments – the time of the story and the time of the narrator – in
order to interpellate the reader into the novel's blended aesthetics
that establish continuity over time.

The narrator and Adam Bede, for instance, have a conversation
with one another in a shared present moment, collapsing the boundaries between story and narrative, past and present. Through this

conversation, the narrator transforms what Gérard Genette calls 'the double temporality of the story and the narrative' into a single, continuous development as it blends the daily habits of the past with the expectations of modern institutions.[43] This blending has a contradictory effect, however, because although it produces a path-dependent historicist narrative, it also highlights the people and practices that cannot easily be integrated into the narrative's present. Hetty, for instance, seems trapped within the time of the story because of her inability to read. Unable to move seamlessly between past and present, Hetty shows the seemingly insurmountable differences between past and present: most notably, increased literacy.

Adam's conversation with the narrator in the oft-noted Chapter 17 – 'In which the story pauses a little' – demonstrate that the novel's blended aesthetics, which merge individual and institutional desires, past and present, produce a form of history defined through institutional continuity. For many scholars, this chapter functions as an interruption within the novel – a portable essay on realism that can be easily separated from the story in which it is embedded. However, this chapter actually merges the story and the discourse into a continuous, historical development – integrating past and present, characters and readers, to establish a sense of progression.[44] In other words, although literacy produces radical breaks between past and present, these metaleptic moments affirm a sense of historical continuity where literacy is a continuous development rather than a rupture.

The chapter begins by distinguishing the two narrative levels through historical differences. When a contemporary lady reader exclaims, 'This Rector of Broxton is little better than a pagan!' the narrator answers by historicising: 'Sixty years ago – it is a long time, so no wonder things have changed – all clergymen were not zealous' (*AB* 175). But the narrator quickly shifts from addressing a reader to talking directly to Adam, reporting a conversation between them 'in his old age' (*AB* 179).[45] By moving between a conversation with readers and a conversation with a character, the narrator brings readers and characters into the same narrative space and implies that Adam can answer the reader's questions. Acknowledging historical difference but collapsing historical distance, this conversation interrupts the narrative to reinforce the continuity between the characters in the story and the readers who read it.

More implicit sites of metalepsis also reinforce the continuous history that emerges from the conversation with Adam Bede by suggesting that human emotions often transcend their specific historical locations. The narrator's frequent use of the pronoun 'our' blends past and present into a single temporal development in part by consolidating a transhistorical subject position. When describing Seth Bede's love for Dinah Morris, the narrator shifts from Seth's particular feelings to a shared emotion as they describe how 'our emotion in its keenest moment passes from expression into silence; our love at its highest flood rushes beyond its object' (*AB* 37).[46] The narrator then articulates the historical continuity that the 'our' already implies, saying, 'This blessed gift of venerating love has been given to too many humble craftsmen since the world began, for us to feel any surprise that it should have existed in the soul of a Methodist carpenter half a century ago' (*AB* 37). Adam's sorrow evokes similar continuity as the narrator again moves from the particular to the general, writing: 'In our times of bitter suffering, there are almost always these pauses, when our consciousness is benumbed to everything but some trivial perception or sensation' (*AB* 404). Validating the importance of 'pauses' in life as well as in plotted narratives, the narrator uses this temporary break to assert the continuity between the past and present as well as between the novel's two narrative levels.

By contrast, Hetty is a figure of historical discontinuity – an anachronism that represents the differences between past and present that must be overcome for synthesis, integration and blending. After telling of Hetty's feelings for Arthur, the narrator reminds the reader: 'All this happened, you must remember, nearly sixty years ago, and Hetty was quite uneducated – a simple farmer's girl, to whom a gentleman with a white hand was dazzling as an Olympian God' (*AB* 100). Anticipating rather than responding to readers' questions, the narrator implies that Hetty's behaviour needs contextualisation because readers might easily forget that girls from the previous generation would lack education.[47] Unlike the interruption in Chapter 17, the narrator's work to historicise Hetty's behaviour occurs throughout the novel: historical context almost always accompanies descriptions of her interior life. Her emotions, it seems, do not blend with the readers' emotions, remaining distanced and historically rooted instead.

Such contextualisation – and distancing – ultimately associates futurity with literacy.[48] Unlike 'the lady readers' (*AB* 175) that Eliot's narrator addresses, 'Hetty had never read a novel: if she had ever seen one, I think the words would have been too hard for her: how then could she find a shape for her expectations?' (*AB* 136). Novels 'shape' expectations in institutional terms – implicitly teaching readers to fashion futures that acknowledge institutional constraints.[49]

Unable to read these novels, Hetty's sense of the future lacks institutional form. Hetty is not technically illiterate; she slowly reads
Arthur's letter, stumbling over his gentleman's handwriting, and
understands what it says. However, Hetty repeatedly refuses to use
her literacy – however limited – to learn more about the world. Even
after reading Arthur's letter, Hetty clings to her memory of Arthur's
love as opposed to the words in 'the cruel letter' (*AB* 371). Not being
well-read, she is unable to blend with other historical moments and
to fashion a 'probable future':

> She knew no romances, and had only a feeble share in the feelings which
> are the source of romance, so that well-read ladies may find it difficult
> to understand her state of mind. She was too ignorant of everything
> beyond the simple notions and habits in which she had been brought
> up, to have any more definite idea of her probable future than that
> Arthur would take care of her somehow, and shelter her from anger
> and scorn. (*AB* 372)

Here, reading becomes a bridge between 'the simple notions and
habits in which she had been brought up' and the modern perspective necessary for her to be understood by 'well-read ladies'.

Excluding Hetty from the future of the community because she
does not read 'romances' like modern 'well-read ladies' validates
these feminine novelistic genres as participating in the consolidation of more masculine educational institutions. Engaging in ongoing debates about whether novel reading is useful or frivolous, even
dangerous, Eliot legitimates 'the woman reader', regardless of the
genres that she reads, by suggesting that romances create a 'probable future' grounded in institutions. Such faith in romances is surprising, given Eliot's own suspicion of such reading in 'Silly Novels
by Lady Novelists'.[50] But Eliot does not contrast her realism with
romance, her serious novel with silly ones; she suggests that 'well-
read ladies' would not understand Hetty's state of mind because
they would imagine the future differently. Thus, Hetty's exclusion
from the community is historical – suggesting that her illiteracy is a
thing of the past that must be historicised in order to be understood
by modern readers – and pedagogical – suggesting that reading
overcomes the distance between past and present by establishing
a shared 'state of mind'. Reading creates and abolishes historical
distance – it marks Hetty as historically different from the readers
of Eliot's novel but nevertheless allows these very readers to connect with her and the past she represents. Like Eliot's review of

Mary Wollstonecraft and Margaret Fuller, these readers can make Hetty, however anachronistic, become present once more.

Thus, Eliot's representation of reading in *Adam Bede* ultimately has two distinct effects. The novel demonstrates that reading teaches people to imagine institutional futures but also shows how the very act of reading can forge transhistorical connections that disrupt the future-oriented emphasis of modern institutionalism. After all, in a few brief moments, Eliot acknowledges that Hetty's experience of 'womanhood' actually connects her to the lady readers who question her actions (*AB* 221). These moments are often uncomfortable, for the narrator writes, 'it is too painful to think that she is a woman, with a woman's destiny before her' (*AB* 249).[51] While 'woman's destiny' might be specific here – suggesting pregnancy and childbirth – it also ultimately extends beyond this specific reference to reveal women's uncomfortable relationship to history. Fashioning a future has little meaning here: Hetty must confront her destiny as a woman. Facing a 'woman's destiny' means resigning oneself to other people's futures – just as Dinah learns to accept marriage and stop preaching. As Dana Luciano warns, establishing motherhood as 'the temporal destiny of the female body'[52] works to extend 'an essential *identity* between past and present into the future'.[53] In this way, 'woman's destiny', however specific, represents a form of futurity that replicates rather than develops out of the past. To the extent that Hetty is 'a woman' as opposed to a historically located 'simple farmer's girl', she represents experience that transcends her historical position.

Georg Lukács would be sceptical of such claims to 'destiny' in opposition to history. After all, he praises Walter Scott's realism for creating 'historical-social types', not social types seemingly at odds with history.[54] Many twentieth- and twenty-first-century feminists would also bristle against the narrator's ahistorical account of 'woman's destiny', arguing, as Joan Wallach Scott does, that 'there is no essence of womanhood (or of manhood) to provide a stable subject for our histories'.[55] But the narrator's ahistorical account of Hetty's 'woman's destiny' actually does important historical work by showing women's uneasy relationship to modern institutionalism. Highlighting the differences between Hetty as a symbol of historical alterity (a necessary anachronism that reveals the increased literacy associated with modernisation), and Hetty as a site of historical stasis (an unnecessary anachronism that forges transhistorical relationships between women), the novel reveals the fundamental discordance of historical time. This discordance suggests 'historical-social types' are unevenly distributed: certain social positions are defined in opposition to history.[56]

From this perspective, Hetty's lack of agency – her failure to be what Harry Shaw calls 'an active bearer of personal experience' – is precisely what connects her to the 'lady readers' whose literacy separates them from Hetty's state of mind.[57] As readers who use their modern education to be aware of probable futures, they, like Adam, appear to be good institutional subjects. But, as women, they also share Hetty's powerlessness in the face of destiny. I do not mean to suggest that women had no power in the Victorian period or even that Hetty has no power in this narrative, but rather contend that the realist novel shapes a particular form of feminine subject that both consolidates and questions modern institutionalism. In *Adam Bede*, women characters can choose a romantic partner, but as Hilary Schor argues, they do not always have 'the chance to fulfill that striving after something original only they can see'.[58]

Despite the narrator's historicising, the reader can interpret Hetty's actions not as the result of her limited literacy or even her moral failings, but rather as the expression of a desire to seek out a future that is not preordained – to escape her destiny. After all, Hetty is one of the very few characters in the novel who is open to the possibility of an unknown future; she tries – and fails – to find a future that does not replicate the past. As the narrator tells the reader, 'she could never stay here and go on with the old life – she could better bear something quite new than sinking back into the old everyday round' (335). Her attempt to seek something new ultimately fails because she cannot confront the 'difficulties' that accompany forging one's own path (335). The painful, transhistorical connections between women that emerge at odds with the path-dependent narrative of modernisation allow Hetty to become a figure that points to new futures rather than one who remains entirely rooted in the past or defined through the present. In this way, Hetty's untimeliness not only represents that which must be excluded in the name of progress, but also, in brief, painful moments that the novel ultimately closes down, imagines politics otherwise where women yearn after the unknown instead of following the narrow path of the known.

The Mill On The Floss: Reading and Distance

Like *Adam Bede*, *The Mill on the Floss* both associates literacy with modern institutionalism and uses literacy to foster transhistorical relationships that question path-dependent modernisation. Adopting the *Bildungsroman* form, the novel describes the failed education of the two Tulliver children – Tom receives an outdated education and Maggie receives none – and dramatises their attempts to reconcile their ties to the past with their desires for the future. Tom Tulliver economically advances but stubbornly maintains his father's dislike of the Lawyer Wakem and thus has difficulty imagining any personal future. In turn, Maggie Tulliver seems to be awakened to the possibilities of a larger, less constraining world only to return to St Oggs 'to be rescued from more falling' (*MF* 479). The novel ends with the reunion of Tom and Maggie as they futilely try to escape the flood and, in death, seem to return to their days of childhood: 'the days when they had clasped their hands in love, and roamed the daisied fields together' (*MF* 521).

Scholars have long tried to resolve the novel's emphasis on modernisation with its regressive ending. Feminist theorists suggest that the novel reveals the difficulty of plotting a female protagonist, building on Gillian Beer's claim that Maggie is 'trapped in time' because social and historical change occurs at a slower rate than her own personal development.[59] Certainly, the novel's ending shifts from history to destiny, seemingly validating deterministic rather than contingent forces. But the novel's regressive ending does not necessarily suggest that Maggie is trapped by time: it demonstrates the radical potential of anachronism. Her retreat to the past at the end of the novel echoes her anachronistic reading throughout the novel, mobilising the possibilities of other historical moments as it represents the limits of path dependency as a model of history.

Literacy and education are key sites where linear modernisation and anachronism collide within the novel. They reveal the 'onward tendency of human things' by distinguishing the era of 'modern' education – or the time of the discourse – from the 'dark ages' that precede modern education – the time of the story (*MF* 272–3, *MF* 167). In the story, characters lack standardised literacy: Tom struggles 'not only with the Latin grammar but with a new standard of English pronunciation' (*MF* 134), Maggie reads haphazardly and Mr Tulliver spells according to personal preference. Thirty years later, however, in the 'instructed times' of the narrator and reader, standard English and standardised systems of education have become normal (*MF* 70).

As is the case in *Adam Bede*, Eliot distinguishes between strong and weak institutions, in part by contrasting the Dodsons' habitual family practice with Mr Tulliver's vague desire for Tom to get ahead in business by becoming 'a scholard' (*MF* 16). 'Puzzled' by modernity and victimised by the law, Mr Tulliver wants Tom to use institutions rather than be confused by them and to become 'a match for the lawyers' (*MF* 19). But such vague ambition for his son contradicts the Dodson family's 'particular ways of doing everything" (*MF* 43). The Dodson's habits are 'a peculiar tradition' rather than a modern institution (*MF* 44). In the time of the story, at least, this tradition is far stronger than Mr Tulliver's impulse to use institutions to advance.[60] By the time of the discourse forty years later, the relative strengths of institutions and traditions have reversed: the Dodsons' habits seem out of date, while education has become standardised and normalised. If the *Bildungsroman* plot fails because neither Maggie nor Tom achieve maturity, the narrative nevertheless achieves the genre's purpose: integrating 'peculiar traditions' of particular families into institutional time.[61]

Both the traditions of Dodson family and the modern institutions that render such traditions obsolete produce gendered structures that distinguish between boys and girls, men and women. The opening book, 'Boy and Girl', narrates how family structures reinforce gender differences, while the second book, 'School-time' suggests that the very educational institutions that will transform traditional family structures reproduce its gendered exclusions. Narrating the relationship between two seemingly stark divisions – past and present, boys and girls – Eliot suggests supposed 'separate spheres' can challenge modern institutionalism's vision of a shared future by showing the temporal discordance of the present. Women's untimeliness, for Eliot, is not simply a problem that modern institutionalism has to solve, but also a way of forging alternative relationships between past and present, and imagining the future otherwise.

Anachronistic Literacies

The Mill on the Floss expands *Adam Bede*'s brief questioning of path dependency by representing literacy not simply as a way to 'get for'ard in the world', but also as a method of disrupting the onward flow of linear time (*AB* 245). In *The Mill on the Floss*, non-standard forms of literacy make characters appear anachronistic to modern readers, but also enable forms of reading that push against modern institutionalism's emphasis on futurity. Anachronistic literacy, in this novel, is a mode of connecting to the past – a form of relationality – that undermines path dependency by showing that there are multiple lived relationships to the past.

Mr Tulliver's written vow in the family Bible is one example of anachronistic literacy because it promotes stasis rather than linear sequence. Vowing both to 'serve [Wakem] honest' and 'wish evil may befall him', Mr Tulliver betrays his incomplete submission to institutions (*MF* 267). He acknowledges that the law and his marriage are too much for him and thus he needs to work at the mill under Wakem to support his family, but he nevertheless uses writing to insist that vengeance rather than submission should extend into the future. As Leah Price suggests, his writing 'unread[s]' the Bible by privileging the book's function as a material and social object over its meaning as a written text.[62] The language of the vow ensures the continuance of the past and negates the present arrangement of power. Mr Tulliver instructs Tom: 'Write as you'll remember what Wakem's done to your father, and you'll make him and his feel it, if ever the day comes. And sign your name Thomas Tulliver' (*MF* 267). Mr Tulliver uses writing's permanence to ensure that his hatred of Wakem will continue even as the impersonal law acquires force so that such personal feelings have no place. Resisting the newly consolidated institutional path, his literacy, like his life, seeks to perpetuate the past rather than project the present into the future.

In turn, Maggie's reading of Thomas à Kempis's *The Imitation of Christ* collapses past and present in order to unsettle existing social arrangements. In this scene of reading, writing from the 'far-off middle ages' acquires the immediacy of a voice in the present (*MF* 290). Eliot describes the book's age in great detail, noting 'strong pen-and-ink marks, long since browned by time' (*MF* 289) and referring to it as 'the small old-fashioned book' (*MF* 291). When Maggie begins to read, however, she is 'hardly conscious that she was reading – seeming rather to listen while a low voice said' (*MF* 290). Critics' understanding of Maggie's character often depends upon how they interpret this scene. Margaret Homans suggests that it is a scene of literal and feminine reading, where Maggie demonstrates her increasing femininity by mistakenly finding satisfaction in Thomas à Kempis's argument for renunciation.[63] By contrast, Sara Ahmed claims that reading Thomas à Kempis allows Maggie to 'deviate from well-trodden paths'.[64] By allowing this voice from the middle ages to guide her, Maggie performs an anachronistic way of being in the world that refuses the assumptions of path dependency. Maggie is directed by a 'quiet hand' from the past rather than the assumptions of the present (290).

The novel presents Maggie's anachronistic literacy as a response to her exclusion from institutions that might make her feel more at home in the world. Just before she picks up the book, the narrator indicates that Maggie's loneliness partly results from her position outside of institutional integration or blending:

> Poor child! as she leaned her head against the window-frame, with her hands clasped tighter and tighter, and her foot beating the ground, she was as lonely in her trouble as if she had been the only girl in the civilized world of that day who had come out of her school-life with a soul untrained for inevitable struggles – with no other part of her inherited share in the hard-won treasures of thought, which generations of painful toil have laid up for the race of men, than shreds and patches of feeble literature and false history – with much futile information about Saxon and other kings of doubtful example – but unhappily quite without that knowledge of the irreversible laws within and without her. (*MF* 288)

Eliot suggests that 'school-life' might prepare people for 'inevitable struggles' by connecting them with their 'inherited share in the hard-won treasures of thought'. Thus, she articulates the goal of education: to teach people 'irreversible laws' and blend them with cultural traditions so that they never feel alone but also never expect too much. What is telling, here, is that Maggie's isolated position is shared – although she feels 'as if' she is 'the only girl' who struggles, she is actually a representative girl *because* she struggles (*MF* 288). In this moment, it is hard for readers to remember that Maggie has had a 'school-life' at all, for while the novel carefully recounts Tom's failure at Mr Stelling's, it sums up Maggie's school days in a few meagre sentences.

The very fact that Maggie is not integrated into the 'civilized world' through 'school-life', however, allows Maggie to undermine laws that seem to be 'irreversible' through anachronistic literacy. By reading Thomas à Kempis as a contemporary, Maggie not only collapses historical distance, she imagines futures at odds with the institutions that have isolated her. Instead of teaching her to submit herself to external laws, this reading presents 'a sublime height to be reached without the help of outward things' (*MF* 290). Moreover, Maggie's reading cultivates relationships that do not cohere into institutional forms: 'She knew nothing of doctrines and systems – of mysticism or quietism; but the voice out of the far-off middle ages was the direct communication of a human soul's belief and experience, and came to Maggie as an unquestioned message' (*MF* 291). This 'direct communication' offers lessons of mysticism and quietism but not systems. Because the book can function as a 'voice' rather than a doctrine, it can make the past present and, just as importantly, cultivate visions of the future that do not simply extend the present. Making the past immediate creates an affective tie to the past that thwarts the power of both the educational institutions she is excluded from and the familial traditions in which she is immersed. This book 'works miracles to this day' while 'expensive sermons and treatises, newly issued, leave all things as they were before' (*MF* 291). This juxtaposition between the old and the new, effective and ineffective texts validates untimely relationships to the past rather than institutional structures that blend the past and present and merge individual desires and organisational forms.

Although anachronistic literacy always disrupts the logic of path dependency, it does not always lead to better politics. In the wrong hands, anachronistic literacy extends the reaches of institutions. In *Romola* (1863), for instance, the scholar Baldassarre is also distanced from a cultural tradition. Unlike Maggie, however, whose gendered 'school-life' excludes her from the 'hard-won treasures of thought', Baldassarre's exclusion results from amnesia – his inability to remember either the past or how to read. Carrying the heavy burden of 'an unremembered past' with him to Florence, he seeks revenge for his foster-child Tito's betrayal (*R* 267*)*. Cut off from his past and his Greek homeland, he represents radical discontinuity until 'the black marks become magical' and he can read once more. Reading connects Baldassarre with his past, his experience and the world, allowing him to transcend the constraints of his current material circumstances. In the words of the novel:

> He was once more a man who knew cities, whose sense of vision was instructed with large experience, and who felt the keen delight of holding all things in the grasp of language. Names! Images! – his mind rushed through its wealth without pausing, like one who enters on a great inheritance. (*R* 334–5)

In the moments when he can read, he has access to the 'great inheritance' that literacy provides. Reading restores a continuous tradition, reintegrates Baldassarre with cultural knowledge, and, surprisingly, makes him young again: when reading, 'he forgot that he was old' (*R* 334). When he lapses into illiteracy, he once again becomes rooted in his present condition – trapped in 'the rugged face and the coarse hands' that lead him to be locked up again (*R* 353). Through Baldassarre, Eliot implies that literacy enables people to use the past to resist contemporary social constraints while still associating literacy with historical continuity.

In fact, for Baldassarre, reading encourages a sense of mastery that underlies imperial structures rather than questioning modern institutionalism. Cultivating a 'sense of mental empire', his reading transforms the city from 'a weary labyrinth' he must navigate to mere 'material that he could subdue to his purposes' (R 334). This description of reading evokes Elaine Freedgood's argument against realism – that reading realist novels teaches us 'the practices of space and time that allow us to imagine expansion and colonization – of territory, of the future, of other minds'.[65] This sense of mastery – and magic – differs from Maggie's anachronistic reading where access to the past encourages transgressive, transhistorical relationships. For instead of teaching her to *use* or *subdue* history, Maggie's reading highlights how we learn from unexpected places and unexpected people – from pasts that remain at odds with modernising institutions, from people that we will never meet. Armed with her own sense of the future, Maggie can accept her role in the family – even convince her mother that she was 'growing up so good' – without accepting her family's more path-dependent approach to futurity (R 294). Her relationship with the old-fashioned book indirectly leads her to validate her relationship with Philip, upholding friendship in the face of familial expectations.

Middlemarch and *Romola* offer additional qualifications of Maggie's anachronistic literacy, suggesting that although untimely reading can open up radical relationships to the past, it can also work to extend institutional power. For the scholars Edward Casaubon and Bardo de' Bardi, literacy allows them to escape from the present but ultimately confirms and consolidates modern institutionalism. While in Rome – 'the city of visible history' – Dorothea's emotional and intellectual life expands through the 'incongruities' of untimely encounters (M 182). By contrast, her husband, Casaubon, reveals how his reading of old texts fails to create new possibilities: he maintains 'a measured official tone, as of a clergyman reading according to rubric' (M 185). He is at home in the abstract authority of institutions as he is 'among the tombs of the past' (M 394). He uses institutions to extend his patriarchal authority beyond the timespan of his life, adding a codicil to his will to prevent Dorothea from marrying Will Ladislaw. Instead of imagining futures that break from the existing institutional path, Casaubon's anachronistic literacy works to limit Dorothea's 'future action' (M 449).

In *Romola*, Bardo de' Bardi's anachronistic literacy also contributes to women's exclusions from educational institutions. Dwelling with books and thinkers from the past, the old scholar retraces established paths rather than forging new ones. He recognises that his 'blindness acts like a dam, sending the streams of thought backward along the already travelled channels and hindering the course onward' (*R* 52). Desiring to push 'the course onward', Bardo laments the fact that he relies on his daughter, Romola, to guide him. If his son had stayed with him, he thinks, 'I might have gone on and seen my path broadening to the end of my life. . . . But it has closed now' (*R* 52). Lamenting the narrowness of his path, Bardo nevertheless quite consciously narrows Romola's by refusing to allow her to participate in his scholarship. Her 'feminine mind' means that her future lies in marriage rather than scholarship (*R* 54). The irony, of course, is that when retracing the frequently travelled course with Romola, he never learns that she is the perfect person to broaden his path.

The fact that anachronistic literacy can either unsettle path dependency or extend institutional power demonstrates how modern institutionalism does not simply define modernity through institutions, it controls how people relate to the past. Thus, characters like Maggie Tulliver are important because they remain untimely, at odds with present social conventions and the dominant vision of the future precisely because reading allows them to reanimate forgotten pasts. In a novel that otherwise promotes a continuous relationship with the past – Maggie famously tells Stephen, 'If the past is not to bind us, where can duty lie? We should have no law but the inclination of the moment' – Maggie's anachronistic literacy refuses the governing logic of path dependency (*MF* 475). Her reading resists the narrowness of the established institutional path. In the final section of the book, the community reacts 'with that fine instinct which is given her for the preservation of Society', insisting that Maggie must either remain an outcast or marry Stephen Guest (*MF* 491). Confronted with such narrow options, Maggie's desire to make amends has no place. Tom's surprise at the end of the novel, his utterance of recognition – 'Magsie!' – suggests that feeling his childish love for her again not only restores their relationship, but validates her desire to move backward when the community tells her she must only move forward. The final line of the book, 'In their death they were not divided,' shows how they ultimately overcome the divisive logic of separate spheres, of distinct temporal structures (*MF* 522). Validating regressive returns rather than reproduction, this union of boy and girl, brother and sister enacts a queer temporality where death is not simply a temporal trap, it reconfigures temporal and social relations. By refusing path dependency even as she validates the power of the past, Maggie, in her death as well as her life, shows the importance of imagining alternative paths.

Ultimately, like William Carleton and Charles Kickham, George Eliot produces provincial novels that work in two directions. On the one hand, they 'absorb the forces of change' through path-dependent narratives that blend individual desires with institutional futures, provincial pasts and modern presents. On the other hand, however, they use anachronistic literacy to collapse the distance between past and present and disrupt modern institutionalism's emphasis on futurity. Eliot's realism is 'paradigmatic' not because it integrates characters and readers into a shared form, but rather because of its formal and political contradictions.

Notes

1. Eliot, 'The Natural History of German Life', p. 130.
2. Eliot, *Middlemarch*, p. 4. Cited in the text hereafter, abbreviated as *M*.
3. Duncan, 'The Provincial or Regional Novel', p. 331.
4. Eagleton, *Heathcliff and the Great Hunger*, p. 147. As James Murphy argues, this use of *Middlemarch* as a metonym for Victorian realism began as early as 1891 with Rosa Mulholland (*Irish Novelists and the Victorian Age*, p. 2).
5. Elaine Freedgood, for instance, argues that *Middlemarch* institutionalises the literary novel in opposition to the commercial novel (*The Ideas in Things*, p. 117, p. 114). J. Hillis Miller, arguing that *Middlemarch* is a 'realist masterpiece', reads it as 'an example of form as difference in its effect on readers' ('Narrative and History', p. 470). For him, Eliot's novel integrates difference through its diffusiveness, which ultimately extends to readers.
6. Buzard, *Disorienting Fiction*, p. 281.
7. St Clair, *The Reading Nation in the Romantic Period*, p. 103.
8. Williams, *The Country and the City*, pp. 168–9.
9. Eliot, *Adam Bede*, p. 174. Hereafter cited in the text, abbreviated as *AB*.
10. Elaine Freedgood makes one version of this argument when interpreting *Middlemarch*, contending that the novel's central project was 'the standardization of meaning' and thus part of the work of the novel is to exclude readers who lack the proper education (*The Ideas in Things*, 117). Nathan Hensley suggests institutions are an *end* of the narrative, arguing that 'It narrates the birth of a self-consciously modern social formation understood to be governed by "law"' (*Forms of Empire*, p. 39).

11. Recently, Caroline Levine has demonstrated how the concept of path dependence can help us understand the 'staying power' of historical periods in literary studies (*Forms*, p. 59).

12. Haydu, 'Reversals of fortune', p. 29.

13. Eliot, *Daniel Deronda*, p. 355.

14. Sedgwick argues that 'the space and time of women's work are ideologized as not only separate but anachronistic in relation to the realm of "real" work' (*Between Men*, p. 145). In an American context, Dana Luciano also studies the distinct temporalities of separate spheres, associating mother figures tied to the domestic with both 'timelessness and anachronism' (*Arranging Grief*, p. 123). Rita Felski claims that woman 'is a recurring symbol of the atemporal and asocial at the very heart of the modern itself' in *The Gender of Modernity*, p. 38.

15. 'Margaret Fuller and Mary Wollstonecraft', p. 333.

16. Ibid. p. 333, p. 332.

17. Ibid. p. 333.

18. Ibid. p. 332.

19. Ibid.

20. Freeman, *Time Binds*, p. xvii.

21. Eliot, 'Margaret Fuller and Mary Wollstonecraft', p. 337.

22. Ibid.

23. Sedgwick, *Between Men*, p. 140.

24. Recently, Tricia Lootens thinks through such contradictions in *The Political Poetess*. She offers a provocative new alternative to the legacy of separate spheres, where 'the "private sphere" is not the "feminine" sphere. It is, rather, a mortal, masculine, martial refuge, held sacred by the labours of feminine custodians; and as such, it teaches a Morality that takes form, both as temporally contained by, and as redemptively, transcendently in excess of, Politics writ large' (p. 14).

25. Ahmed, *Living a Feminist Life*, p. 6.

26. Kristeva, 'Women's Time', p. 354.

27. Grosz, 'The Untimeliness of Feminist Theory', p. 48. Elizabeth Grosz further elaborates her insistence on the politics of the untimely in *The Nick of Time*, where she provocatively begins by noting that academic institutions have forgotten the importance of the body and time, and contends that feminist, antiracist and postcolonial discourses 'are about inducing the untimely' (p. 2, p. 14). She suggests that 'the more clearly we understand our temporal location as beings who straddle the past and the future without the security of a stable and abiding present, the more mobile our possibilities are, and the more transformation becomes conceivable' (p. 14).

28. Eliot, *The Mill on the Floss*, p. 474. Cited in text hereafter, abbreviated as *MF*.

29. Markovits, 'George Eliot's Problem with Action', p. 786.

30. Eliot, *Felix Holt*, p. 43.

31. Ibid.
32. Ibid. p. 490.
33. Here, I differ from Rachel Bowlby who argues that 'historical distance provides a means of maintaining or creating an image of settlement and relative changelessness' in 'Versions of realism in George Eliot's *Adam Bede*', p. 418.
34. Eliot, *Romola*, p. 497. Cited in the text hereafter, abbreviated as *R*.
35. Flint, *The Woman Reader, 1837–1914*, p. 18.
36. 'Silly Novels by Lady Novelists', p. 154.
37. Ruskin, *Sesame and Lilies*, p. 103.
38. Luciano, *Arranging Grief*, p. 35.
39. Miller, *Reading for Our Time*, p. 6.
40. Many scholars consider Hetty's exclusion: Terry Eagleton suggests that she is excluded because of her disruptive egotism in *Criticism and Ideology*, p. 115; Elizabeth Helsinger argues that she is excluded because she represents a gendered memory in *Rural Scenes and National Representation*, p. 3, and Harry Shaw attributes her exclusion to her failure to be 'an active bearer of experience' in *Narrating Reality*, p. 226.
41. Sedgwick, *Between Men*, p. 138.
42. Mill, 'The Subjection of Women', p. 477. John Stuart Mill describes 'weak' institutions in part to account for how institutions 'which place right on the side of might' endure even in an era of liberal institutions.
43. Genette, *Narrative Discourse*, p. 235.
44. As Fredric Jameson argues in *The Antinomies of Realism*, Eliot seeks 'to affirm historical continuity (as against the radical breaks of modernity)' (p. 120).
45. Robyn Warhol also reads this chapter of *Adam Bede*, demonstrating that the conversation between Adam Bede and the narrator emphasises the characters' reality in 'Toward a Theory of the Engaging Narrator', p. 815.
46. Sarah Allison implicitly connects such statements with metalepsis, claiming that what she calls the 'commentative clause', or moments when the narrator shifts from past to present tense, stitches 'together narrated story and discourse' in *Reductive Reading*, p. 65.
47. As Harry Shaw argues, 'Eliot wants to explore the possibility that there have been times and places in our own tradition that have produced rural folk who *simply don't think in the ways her implied readers do*' (*Narrating Reality*, p. 226).
48. Elizabeth Helsinger also considers Hetty's exclusion, contrasting Adam Bede's history, which represents social transformation, with Hetty's history, which depends upon personal memory. For Helsinger, Hetty reveals to two disparate functions of history within *Adam Bede* – to represent the past and explain how the past became present (*Rural Scenes and National Representation*, pp. 222–3).

49. Ascribing this power to novels, Eliot, like Austen before her, 'proposes a form of authority – a form of political authority – that works through literacy rather than through traditional juridical means to maintain social relations'. Armstrong, *Desire and Domestic Fiction*, p. 157.

50. Bowlby, 'Versions of realism in George Eliot's *Adam Bede*,' p. 421.

51. The longer passage in which this sentence appears encourages both sympathy towards Hetty and judgement of her. It begins by saying 'it is impossible to be wise on the subject of earrings as one looks at her' – indicating that readers, like Hetty, would be silly about earrings. But it concludes by presenting Hetty as 'a woman spinning in young ignorance a light web of folly and vain hopes which may one day close round her and press upon her', which separates her from readers once more (p. 249).

52. Luciano, *Arranging Grief*, p. 59.

53. Ibid. p. 60.

54. Lukács, *The Historical Novel*, p. 35.

55. Scott, *The Fantasy of Feminist History*, p. 11. Eliot, herself, also warns against generalising a shared conception of 'womanhood'. She celebrates Margaret Fuller because she demonstrates 'the folly of absolute definitions of woman's nature and absolute demarcations of woman's mission' ('Margaret Fuller and Mary Wollstonecraft', p. 335). She also begins *Middlemarch* by reflecting on the 'inconvenient indefiniteness' of women, suggesting that their lives cannot be represented through the generalising abstraction: 'the social lot of women' (p. vii).

56. This fact is true in Lukács's own account where James Fenimore Cooper's novels reveal their historical faithfulness by representing Indians as doomed to die (*The Historical Novel*, pp. 64–5).

57. Shaw, *Narrating Reality*, p. 226.

58. Schor, *Curious Subjects*, p. 29.

59. Beer, 'Beyond Determinism', p. 89.

60. Nathan Hensley argues that the Dodson family's emphasis on kinship represents a 'countryside premodernity' that will be replaced by modern liberal individualism (*Forms of Empire*, p. 54).

61. Jed Esty's account of the novel in *Unseasonable Youth* is helpful here, claiming that it registers 'the potential losses for women when male institutions replace female-regulated customs' (p. 59).

62. Price, 'Reader's Block', p. 234.

63. Homans, *Bearing the Word*, p. 124.

64. Ahmed, 'Willful Parts', p. 248.

65. 'Hetero-ontologicality, or Against Realism', p. 92.

Part III

Untimely Improvement

Chapter 4

Charles Dickens's Reactionary Reform

'You may make anything an Institution if you like.'[1]

Charles Dickens, the great novelist of social reform, famously pits characters against ever-encroaching institutionalism. Betty Higden bravely struggles to escape the workhouse in *Our Mutual Friend* (1865) as she seeks to die free of 'the Parish' and its corresponding institutions; Arthur Clennam confronts the Circumlocution Office and its empty bureaucratic forms in *Little Dorrit* (1857); and Oliver Twist challenges the logic of the workhouse by asking, however reluctantly, for more food.[2] Dickens stages these conflicts between individuals and institutions to reform institutions through an expanded social relationality.[3] In the nineteenth century, government institutions increasingly defined social relations through impersonal bureaucratic procedures while industrial capitalism defined social relations through monetary exchange – or what Thomas Carlyle called the cash nexus.[4] By contrast, Dickens represents social relationships that exceed these procedures and prescriptions: interpersonal connections that work across institutions such as prisons, schools, bureaucratic offices and courts of law; domestic relationships that extend beyond the heteronormative family unit; and anachronistic ties to the past that institutions obscure in their drive towards futurity.

Focusing on Dickens's social reform efforts, I argue that his novels produce what I call 'reactionary reform', a vision of the future that is actually the return of an anachronistic past. Paradoxically suggesting both a conservative desire to revert to the past and a commitment to progressive reform, 'reactionary reform' captures the complexity of Dickens's politics. Progressive and conservative, oriented towards the future and the past, Dickensian reform seeks to improve institutions by critiquing institutional time.[5] His novels reanimate anachronistic pasts to thwart modern institutionalism's narrow vision of the future.

However, Dickens also problematically naturalises the boundaries of the nation-state and suggests that minority and colonised subjects are outside of history and at odds with institutionalism altogether. These contradictions explain why critics are so divided about the politics of Dickens's novels. For Foucauldian scholars like D. A. Miller, Dickens's attempts to reform institutions only spread disciplinary power, while liberal scholars such as Lauren Goodlad, Bruce Robbins and Amanda Anderson suggest, in quite different ways, that Dickens's reform efforts are both productive and progressive.[6] Rather than choosing between these critical positions, I use the concept of reactionary reform to draw attention to the faultlines within Dickens's reform efforts.

Race and empire are two such faultlines, as Dickens's English characters can reanimate anachronistic pasts that reform institutions while colonial subjects appear as racialised abstractions outside of the expanded social and historical relationality that he imagines.[7] For this reason, his critique of institutional time, however important, does not go far enough. While Dickens suggests that English institutions require reactionary reform, he represents colonial subjects such as Indigenous and Irish peoples as reactionary but incapable of reform. These racialised and colonised subjects are excluded from but nevertheless constitutive of Dickens's vision of institutionalism. Empire fundamentally shapes Dickens's social reform efforts, but he presents English institutions as bounded national forms to disavow their imperial effects.

Thus, unlike other critics who understand 'The Noble Savage' to be an anomaly in Dickens's writings, I argue that the same racialised logic underlies his novels.[8] He upholds the logic of empire by limiting who can participate in and reform British institutions. In this way, instead of embracing the 'portable domesticity' associated with settler colonialism which seeks to extend English institutions to colonial settlements, Dickens creates stark boundaries that distinguish between Britain and its colonies, modern institutional subjects and racialised others.[9] In doing so, Dickens shows that the violence of modern institutionalism is twofold: it forcefully integrates colonial subjects into imperial institutions (exporting British institutions to the colonies) and it actively excludes these subjects from constructions of social, political and historical life (refusing to view Britain in relation to its colonies).[10] In England, Dickens argues for the inhabitation of institutions by British subjects in order to create an expanded social relationality; outside of England, he supports forms of settlement that actively deny colonised people either pasts or futures.

As I argue throughout this book, institutions mediate the past, present and future and define them in institutional terms. Dickens was especially aware of how Victorian institutions – schools, prisons, factories and courts of law but also families, charitable organisations and the free market – require subjects to relinquish their attachments to the past and assimilate into institutional time. Through anachronisms, Dickens questions this future-oriented temporality, showing how relationships to the past not only endure within institutions, but also can animate otherwise possibilities. *Dombey and Son* (1848) concludes with Old Sol's surprisingly successful investments which indicate that 'instead of being behind the time in those respects, as he supposed, he was, in truth, a little before it'.[11] In *Little Dorrit*, Amy Dorrit's marriage with Arthur Clennam depends upon a return to her origins – the Marshalsea prison and her name, 'Little Dorrit'. In each instance, an anachronistic orientation towards obsolete origins – Old Sol's old-fashioned economics, Amy Dorrit's attachment to her birthplace – activates social relationships that challenge modern institutionalism's emphasis on futurity. For Dickens, development is untimely because growth results from anachronistic attachments.

Anachronisms reconfigure institutional rhythms and relations by fostering what Roderick Ferguson calls 'visions that are in the institution but not of it'.[12] Dickens's reform efforts within England thus employ anachronism to disrupt institutional settlement – fixed arrangements, permanent structures and legal agreements – in order to suggest a logic of inhabitation. Settlement, whether it refers to a form of consensus or a colonial practice, creates permanence by erasing origins in the name of a shared futurity. To settle an argument, for instance, is to relegate the conflict to the past. Inhabitation, by contrast, implies a more temporary and transient act: 'the action of inhabiting'.[13] Inhabiting an argument means imagining the conflicting perspectives as ongoing and unresolved. Dickens articulates the differences between these two logics in *Hard Times* (1854) by juxtaposing Mr Gradgrind, who accepts utilitarian institutions as a settled system, with Sissy Jupe, who inhabits these institutions while refusing to allow them to erase her origins or shape her future.

Colonial settlements – whether the 'happy settlement, on the banks of the African rivers' that *Bleak House*'s Mrs Jellyby supports, the Australian settlements that *David Copperfield*'s Mr Micawber helps govern, or the American settlements that Martin Chuzzlewit imagines – also clarify the difference between the logic of settlement and that of inhabitation.[14] The violence of colonial settlement results in part from its projection of permanence: merely inhabiting a settlement only to question whether it ever could last, as Martin Chuzzlewit does, has the potential to undermine settler colonialism.[15] In all of Dickens's novels, anachronisms can unsettle institutions' projection of permanence by restoring historicity to them. Anachronisms can activate origins at odds with institutions and encourage a logic of inhabitation as opposed to settlement.

However, Dickens cannot resolve the contradictions of reactionary reform into a coherent political vision because realism depends upon movement between anachronisms and institutions, history and ahistorical abstractions. Like reform, realism requires managing relationality as it depicts – but also delimits – social and historical relationships. Realist novels foster relationships between characters and structures, fictional and historical worlds, and distanced and immersive perspectives. Harry Shaw claims that realism creates these connections through its '*historicist metonymy*' or 'real-world relationships' that show 'cause and effect'.[16] Shaw builds on Roman Jakobson's distinction between metaphor, which creates connections through similarity, and metonymy, which creates connections through contiguity, making the case that the realist novel constructs a 'web of causality' that offers the experience of living in a historical world.[17] For Shaw, metonymy's contiguity produces historicist contingency. And yet, as Elaine Freedgood reveals, metonymic relationships are profoundly uneven: in many places, realist metonymy suggests transparent, literal meaning rather than networked relations and thus obscures historical relationships even as it evokes them.[18] For this reason, Freedgood traces the metonymic associations we tend to ignore as she historicises things – mahogany furniture, cotton, Negro Head Tobacco – in the Victorian novel.

Thus, realism's 'web of causality' often runs into dead ends – not simply the things that Freedgood reads, but people who appear outside of the logic of cause and effect and thus outside of futurity. Although Dickens's reactionary reform depends upon activating relationships to anachronistic pasts, he uses metaphor to ensure that minority subjects, like *Dombey and Son*'s 'Native', remain abstractions at odds with both history and institutions.[19] Because it is less dependent on contiguity or external context for meaning, the substitutional logic of metaphor tends towards abstraction, yielding concepts rather than material things or historical people.[20] But, for my purposes, the distinction between metaphor and metonymy is less important than the distinction between forms of representation that expand social and historical relationality and forms of representation that close it off. In novels that otherwise uncover unknown pasts and hidden connections, minority and colonised subjects are often historical dead ends in Dickens's novels. Biddy in *Great Expectations* (1861) evokes Irishness, but because she functions as a metaphoric origin for Pip, her own Irish origins remain obscure and unhistoricised. Tom Gradgrind's 'comic livery' or blackface at the end of *Hard Times* is another dead end.[21] Dickens encourages a metaphorical reading of blackness by suggesting that in taking on this disguise, Tom reveals his moral distance from the characters who seek to save him. At this moment of disgrace, 'the whites of his eyes . . . were the only parts of his face that showed any life or expression, the pigment upon it was so thick' (*HT* 284). The little remaining whiteness – his eyes – is Tom's only hope for redemption as Dickens implies that blackness is at odds with human relationality altogether.[22] Dickens's novels at once celebrate the expanding 'real-world relationships' that exceed institutional settlement and transform these historical networks back into settled forms that restrict the kinds of human and historical relations readers imagine.[23]

The political contradictions within Dickens's reactionary reform ultimately highlight realism's formal and political divisions. Dickens's metaphoric representation of Irish and Indigenous peoples reveals his contradictory approach to anachronisms. While some anachronisms work to restore historicity to the novels' settlements, others show the limits of institutional reform as they confuse institutional settlement with history.

Institutional Settlements

'Institutions are settlements', claims the sociologist John L. Campbell.[24] For Campbell, the idea of settlement captures how institutions create stability by producing consensus instead of ongoing conflict. Settlement is achieved through the distinct temporality of institutions which move towards futurity on the one hand and erase origins on the other. Institutions create a sense of permanence by establishing a vision of a shared future that institutional subjects, regardless of their individual differences, work to achieve. For many sociologists, such ability to create a sense of shared purpose – and shared futurity – is the very strength of institutions: they create agreement from conflict and disorder.

Dickens, by contrast, is wary of how institutional settlement requires relinquishing individual origins and pre-existing attachments. Tattycoram, the rebellious orphan in *Little Dorrit*, is angry precisely because her institutional identity as a foundling at the Foundling Hospital obscures her individual history.[25] Each of her names – Harriet Beadle (given to her by the Foundling Hospital), Harriet Coram and Tattycoram (given to her by the Meagles who adopt her) – implies that she originates at the institution. 'Tattycoram' – the nickname she objects to – refers to 'a blessed creature of the name of Coram', who was the 'originator of the Institution', but its more 'playful' form also suggests a more private institution – the family.[26] Whether she is called Harriet Coram or Tattycoram, her name ensures that the Foundling Hospital or the Meagles – not her individual history – becomes the origin of her identity. Of course, at the Foundling Hospital, family names might be unknown or, if known, might threaten familial institutions by acknowledging the prevalence of unwed mothers and extramarital affairs. But such erasure is not limited to that particular institutional context: Gradgrind's educational system in *Hard Times* and the Chancery in *Bleak House* (1853) have a similar effect. Dickens's reactionary reform questions the temporality of settlement by uncovering origin stories that institutions obscure.

The temporal structure of settlement that constructs a shared future out of disparate individuals has a particularly sinister force in settler colonial institutions: it produces what Patrick Wolfe famously calls the 'logic of elimination' upon which settler colonialism depends.[27] Here, the erasure of origins is not merely figurative, but literal: Indigenous peoples are either killed or displaced and their claims to the land are denied. In the words of Catherine Hall, in the nineteenth century, 'settlement meant dispossession'.[28] Settler colonial institutions – especially the state, legal institutions and schools – further erase Indigenous peoples by assimilating them into the very structures that refuse to recognise them. As Glen Coulthard argues, these institutions ask that Indigenous peoples 'come to *identify*, either implicitly or explicitly, with the profoundly *asymmetrical* and *non-reciprocal* forms of recognition either imposed on or granted to them by the colonial-state and society'.[29] This assimilative logic refuses to recognise Indigenous peoples' own histories, which predate colonial settlement, as well as the present-tense existence of Indigenous peoples. Through their erasure of the past and narrow vision of the future, settler colonial institutions rewrite history as settlement in two ways: first, by suggesting that history begins with colonial settlement, and second, by creating a settled trajectory for history where the present tense of settler colonial institutions extends into the future.[30]

In the Victorian era, the two signature temporal moves of institutional settlement – erasing the past and prescribing the future – fuelled the expansion of British settler colonialism in Canada, Australia, New Zealand and South Africa through institutions like the state.[31] In 1883, the historian J. R. Seeley asserts the importance of institutions when he differentiates between Britain's colonial relationship with India and the stability of its 'colonial Empire', or settler colonies.[32] Seeley declares that 'Greater Britain is a real enlargement of the English State; it carries across the seas not merely the English race, but the authority of the English Government.'[33] For Seeley, British settler colonies differ from other British colonies precisely because they uphold the authority of English institutions. The state can be transported to these colonies because settler colonial violence erases Indigenous peoples, often by killing or removing them, in order to transform their land into a space of opportunity. Figured as 'the unoccupied territory of the globe', the territory only becomes 'unoccupied' through a genocidal project of elimination.[34] But the state is also necessary for the very process of settlement – as Seeley argues, 'Without the State the settler would run the risk of being murdered by Indians'.[35] Erasing origins on the one hand and securing a future that naturalises settler colonialism on the other, the institutions of Greater Britain extended the reach of the British state in ways that sought to ensure that Indigenous peoples had no future.

Charles Dickens's *Bleak House* questions the temporal and political dimensions of institutional settlements in both domestic and colonial contexts. While the Chancery plot shows the danger of waiting for a settlement from the courts, Mrs Jellyby's telescopic philanthropy concerns itself with 'the happy settlement, on the banks of the African rivers, of our superabundant home population' (*BH* 44). The novel implies that the problem with both legal and colonial settlements is that a strong faith in a promised future makes people neglect the present and their prior attachments. Trusting a settlement from the courts, Richard Carstone cannot live 'a very settled life' and thus abandons his old friends; and trying to encourage English families to settle in Africa, Mrs Jellyby neglects her family (*BH* 555). In both instances, accepting institutional futurity means erasing one's personal history. As *Bleak House*'s Richard Carstone phrases it, institutions put 'us on unnatural terms, with which natural relations are incompatible' (*BH* 554).

And yet, Dickens's emphasis on 'natural relations' as a mode of institutional reform is very much mediated and delimited by the nation and the family – it does not extend to the natives of Borrioboola-Gha that Mrs Jellyby seeks to educate. This fact is not surprising: Dickens's explicitly racist essay, 'The Noble Savage', declares that Indigenous peoples should be 'civilised off the face of the earth', and both *David Copperfield* and *Great Expectations* celebrate the possibility of starting a new life and acquiring wealth in Australia.[36] Dickens questions institutional settlement, but his vision of institutional reform reinforces settler colonialism by representing particular groups of people as outside of history and futurity.

Reactionary Reform

Within England, Dickens seeks to reform modern institutions by activating origin stories that thwart modern institutionalism's emphasis on futurity. In *Hard Times*, Sissy Jupe attends Gradgrind's school while maintaining her attachment to her father and Sleary's Circus. This attachment, which Gradgrind's educational system continually tries to root out, leads to a productive temporal discordance with – rather than assimilation into – the school. Similarly, in *Bleak House*, Esther's past-tense narrative offers remembrance as a mode of reform. Narrating the origin stories that institutions erase, Dickens reactivates anachronistic English pasts in order to unsettle institutional futurity.

Both *Hard Times* and *Bleak House* capture institutions' drive towards futurity by representing institutional portability as out of control: institutional forms reproduce themselves in public and private spaces, transforming difference into similarity. *Hard Times* exemplifies such portability, where Thomas Gradgrind's angular house, 'Stone Lodge', mirrors the stoniness of the schoolroom and both become a part of the standardised, regularised Coketown, 'a triumph of fact' (*HT* 28). In *Bleak House*, diffuse fog rather than rigid geometry displays institutional portability across diverse spaces and places – for if there is 'fog everywhere' (*BH* 11), the High Court of Chancery lies 'at the very heart of the fog' (*BH* 12). These landscapes show the pervasiveness of institutional forms – Gradgrind's 'facts' and the Chancery's fogginess intrude on domestic scenes and distant locations as they shape disparate characters.

These two novels locate institutional power in the construction of futurity. Institutions acquire power by approaching the future as an extension of the present.[37] The Chancery in *Bleak House* defers futurity, while in *Hard Times*, Gradgrind's educational system produces a foreclosed futurity – an endless present softened neither by memories of the past nor hopes for the future.[38] They are two sides of the same coin: in both, an expanded present limits the possibilities of historical change. Christopher Castiglia contends that this distinct form of futurity defines institutionalism as 'an abstract structure that apparently guarantees a stasis of order across and despite the historical changes endemic to generation'.[39]

In *Hard Times*, Gradgrind's system is able to expand precisely because the future is only an extension of the present. It disperses institutional forms across space – 'the jail might have been the infirmary, the infirmary might have been the jail, the town-hall might have been either' (*HT* 29) – but also extends itself across time. By paying attention to abstractions rather than contingencies, Gradgrind's system makes the future known in the present. Not surprisingly, this form of futurity is represented by 'a deadly-statistical clock in it, which measured every second with a beat like a rap upon a coffin-lid' (*HT* 99). It carefully measures the onward march of time while implying that this march will bring nothing new – only death.

The 'monotonous vault' of Gradgrind's schoolroom thus represents institutional futurity in this novel: repetition without difference. By rooting out fancy and imagination, Gradgrind's school not only suppresses childhood, creativity and sentiment, but refuses any hope for historical change. The system is damaging precisely because it renders its subjects 'deaf to the call of time' (*HT* 12). Claiming to 'know the value of time', these institutions only recognise time that is used to perpetuate the institution (*HT* 36).[40] Thus, when the labourer Stephen Blackpool calls 'the Institutions of [his] country a muddle' and concludes 'the sooner I am dead, the better', he betrays the logic of institutional time: that death is often the only change that institutional subjects can imagine (*HT* 79). With 'no other law', there is no reason to hope for a future that looks any different from the present (*HT* 79).

The varied uses of the verb 'to settle' in the novel demonstrates how this apparent monotony depends upon the temporal structure of institutional settlement that I have characterised throughout this chapter. Because utilitarian institutions always already know the future, social questions are easy to answer without taking into account particular historical circumstances: Gradgrind 'could settle all their destinies on a slate, and wipe out all their tears with one dirty little bit of sponge' (*HT* 99). Gradgrind believes that utilitarian institutions are settled facts, and thus can 'settle' destinies without engaging with people's distinct histories and experiences. Venturing into 'one of the dwellings of the Coketown Hands; for the first time

in her life', Louisa realises that she never understood these workers to be human individuals, but rather 'something to be worked so
much and paid so much, and there ended; something to be infallibly
settled by laws of supply and demand' (*HT* 160). Here, the temporal
structure of settlement erases the very humanity of the Coketown
Hands. Understanding them as 'something to be infallibly settled'
rather than people with lives and histories, Louisa integrates them
into the institution in ways that delimit social relationality.

Mr Bounderby, so fond of describing his woeful 'antecedents',
reinforces this structure of settlement by using fictitious origin stories to consolidate institutional futurity (*HT* 23). Telling
hyperbolic tales of the hardship that he has overcome, Bounderby
becomes 'the Royal arms, the Union-Jack, Magna Charta, John
Bull, Habeas Corpus, the Bill of Rights, An Englishman's house
is his castle, Church and State, and God save the Queen, all put
together' (*HT* 49). This catalogue of English institutions suggests
that Bounderby's self-narrative has national significance. The fiction that he repeats – that he is a self-made man who has overcome his origins – not only erases his own history, but becomes
a method through which to diminish his workers' origin stories.
The very repetition of this narrative implies that anyone can succeed in the system. But Dickens believes otherwise, and shows how
laws maintain existing social arrangements by making 'one side
unnat'rally awlus and for ever right, and toother side unnat'rally
awlus and for ever wrong' (*HT* 154). Unlike Bounderby, Dickens
believes that the workers' origin stories and individual histories
matter because they can disrupt the temporality of 'awlus' – the
endurance of the same. Bounderby, by contrast, has no capacity
for change. At the end of the novel, his mother exposes him as a
fraud, and yet he continues to project 'himself after his old explo-
sive manner into his portrait – and into futurity' (*HT* 295). If his
exposure is central to the novel's plot, it does little to change Mr
Bounderby's character. Found to be a bully and a liar, Mr Bounderby relentlessly carries on, repeating his old actions in the name
of institutional futurity.

In *Hard Times*, realism's divided time suggests two opposing
forms of relationality: one where institutions mediate all relations
and one where natural relations, at odds with institutions, endure.[41]
Anachronisms make such temporal division visible, at once highlighting the problems with institutional futurity and opening up spaces to
imagine new futures. In systems where the future is known, moving
towards futurity feels like stagnation. Louisa Gradgrind perhaps best

captures the affect of institutional futurity – premature exhaustion. Although the narrator and her father track her steady growth and development from a child in the Gradgrind school to 'quite a young woman', Louisa only feels endless stagnation (*HT* 96). Telling her father, 'I have been tired a long time' while still a child, Louisa shows the world-weariness that results from being part of a system that defines the future in terms of the present (*HT* 20). For subjects who accept existing institutions as a settled fact, futurity means duration rather than diachronic change: to think of the future is only to think, as Louisa does, 'how short my life would be, and how little I could hope to do in it' (*HT* 59).

Although Louisa exemplifies the feeling of foreclosed futurity, she also appears as an anachronism that disrupts the monotony of the system. She takes 'step by step, onward and downward, towards some end, yet so gradually, that she believed herself to remain motionless' (*HT* 169). Here, time is divided into what it does (brings Louisa closer to 'some end') and how it feels ('motionless'). From Gradgrind's perspective, this feeling, like all others, is irrelevant: whether you feel motionless and sad, or mobile and happy, the result is the same – the extension of the system across space and time. But for Louisa, the feeling of stagnation points towards new possibilities. For if her sense of stagnation sometimes obscures reality (it makes her vulnerable to Mr Harthouse's and Mrs Sparsit's machinations and encourages her to accept Mr Bounderby's marriage proposal), it also reveals the ways in which institutional time is not actually as unitary and monotonous as the novel implies. When Louisa confronts her stagnation, she also confronts her 'doubts and resentments' – the belief that there are other modes of being, other definitions of futurity that she cannot quite access (*HT* 169). Caught between the novel's two temporalities, Louisa's character registers their incongruity: her actions are determined by the institutions she is subjected to, and yet she still believes that some individuals retain the possibility of 'doing' something.

Sissy Jupe is even more anachronistic as a character: 'altogether backward, and below the mark' when viewed through the lens of Gradgrind's educational programme (*HT* 94). Sissy joins the Gradgrind school and family after her father leaves her, presumably because he wants her to get an education rather than travel with Sleary's Circus. Gradgrind takes charge of her on the condition that she cuts off all ties with her friends from the Circus in order to assimilate into his system. But Sissy fails to meet this expectation just as she fails to meet the other expectations of Gradgrind's educational programme.

In the face of an educational institution that defines itself entirely through the present and future, she remains oriented towards the past and attached to her old friends. She inhabits the institution without accepting its temporal rhythms or restricted relationality. While the institution defines her father as an obstacle to be overcome and then forgotten, Sissy imagines him as the future. Gradgrind claims that her residence with him is the beginning of 'your history', but she refuses this radical break with her origins (*HT* 53). She does not 'run away' from the Gradgrind system precisely because she hopes that her father will return, having 'faith that he would be made the happier by her remaining where she was' (*HT* 60). Defying all logic, she even keeps the bottles of nine oils that her father sent her for when he left, hoping someday that they will be of use to him (*HT* 292). By maintaining this intense attachment to her origins, Sissy ensures that although her present is shaped by the institution, her future is not.

As an anachronism, Sissy transforms the shared time of modern institutionalism into a heterogeneous historical time. This temporal transformation resists the impulse to find 'an "outside" to institutional power' by showing that even while subject to institutional power, one can thwart institutional futurity.[42] For Michel Foucault, knowing how power works means knowing one's own complicity within the 'multiplicity of force relations' – that is, relations that exceed bounded forms.[43] Although such an approach to power threatens to be totalising, it also creates opportunities for what Roderick Ferguson calls 'ruptural possibilities' or 'visions that are in the institution but not of it'.[44] Immersed in circuits of power established through institutional arrangements, people can still imagine the future otherwise by inhabiting institutions in ways that reorient their circuits of meaning and formal arrangements.

Sissy is a visible symbol of realism's contradictions, reminding readers that if the Gradgrind system seeks settlement, history remains heterogeneous. As an anachronism, Sissy reveals the temporality that the institution legitimates – normative rhythms that designate her as 'backward, and below the mark' because she fails to improve over time – but also alludes to a multivalent historical time that necessarily exceeds the institution (94). Her untimely development shows that *Hard Times* opens up the possibility of futures not sanctioned by institutions.

The novel's resolution, which validates Sissy's anachronistic presence, suggests that Dickens's vision of the family is ultimately more queer than his vision of the nation: the family, unlike the nation, can encompass social difference and different forms of relationality.

Because Sissy's children help transform Louisa by allowing her to grow 'learned in childish lore', it may seem as if Louisa's happiness depends upon being integrated into reproductive futurity, what Lee Edelman calls 'the communal realization of futurity, the fantasy structure, the aesthetic frame' (*HT* 297).[45] But Sissy continues to validate forms of untimely development that insist on what José Esteban Muñoz calls a queer 'futurity that exists beyond the self or the here and now'.[46] In other words, even as the novel seems to imagine the reproductive futurity that Lee Edelman critiques, it also redefines it by questioning the heteronormative family unit and embracing untimeliness. Sissy's belatedness allows her to cultivate a form of futurity that is communal but not institutional (*HT* 95). For although Sissy represents, among other things, the importance of family in a system of fact, her family is a 'queer sort of company' (*HT* 37). She nourishes family ties within the Gradgrind home while declaring that she is not 'related to the family' and maintains her connections to the Sleary circus even at a distance (*HT* 237). Sissy's children are important to Louisa not because they are Sissy's children, but because they encourage Louisa 'to know her humbler fellow-creatures' (*HT* 297–8). Because this relationality exceeds the institutional expectations of school on the one hand and the heteropatriarchal family on the other, Sissy enables institutional reform.

The speculative style of the novel's ending reinforces the sense that resisting institutional settlement ultimately hinges on a different stance towards futurity. For if monotony results when you accept the 'deadly-statistical clock . . . which measured every second with a beat like a rap upon a coffin-lid', speculating on the future is a way to refuse the deadening effects of such measurements (*HT* 99). At the close of the novel, the narrator asks 'how much of futurity' each character sees, before distinguishing between events that were 'to be' and 'never to be' (*HT* 297). This ending is at once speculative and concrete, fanciful and factual, as it shifts between projecting possible futures and confirming whether in fact these futures were 'to be'.

This ending is formally interesting because it insists upon the very temporal division that is so central to the narrative – between predetermined fate and historical unfolding, the present and the future. The narrator declares what is to be and never to be for characters, but remains elusive about whether characters 'see these things' themselves (*HT* 298). Dickens concludes by declaring: 'Dear reader! It rests with you and me, whether, in our two fields of action, similar things shall be nor not. Let them be! We shall sit with lighter bosoms on the hearth, to see the ashes of our fires turn grey and cold'

(*HT* 298). While such a conclusion is certainly moralising – it encourages the reader to choose Sissy's domestic future as it warns against utilitarianism – it does more than teach readers to choose domesticity over institutionalism or fantasy over fact (*HT* 298). Saying 'it rests with you and me' acknowledges not only agency to work towards a future but also the value of letting things be and sitting 'with lighter bosoms on the hearth'. Alluding to the many times that Louisa sat by the fire with a heavy heart, unable to read the future, this detail evokes repetition that leads to difference. To thwart institutional settlement, which produces a future that only extends the present, one only needs to be present in new ways.

In *Hard Times*, progressing through time feels like stagnation because the future is known, while in *Bleak House*, progressing through time feels like stagnation because the future is repeatedly deferred. Haunting the Court of Chancery expecting a judgement, characters like Miss Flite and Richard Carstone trust this deferred futurity. Every day is a disappointment, and yet these disappointments only further commit the characters to the future that the institution promises. Miss Flite's madness and Richard's premature ageing register the damaging effects of this prolonged present, but are not enough to shake their belief in institutional futurity. Miss Flite repeatedly declares, 'I expect a judgement. Shortly' (*BH* 43), and Richard insists that 'it can't last forever' (*BH* 554). Their conviction that the court will produce a judgement shows how faith in institutionalism traps people in the very institutions that harm them.[47] Foreclosed and deferred futurity ultimately have the same effect: they create an ever-expanding present and ensure that the future brings repetition rather than change.

Ada's commitment to her marriage and family life echoes Richard's approach to the Chancery: despite the dismal circumstances of her present, she says, 'I still look forward. I look forward a long while, through years and years', hoping for the day that her daughter 'may be proud of him and a blessing to him' (*BH* 859). It is a moment of reproductive futurity – her child will, one day, be proud of her father and thus redeem his current actions – but also of deferral: unable to justify her marriage in the present, Ada looks to a future that might not happen for 'years and years'. Like Miss Flite and Richard, she seeks redemption from the very institution that is entrapping her – marriage and the family.

While the deferred futurity of the Chancery suit is illusive, the deferred futurity of professions appears to be sensible, rational and real to many critics. Arguing that *David Copperfield* depicts the 'appropriate tempo for the new breed of professional who must not anticipate "ends" . . . but rather devote himself to the task at hand', Jennifer Ruth suggests that Dickens's novels demonstrate the value of professionalism by reproducing the time-discipline of the factory.[48] Richard fails in his chosen professions because he does not learn this time-discipline – he cannot wait through 'years of considerable endurance and disappointment' to achieve professional success (*BH* 246). Accepting the 'probation' of the suit where he only needs to wait for a judgement, he refuses the 'probation' of a profession where he must wait and work (*BH* 248). Bruce Robbins suggests that this is one of the central paradoxes of *Bleak House*: although it is critical of institutions, it nevertheless encourages readers to embrace professionalism.[49]

D. A. Miller is more cynical about the promise of professionalism, but he, like Ruth and Robbins, makes the case that the novel form encourages readers to trust deferred institutional futurity. Like the Chancery suit, the novel produces a seemingly endless present. But unlike the suit, the novel ultimately achieves closure by redeeming Richard, marrying off characters, and teaching readers to 'wait *and see*'.[50] In his words:

> We read the novel under the same assumption that Richard makes about the suit, that 'the longer it goes on, . . . the nearer it must be to a settlement'; and if the assumption is to be validated in the one case as it is discredited in the other, the novel is under obligation to make good its promise by issuing in judgments and resolutions.[51]

For Miller, *Bleak House* channels disciplinary power by encouraging readers to accept the deferred futurity upon which institutions depend. In this way, Miller suggests that the novel critiques the workings of the Chancery while also presenting public institutions as capable of reform precisely because they, like the novel, can create settlement: protected spaces in which we can wait for the future that institutions promise.

By contrast, I argue that Dickens questions the narrow relationality that results from trusting the future promised by either the legal system or professionalism. Whether successfully navigating the law, like Mr Tulkinghorn, or becoming a victim of the law, like Mr Grindley, the effects of accepting institutional futurity are the same: it replaces 'old associations' – friendships, family relations, personal attachments – with a narrow sense of duty (*BH* 372). Mr Tulkinghorn, a consummate professional, pursues his ends 'doggedly and steadily, with no touch of compunction, remorse or pity . . . immovable in what he has made his duty' (423), while the vampiric Mr Vholes discharges his 'professional duty' and insists that this duty entirely determines 'our present relations' (*BH* 581). Institutions substitute a duty that is 'made' – constructed by one's profession or institutional position – for a duty that is given by one's human nature. The effect of this substitution is the erasure of history, origins and one's personal past. Mr Grindley, a victim of Chancery, reflects on this substitution as he addresses his fellow-sufferer, Miss Flite: 'Of all my old associations, of all my old pursuits and hopes, of all the living and the dead world, this one poor soul alone comes natural to me, and I am fit for. There is a tie of many suffering years between us two, and it is the only tie I ever had on earth that Chancery has not broken' (*BH* 372). Tellingly, the Chancery not only destroys his 'old associations' but also his 'old pursuits and hopes'. Mr Grindley's plight shows that accepting institutional futures means renouncing one's own vision of the future.

In order to reform social institutions like the Chancery and domestic institutions like the family, Dickens reorients this futural drive towards anachronistic pasts. Esther's past-tense narrative is central to this project, as she interrupts the forward progress of the plot to assert her continued connection to the past.[52] In contrast with the Chancery's relentless futurity, Esther's story is what Hilary Schor calls a 'story of origins'.[53] The first chapter of her narrative, 'A Progress', introduces Esther through temporal contradiction: growing up requires a constant negotiation with her origins because her 'life begun with . . . a shadow on it' (*BH* 26). In stark opposition to Esther's name, 'Summerson', and the developmental trajectory that the chapter title suggests, this 'shadow' introduces gothic tropes that reactivate seemingly dead pasts such as her parentage. Uncovering this shadow unsettles established institutional roles. The reader learns, for instance, of Lady Dedlock's doubleness: the way she functions both as 'Lady Dedlock, brilliant, prosperous, and flattered' and a 'wretched mother, conscience-stricken, underneath that mask' (538). Through this doubleness, the novel implies that accepting institutional futures – in this case, the aristocratic position as Lady Dedlock – masks but does not completely erase the past. The reader also learns that Esther is not confined to the social position that her birth assigns her. Alluding to her illegitimacy, her aunt declares, 'you are different from other children . . . you are set apart' (*BH* 26). The 'progress' of the story begs to differ: Esther becomes the ultimate connector, a character that brings people together instead of being 'set apart'.[54] Uncovering origins activates relationships that exceed institutional roles and, ultimately, unsettle institutional futurity.

Esther models proper relationality throughout the novel as she lets 'that circle of duty gradually and naturally expand itself' (*BH* 117). Each new character becomes a part of her 'circle of duty': Ada, Richard, her guardian, the Jellyby children, Miss Flite, Charley, even Lady Dedlock. She solidifies social connections by emphasising the origin of such relationships. For instance, she accompanies the letter establishing the fact that she will be Ada's companion with the declaration, 'Never, never, never shall I forget the emotion this letter caused in the house' (*BH* 35). Similarly, when Charley becomes her servant, Esther tells her, 'O Charley dear, never forget who did all this' (*BH* 356). At the close of the novel, Esther even asserts that she will remember the unknown reader she addresses in an ironic form of pre-emptive remembrance. Such an emphasis on remembrance only becomes a problem when Allan Woodcourt proposes. Despite her love for him, Esther must treasure his proposal as a 'remembrance' because she has already promised herself to her guardian (*BH* 867). Transforming a future she wants into a past that she treasures shows Esther's firm attachment to origins: her 'circle of duty' expands precisely because she remains oriented towards the past.

Esther's 'naturally' expanding duty is not entirely at odds with institutions but instead depends upon a logic of inhabiting institutions – that is, dwelling within them without accepting the narrow social relations and temporal orientations they establish. As the novel moves between her narrative and the omniscient narrator's story, it emphasises how Esther subtly changes structures by inhabiting them. The self-effacing, even self-denying, style of her narrative does not settle facts or project permanence, but rather asserts opinions that are open to revision, contestation and history. Parenthetical statements pepper her narrative, qualifying her observations and betraying the limits of her own perspective and, in many cases, the limits of other people's perspectives. Visiting the brickmaker's family, Mrs Pardiggle talks with 'much volubility about the untidy habits of the people' but Esther adds in an aside: '(though I doubted if the best of us could have been tidy in such a place)' (*BH* 118). Asserting that historical circumstances matter, Esther shifts from Mrs Pardiggle's abstraction, 'the people', to the particular location, 'such a place'. This qualification of generalised statements allows Esther to transform settled structures into social relations through acts of inhabitation. As Ada insists at Mrs Jellyby's house: 'You would make a home out of even this house!' (*BH* 52). Like Sissy Jupe, Esther's ability to make a home out of a house exceeds the logic of the heteronormative family unit. Esther uses the word 'home' to refer to both Bleak Houses – her guardian's house and the house he gives to her and Allan Woodcourt. For this reason, home, for Esther, expresses a social relation that encompasses disparate spaces and includes diverse forms of relationality. Growing up between these two homes, Ada's son declares that 'he has two mamas', showing how social relationships can redefine social roles (*BH* 913).

Bleak House's omniscient narrator voices this logic of inhabiting institutions by questioning the Dedlocks' fear of external threats and insisting that what they need is 'habitation' (*BH* 590). In 'National and Domestic', a chapter which links the failed governance by the Coodle and Doodle factions to the Dedlocks' deadening estate, the narrator subtly undermines Sir Leister's fear that 'the floodgates of society are burst open, and the waters have – a – obliterated the landmarks of the framework of the cohesion by which things are held together' (*BH* 600).[55] This metaphor of a flood that destroys seemingly permanent 'landmarks' differs starkly from the narrator's own diagnosis of national and domestic matters: 'the great house, needing habitation more than ever, is like a body without life' (*BH* 593). For the narrator, 'the framework of the cohesion by which things are held together' endures, but, without people, it is a form without followers, a structure without spirit. The only inhabitants are 'the pictured forms upon the walls' – spirits from a time when the house was a body with life (*BH* 590). The problem, it seems, is not that divisions are dissolving into chaos, but rather that they are enduring beyond their proper lifespan. The solution is simple: to restore 'life' to this lifeless form, people rather than pictures must inhabit the 'dreary and solemn' house (*BH* 590).

The Dedlocks are anachronistic – ghostly remainders of a time of aristocratic authority when, in the words of Pam Morris, 'affairs of state are affairs of family'.[56] So, too, is the Chancery, which 'languidly' endures beyond its usefulness (*BH* 12).[57] But Dickens does not simply critique the Deadlocks and the Chancery as anachronisms, he mobilises them in the name of reactionary reform – a future that emerges from a return to the past. These 'over-sleeping Rip Van Winkles' need to be woken up (*BH* 17). But waking up, for Dickens, does not mean replacing these anachronisms with more modern forms; instead, it means restoring historicist relations to forms that seem to exist outside of time.

While the Chancery remains asleep throughout the novel – the only return to origins comes when the Jarndyce and Jarndyce suit is absorbed in costs – the Rouncewell sons do the work of waking up Chesney Wold. The sons of the estate's dedicated housekeeper each represent a new future: the ironmaster suggests the future of industry, while George suggests a future that emerges from attending to anachronisms. Having left the Dedlock estate, the ironmaster begins the work of restoring historicity to the lifeless structure by drawing 'a parallel between Chesney Wold, and . . . a factory' (*BH* 419). He shows that the estate is not a bounded form that endures outside of time, as Sir Leicester might imagine; instead, it is connected through historical relationships and shared inhabitants to the very forward-moving projects that the ironmaster enacts and Sir Leicester deplores (*BH* 419). In turn, George Rouncewell restores life to the estate by returning to it after a career in the army and inhabiting it as a 'familiar recollection' (*BH* 827). Taking up his old position as 'another self' to Sir Leicester, George reactivates memories of the past that encourage Sir Leicester to indulge in domestic feelings that do not serve national interests.[58] Whether leaving Chesney Wold or returning to it, forging a new future or reactivating the past, both the ironmaster and George animate social and historical relationships that show that the estate is not a settled form, but a structure that requires inhabitation. Thus, Dickens suggests that readers do not need to decide between Chesney Wold and the factory as two alternate futures for the nation, but rather should recognise the relationship between the two and, in doing so, imagine the future otherwise.

Bleak House, the idealised home at the centre of the novel, demonstrates the untimely circuits of meaning that result from inhabiting institutions. 'Old-fashioned rather than old', the house and furniture is 'pleasantly irregular' (*BH* 79). It suggests John Ruskin's account of the gothic as oriented towards surprise rather than 'symmetry', being 'one of those delightfully irregular houses where you go up and down steps out of one room into another . . . and where you find still older cottage-rooms in unexpected places' (*BH* 78).[59] This irregularity suggests that the house is not a site of protected enclosure, but a place of movement. To learn how to navigate the house's 'unexpected places', one must inhabit it. The outgrowth of such habitation is the recognition that if the house has a 'dreary name', it is not 'a dreary place' (*BH* 40). Bleak House is open to the future not as a repetition or extension of the present, but as difference. Importantly, John Jarndyce's tenure in the house dramatically breaks from his great-uncle Tom's, while Esther's Bleak House – the house that John Jarndyce gives to her and Allan Woodcourt – marks the beginning of a new domestic arrangement.

Hard Times and *Bleak House*, however different, suggest that origin stories thwart institutional futurity precisely because they acknowledge the temporal discordance between individual histories and institutional time. Both Sissy's attachment to her father in the face of Gradgrind's future-oriented education and Esther's 'progress'-as-remembrance activate relationships that transform the future into something other than the repetition of the present. Stony and foggy landscapes give way to temporary dwelling and origins and 'old associations' disrupt the deadening effects of a known institutional future. By activating these origins, natural relations can be restored in ways that foster forms of untimely development.

Race and Relationality

Dickens's novels are transnational but his reform efforts are decidedly national.[60] The Micawbers and the Pegottys leave for Australia in *David Copperfield*, Herbert and Pip leave for the 'land of the Arabian Nights' in *Great Expectations* and Daniel Doyce begins 'directing works and executing labours over yonder' in *Little Dorrit* (*LD* 782).[61] Each of these departures celebrates some kind of escape from ailing British institutions, and thus reinforces the meaningfulness of the boundaries of the nation.[62] These moments also implicitly support British settler colonialism by delimiting the scope of national institutions in ways that disavow their imperial effects. In the Victorian period, many people encouraged the spread of British settler colonialism by seeking to export modern institutionalism to the colonies, transplanting British 'civilisation' to new environments. As J. A. Hobson writes in 1902, 'colonialism, in its best sense, is a natural overflow of nationality; its test is the power of colonists to transplant the civilisation they represent to the new natural and social environment in which they find themselves.'[63] Scholars of British settler colonialism tend to emphasise this approach to empire, claiming that settlers sought to produce 'domestic arrangements that were an extension of Britain's own', and thus make settler colonies an extension of British institutional space.[64] But settler colonialism depends as much upon violent exclusion as it does upon forceful assimilation; it requires what Nathan Hensley calls 'abandonment' as well as 'inclusion'.[65] Thus, Dickens supports settler colonialism in part by presenting reform as a bounded national project that is limited to England, creating a constitutive externality. He shores up the boundaries of the nation in order to contrast British subjects who can reform institutions with racialised and colonised subjects who he understands to be at odds with modern institutionalism altogether.

Dickens's troubling 1852 essay 'The Noble Savage' is important here. This explicitly racist essay calls the savage 'a beastly animal' and indicates that 'his absence is a blessed relief and an indispensable preparation for the sowing of the very first seeds of any influence that can exalt humanity'.[66] Dickens conflates distinct groups of Indigenous peoples – 'Ojibbeway Indians', 'Bushmen', 'Zulu Kaffirs' – to question sentimental accounts of them on the one hand, and to dismiss them through a stereotypical and deeply anti-Indian portrayal on the other.[67] For Dickens, these Indigenous peoples have no future because they have no place in institutions – they perpetuate 'beastly customs' that are at odds with modern civilisation.[68] Celebrating the imperial effects of modern institutionalism, Dickens claims that the savage 'passes away before an immeasurably better and higher power than ever ran wild in any earthly woods, and the world will be all the better when his place knows him no more'.[69] He renders Indigenous peoples anachronistic to ensure that they have no future, explicitly endorsing a settler colonial project of elimination.

Within the essay, the Irish appear as people comfortable with savagery even in the midst of modern institutionalism. Irish people do not face the same project of elimination as Indigenous peoples, but they, like Indigenous peoples, practice 'beastly customs', according to Dickens. He writes that 'several of these scenes of savage life bear a strong generic resemblance to an Irish election, and I think would be extremely well received and understood at Cork'.[70] This assertion of a 'strong generic resemblance' between Irish and Indigenous life contributes to a long history of English analogies that connect Irish and Indigenous peoples to disparage both groups of people. Luke Gibbons tracks such analogies from the fifteenth and sixteenth century, noting that English people found echoes of Irish culture in diverse Indigenous practices such as house-building, fashion and sleeping habits.[71] Such comparisons continued through the nineteenth century. *Fraser's Magazine* publishes an 1844 account 'Of the Red Indian' that remarks:

> When I first gazed on these Indians, an impression, almost amounting to conviction, took possession of my mind, to the effect that the chiefs, braves, squaws, and child before me, were neither more nor less than a party of 'the finest peasantry on the face of the earth' (as Mr O'Connell calls them), who were employed in earning the rent for some flinty-hearted Sassenach landlord.[72]

This 'impression' is a telling one, as descriptions of Indigenous peoples in North America give way to subtle mockery of Daniel O'Connell's nationalist politics. It shows the extent to which Irish people, even after the Act of Union integrated them into the British state, were derided for their nationalist assertions. By understanding Indigenous peoples through the Irish peasantry, the author not only fails to 'see' Indigenous peoples but also refuses to recognise the Irish as modern institutional subjects.[73]

Dickens's essay similarly implies that the Irish remain savages despite their 'modern' elections and institutions. Before mentioning an Irish election, Dickens alludes to 'an Irish House of Commons' – a body that did not exist in 1852. In fact, at the time, many Irish nationalists were fighting to establish this very institutional structure. Dickens, however, acts as if an independent Irish parliament already exists in order to pre-emptively denigrate Irish institutions. Describing a war council of savages, he writes: 'Several gentlemen becoming thus excited at once, and pounding away without the least regard to the orator, that illustrious person is rather in the position of an orator in an Irish House of Commons.'[74] Although Dickens implies that English institutions bring progress and civilisation in the essay, this fictional Irish institution only formalises savagery. Dickens thus reveals the racialised logic that limits his approach to social reform and social institutions: Irish people can participate in modern institutions only if they assimilate into British (as opposed to Irish) institutions and act as British rather than Irish subjects. For Dickens, Indigenous people appear to be at odds with institutionalism altogether.

'The Noble Savage' draws attention to a formal structure at work in Dickens's novels: they question domestic institutions in England but nevertheless seek to legitimate the very racial abstractions upon which these institutions depend. Metaphoric uses of epithets like 'savage' determine which social relations are 'natural' and which are 'unnatural' as they establish the limits of institutional reform. Take, for instance, Dickens's early description of the stony streets and endless brick of *Hard Times*'s Coketown as 'unnatural red and black like the painted face of a savage' (*HT* 28). Here, the figure of the savage represents the 'unnatural' relations that the Coketown institutions such as the school and factory create, while also establishing a firm boundary for who can and cannot be integrated into British institutions. As a figure that draws attention to institutional problems, the 'savage' will never be incorporated into the reformed institutions that Dickens imagines. In the words of Ruth Wilson Gilmore, 'racism is a practice of abstraction, a death-dealing displacement of difference into hierarchies that organise relations within and between the planet's sovereign political territories'.[75] In Dickens's novels, where abstractions are inhabited and institutional networks become discrete forms, this 'death-dealing displacement of difference' occurs when he represents minority subjects as outside of the field of social and historical relationality. Just as the term 'savage' in 'The Noble Savage' is a 'practice of abstraction' that conflates multiple, distinct Indigenous groups and, at times, Irish people, allusions to Indigenous peoples and minority subjects in Dickens's novels work to suggest that these groups of people are outside the scope of institutional reform – and, at times, even outside any future imagining.

With this in mind, *Bleak House*'s central question, 'What connexion can there be?' becomes quite complicated (*BH* 235). The omniscient narrator asks this oft-cited question as he abruptly shifts from the aristocratic scene of Chesney Wold to the slum of Tom-All-Alone's, wondering how these disparate English locations are related to one another. The narrative intervention helps us understand the novel's apparent drive towards integration – visible differences of location and social class will transform into 'connexion' as we read.[76] Yet, as the narrator continues, he subtly shifts his tense and expands the scale of his question, asking: 'What connexion can there have been between many people in the innumerable histories of this world, who, from opposite sides of great gulfs, have, nevertheless, been very curiously brought together' (*BH* 235). This tense shift is telling, for while the sentence ultimately celebrates the ways in which histories have brought disparate people together, the implication is that the connection does not continue. As the passage moves from reflecting on fictional locations in the novel to historical locations in the world, Dickens manages relationality so that national connections endure while global connections have 'brought' people together without continuing to cultivate social ties. Dickens's modification of this question shows that the novel's integrative structure ultimately has limits: global connection is a past-tense phenomenon. In the present and future, connection occurs within national boundaries as people are assimilated into national institutions. Reactionary reform's retrospective orientation reactivates English pasts while denying colonised people and minority subjects futures.

This tense shift helps us understand the strange reversal that occurs at the heart of *Bleak House*: Mrs Jellyby's commitment to African people transforms her own children into 'Wild Indians'

(438). Dickens ironises Mrs Jellyby, suggesting that she mistakenly substitutes private ties with public responsibility, familial bonds with international philanthropy, as he specifies a proper hierarchy of relations: family, then nation, then the world. Mrs Jellyby reverses this hierarchy as her 'duty as a parent' is 'all made over to the public and Africa' (59). This substitution of empire for home ultimately brings the empire home – her family becomes 'Wild Indians'. This designation of 'Indianness' refuses these children any futurity. In the words of her despairing husband, 'the best thing that could happen to them was, their being all Tomahawked together' (*BH* 438).[77] Dickens's abstractions certainly are 'death dealing', for in the context of the novel, to be a 'Wild Indian' is to be without futurity.

In an American context, Jodi Byrd argues that settler colonialism produces a 'transferable Indianness'[78] that reproduces empire by representing 'American Indian lives as ungrievable in a past tense lament that forecloses futurity'.[79] In other words, settler colonialism relegates American Indian lives to the past tense, while cultivating a metaphoric Indianness that continues on as an effect and engine of empire.[80] Dickens participates in an English version of this project as he offers Indianness as a metaphor for foreclosed futurity.[81] In his more 'favorable' portrayal of Indigenous peoples in *American Notes*, Dickens recounts telling the chief of the Choctaw tribe of 'that chamber in the British Museum wherein are preserved household memorials of a race that ceased to be' and concludes, 'it was not hard to see that he had a reference in his mind to the gradual fading away of his own people'.[82] Attributing his own ideas to the chief, Dickens implies that the experience of Indigenous peoples is the same as 'a race that ceased to be'. In this encounter, the 'household memorials' in the British Museum, George Catlin's gallery and James Fenimore Cooper's novels are endowed with Indianness, while the chief is fated to past-tense existence. Although Indigenous peoples live on in the present, they are defined only in terms of the past so that they can be more easily assimilated into British institutions such as the British Museum. Here, Dickens confuses history and settlement by producing a metaphoric Indianness that relegates Indigenous peoples to the past.

Such a metaphoric construction of Indianness has a double effect: on the one hand, it represents Indigenous peoples as outside of the field of relationality because they are consigned to the past tense; on the other hand, it suggests that British subjects, insofar as Dickens endows them with a metaphoric Indianness, confront the same foreclosed futurity. This metaphoric Indianness relocates the empire at home – relations, histories and real Indigenous peoples outside of England's national boundaries no longer need attention. Building on Elaine Freedgood's account of metaphors of slavery in *Great Expectations*, I argue that metaphoric Indianness 'becomes part of the human condition, and in this universal mode, it need not be . . . mentioned in all of its specific instantiations'.[83] In Dickens's novels, Indigenous peoples and British subjects have been 'curiously brought together' to evacuate rather than elucidate historical relationships.

Dombey and Son's 'Native' – the 'dark servant' that Major Bagstock abuses – exemplifies how race limits Dickens's vision of reactionary reform (*DS* 91). In a novel about imperial networks – Dombey and Son's firm famously extends across the globe – the 'Native' has no network except his servile relationship to the selfish Major Bagstock. Like Miss Tox, who is 'quite content to classify' Major Bagstock's servant as 'a "native", without connecting him with any geographical idea whatever', the novel asserts that his classification as 'native' is the only history or origin story that he needs (*DS* 91). Tellingly, he does not even have a name: the narrator describes him, saying, 'The Native, who had no particular name, but answered to any vituperative epithet' (*DS* 290).[84] Lacking both origin and future within the novel, the Native represents the limits of historical relationality. The ability to reform institutions through an expanded understanding of social and historical relationships does not extend to him.

Origin Stories

Ireland often functions in Dickens's novels as it does in 'The Noble Savage' – as an allusion to a place at odds with history.[85] In *Bleak House*, the Irish Famine appears but remains untethered from the novel's plot. In *Great Expectations*, Biddy functions as a historical dead end who evokes Irishness without having an explicitly Irish origin story. These references to Ireland and Irishness show the limits of Dickens's reactionary reform as they demonstrate how the divided time of his novels manages relationality.

In *Bleak House*, the omniscient narrator alludes to Irish history to set it outside of the social and historical relationships that the novel represents. When describing Nemo's room following his death, the narrator declares: 'No curtain veils the darkness of the night, but the discoloured shutters are drawn together; and through the two gaunt holes pierced in them, famine might be staring in – the Banshee of the man upon the bed' (*BH* 151). Together, the Irish folk figure of the Banshee and the allusion to famine refer to the Great Irish Famine that was still ravaging Ireland at this time. But while the historical event this scene gestures to is clear, the connection between this event and the world the novel represents remains murky, in part because of the strange tense, 'famine *might be* staring in'. If, as Gordon Bigelow claims, this reference to Irish famine functions as a 'metonym for poverty', it is a metonym that goes nowhere, creating only dead-end historical relationships.[86] As the novel progresses, we learn about Nemo's origins and relations – he was Lady Dedlock's lover before her marriage and is thus Esther's father – but we never learn why the narrator alludes to either famine or the Banshee at the moment of Nemo's death. The narrator evokes the Irish Famine as a threat – it 'might be staring in' – only to assure the reader that it is not: Nemo dies from opium rather than starvation.

The characterisation of Biddy in *Great Expectations* also alludes to Irishness but ultimately denies historical connections to Ireland. Biddy's name evokes the stage-Irish tradition: the stock comic characters Paddy and Biddy would be quite familiar to Victorian readers from representations on stage and popular stories of Irish life.[87] 'Her Majesty's Irish Mail', an 1859 story in Dickens's *All The Year Round* shows how Biddy operates as a byword for both Irishness and laziness in this period. When the English narrator mistakenly asks if the car is punctual, Biddy responds with representative ridicule: '"Punshill!" says she, showing all her yellow teeth, and flinging her hands with a laugh as she drove on – "punshill is it? What, Jack MacGan punshill! Away win ye!"'[88] The 'yellow teeth' and nonstandard English suggests disorder that refuses the very idea of punctuality. The 1850 *Household Words* article, 'The "Irish Difficulty" Solved by Con Mc Nale' has another Biddy figure, the sister of Con Mc Nale, whose hard work helps him 'solve' the Irish difficulty, that is, habitual laziness, through a commitment to industry and gradual improvement. In this story, Biddy and Con, who is also referred to as Paddy, challenge stereotypes, but because they are sister and brother rather than husband and wife, their domestic success does not lead to reproduction or carry over to the next generation. At the close of the story, the narrator suggests that the 'Irish Difficulty' continues by insisting, 'But all are not so persevering, so knowing, and so fond of work as you.'[89] These characters take on the representative Irish names of Paddy and Biddy, but because they are hard-working, the narrator questions whether they actually represent Irish people.

Mrs S. C. Hall's 1840 sketch of Irish character, 'The Irish in England: The Washerwoman', shows the importance of origin stories to these 'Biddy' stereotypes as she describes 'Biddy Mahoney', 'a specimen of an Irish Washerwoman', to illustrate Irish national character.[90] Like the Biddy of the stage and stories, Hall's Biddy is untidy. She has a fierce pride in her country and, like many comic Irish figures, 'the only thing she cannot bear is to hear her country abused; even a jest at its expense will send the blood mounting to her cheek'.[91] But, unlike the stage-Irish stereotype in which Biddy represents 'everything the ideal Protestant woman was not', Hall's Biddy is self-denying and incredibly hard-working.[92] Although she remains attached to her Irish origins, she is open to the new experiences and systems that England offers her. As the narrator asserts, 'Biddy accommodates herself to every modification of system in every house she goes to.'[93] Hall's movement from describing Biddy's national pride to praising her tireless industry suggests that although Biddy functions as a comic character, her work and worth belies her appearance and attachment to her Irish origins.

Dickens similarly draws on and revises the character of the Irish Biddy in *Great Expectations*, but without ever explicitly mentioning Irishness or Ireland. Early descriptions of Biddy's 'extremities' suggest that she is also untidy: 'her hair always wanted brushing, her hands always wanted washing, and her shoes always wanted mending and pulling up at heal' (*GE* 40).[94] In turn, the incoherent comic song she teaches Pip, 'too rul loo rul, too rul loo rul', suggests that even as Biddy 'improves' and commits to teaching Pip, she remains a comic figure (*GE* 99). But these standard tropes never become explicitly connected to Irishness because Biddy's origins and relations remain unknown and unnarrated in the novel. As Pip puts it, 'Biddy was Mr Wopsle's great-aunt's grand-daughter; I confess myself quite unequal to the working-out of the problem – what relation she was to Mr Wopsle. She was an orphan like myself; like me, too, had been brought up by hand' (*GE* 40). Biddy's Irishness remains murky – a 'problem' that Pip refuses to work out. Instead, Pip defines her as he defines himself: 'an orphan'.

Biddy-as-orphan helps track Pip's dramatic rise and fall, for Biddy's stability – her contentment at home – contrasts with Pip's changing character and expectations. Although Pip values Biddy because she manages 'always to keep up with me', her real worth emerges precisely when she no longer stays apace (*GE* 114). As Pip betrays his home in the name of social mobility, Biddy grows, develops and improves through her connection to home. With his characteristic lack of insight, Pip declares, 'I think you would always improve, Biddy, under any circumstances' (*GE* 258). Of course, Biddy's great strength is taking advantage of her *particular* circumstances – of inhabiting the place where she lives. Tellingly, Biddy's idealised future reactivates the past in a fitting moment of reactionary reform: she achieves a happy domestic life with Joe in Pip's old home and gives birth to a baby named Pip. Even Pip, the protagonist and narrator, gets confused upon his return: 'there, smoking his pipe in the old place . . . sat Joe; and there . . . was – I again!' (*GE* 439). Through the young Pip, a seemingly distant past (Pip's own childhood) becomes the future in ways that make it possible to imagine a *new* future. Presumably, this new Pip will not make the same mistakes as the old Pip.

But there are limits to the reactionary reform that Biddy represents: her origin must remain unknown in order for her to represent a metaphoric origin for Pip. The final section of the novel discloses previously uncharted relations as readers learn that the convict, Magwitch, is Pip's benefactor and Estella's father. This revelation seems to emphasise the smallness of the world, transforming what Jonathan Grossman calls Pip's 'subjective unawareness' into an awareness that he lives in the midst of a global network that he cannot fully comprehend.[95] But the 'problem' of Biddy's relations remain unresolved. Symbolically tied to Pip's home, Biddy seems to originate there, even though the Irish tropes associated with her character repeatedly suggest otherwise.

Although Biddy exemplifies the productive inhabitation of institutions, her character also reinforces history as settlement. By suppressing her origin story even while subtly evoking her Irishness, Dickens again casts 'connexion' as a past-tense phenomenon. Dickens emphasises the curious people who have been 'brought together' without interrogating why or how. Thus, Biddy's Irishness becomes merely metaphoric, detached from any history of Irish emigration to England or historical connections between Ireland and England. She is integrated within the nation – indeed, she even represents attachment to home and 'immobile domesticity' – precisely because her own origins are obscured.[96] While Magwitch's character helps highlight global networks, Biddy's character manages these very networks by suggesting that certain origins can and should be forgotten. The Irish Biddy must not only adapt to English systems, like the washerwoman in Hall's story, but also renounce all claims and attachments to Irish origins. Thus, 'subjective unawareness' becomes a political strategy as well as a cognitive model. In an era of transnational networks, Dickens insists that the nation can continue to function as a bounded form by refusing to trace certain origins and rejecting particular forms of transnational relationality.

Dickens, perhaps more than any other Victorian novelist, reveals the power of anachronism to disrupt institutional settlement. However, in imagining a future that emerges from a return to the past, he restricts the kinds of people and places who have pasts and, by extension, narrowly delimits their futures. I draw attention to the doubleness of Dickens's reactionary reform to emphasise the extent to which the politics of realism emerges from contradictions – between anachronisms and institutions, inhabitation and settlement, and history and metaphor. Dickens's realism does not create a sense of shared time out of difference; in fact, it does not even include all characters in 'the real-world relationships' it represents. The divided time of Dickens's novels productively unsettles institutional futurity by narrating forms of untimely development. However, it also shows that settler colonialism does not simply depend upon exporting Englishness elsewhere; it is legitimated by distinguishing origins that enable reform from origins that are merely historical dead ends, and people who can productively inhabit institutions from people outside of modern institutionalism altogether.

Notes

1. Dickens, *Martin Chuzzlewit*, p. 461.
2. As Betty Higden declares: 'I've fought against the Parish and fled from it, all my life, and I want to die free of it' (Dickens, *Our Mutual Friend*, p. 501).
3. As Amanda Claybaugh argues, reform always requires managing social relationality. In her words, 'the responsibilities entailed by reform, however, establish a new circle of relations among persons who are not yet identified – and who may never be known to one another' (*The Novel of Purpose*, p. 57).
4. In Carlyle's words: 'Cash-payment [is] the one nexus of man to man' (*Past and Present*, p. 170).
5. Andrew Sanders notes that 'Dickensian' is now used to 'express vague dismay at the survival of a defunct Victorian institution', suggesting that Dickens's critique of institutions lives on (*Dickens and the Spirit of the Age*, p. 15). Orwell highlights the contradictions of Dickensian critiques by arguing that Dickens's attacks on institutions made him an institution in 'Charles Dickens', p. 49.
6. D. A. Miller popularised the argument that Dickensian institutions spread disciplinary power in *The Novel and the Police*, pp. 58–106;

more recently, Emily Steinlight and Jennifer Conary emphasise the failure of Dickensian reform. Steinlight argues that Dickens's reform efforts are an exercise in population management in 'Dickens's "Supernumeraries" and the Biopolitical Imagination of Victorian Fiction', p. 229, while Conary suggests that *Bleak House* shows the impossibility of social reform in '"Whether we like it or not:"', p. 207. By contrast, Bruce Robbins, Lauren Goodlad and Amanda Anderson turn to Dickens to support liberal reform, the liberal welfare state and liberal practices of critical detachment. See Robbins, *Upward Mobility and the Common Good*, p. 9, pp. 11–12; Goodlad, *Victorian Literature and the Victorian State*, pp. 86–9; Anderson, *The Powers of Distance*, pp. 88–90.

7. In doing so, I build on Daniel Hack's argument that the nation is consolidated through racial exclusion: 'As we shall see, *Bleak House* does not merely fail to imagine a community that includes Africans, African Americans, slaves, and people of color in general but rather consolidates the national community it does imagine by means of their exclusion' ('Close Reading at a Distance', p. 731).

8. For instance, Kate Flint argues that Dickens's representation of Native American people changes throughout his writing, claiming: 'Whether he depicted Indians in a positive or a negative light depended, above all, on the part he wished them to play in relation to his moral critique of English society' ('Dickens and the Native American', p. 143). Grace Moore argues that 'undue weight' has been accorded to the essay in *Dickens and Empire*, p. 5. By contrast, Laura Peters argues that 'The Noble Savage' is not an aberration but 'part of a continuum of thinking about race' in *Dickens and Race*, p. 55.

9. Myers, *Antipodal England*, p. 9.

10. Nathan Hensley calls these two forms of violence 'inclusion' and 'abandonment' in *Forms of Empire*, p. 90. Also see Christopher Taylor, who suggests that empire's violence emerges as much from its active intervention within colonies as neglect in *Empire of Neglect*. He argues that 'the theory and practice of economic liberalism displaced the idioms and the institutions that loosely structured empire as a polity, unbinding Britain from the inchoate but nonetheless effective normativity of the imperial compact' (p. 2).

11. Dickens, *Dombey and Son*, p. 921. Hereafter cited parenthetically in the text, abbreviated as *DS*.

12. Ferguson, *The Reorder of Things*, p. 18.

13. 'inhabitation, n'. *OED Online*.

14. Dickens, *Bleak House*, p. 44. Hereafter cited parenthetically in the text, abbreviated as *BH*.

15. Tellingly, Martin's failure to settle results from Eden's unyielding, 'unlivable' environment, which further erases Indigenous peoples who previously lived on the land. The settlers attempt to establish a

permanent settlement with houses, bounded fields, even public institutions, but the land swallows up their attempts to shape it: 'There were not above a score of cabins in the whole; half of these appeared untenanted; all were rotten and decayed. The most tottering, abject, and forlorn among them, was called, with great propriety, the Bank, and National Credit Office. It had some feeble props about it, but was settling deep down in the mud, past all recovery' (Dickens, *Martin Chuzzlewit*, p. 328). Through the character of Mr Chollop, Dickens implies that to be able to see Eden as a settlement rather than a swamp, one must also be willing to confuse the principles of freedom with the institution of slavery (Dickens, *Martin Chuzzlewit*, p. 448). As Tamara S. Wagner argues in *Victorian Narratives of Failed Emigration*, this plot questions emigration propaganda in Britain that celebrates America as a new future (p. 102).

16. Shaw, *Narrating Reality*, pp. 103–4.
17. Ibid. p. 107.
18. Freedgood, *The Ideas in Things*, p. 12.
19. In thinking about how minority subjects are metaphoric, I draw on Alex Woloch's account of minor characters which studies 'the interplay between the structured *position* and the thematic *significance* of any character within the narrative totality' (*The One vs. the Many*, p. 199). According to Woloch, it is more likely for minor characters to be thematically or symbolically understood.
20. As Jill Matus argues, although metaphor and metonymy are sometimes indistinguishable, metaphors seek to 'universalize or totalize' ('Proxy and Proximity', p. 310) and 'go out to discover and conquer the world' ('Proxy and Proximity', p. 311), while 'metonymy is positionality made figurative' ('Proxy and Proximity', p. 310).
21. Dickens, *Hard Times*, p. 283. Hereafter cited parenthetically in the text, abbreviated as *HT*.
22. Also see Laura Korobkin, 'Avoiding "Aunt Tomasina"', p. 126.
23. Goodlad, *The Victorian Geopolitical Aesthetic*, p. 10. Also see Jonathan Grossman, who claims that, 'In Dickens's hands, the novel as an art not only could enable his community, whose individuals were increasingly atomized, to come to know their manifold unseen connectedness, but also, more specifically, could help to produce its self-comprehension in terms of a crisscrossing journeying of characters simultaneously circulating all around' (*Charles Dickens's Networks*, p. 6).
24. Campbell, *Institutional Change and Globalization*, p. i.
25. Jenny Bourne Taylor calls her a 'figure under erasure' in 'Received, a Blank Child', p. 349.
26. Dickens, *Little Dorrit*, p. 31. Hereafter cited parenthetically in the text, abbreviated as *LD*.
27. Wolfe, *Settler Colonialism and the Transformation of Anthropology*, p. 27.

28. Hall, *Civilising Subjects*, p. 41.
29. Coulthard, 'Subjects of Empire', p. 439. See also Daiva Stasiulis and Nira Yuval-Davis, who claim that settler colonialism depends upon the belief in a 'common destiny' in 'Introduction', p. 19. Edward Said claims it is grounded in a 'future wish' in *The Question of Palestine*, p. 9.
30. Recently, Mark Rifkin suggests that one of the struggles with narrating Indigenous history is that history so thoroughly relies on 'the temporal frames generated in and by settler governance' in *Beyond Settler Time*, p. viii.
31. James Belich argues that 'representative assemblies and the common law' as well as 'a wide franchise among white men and a strong tendency towards political decentralization' were crucial to the spread of settler colonialism in *Replenishing the Earth*, p.165.
32. Seeley, *The Expansion of England*, p. 13.
33. Ibid. p. 51.
34. Ibid. p. 67.
35. Ibid.
36. Dickens, 'The Noble Savage', p. 337.
37. As Irene Tucker argues, 'So long as the people who predict the future are the people with the institutional power to bring about the predicted conditions, such predictions reveal the interests of the predictors, not any essential (because unchanging) qualities of the state. Knowledge about the future conditions of such a state is thus essentially knowledge of its present, contingent relations' (*The Moment of Racial Sight*, p. 41).
38. As Daniel Wright argues, in *Hard Times* 'the future's shape even within the fictional world of the novel seems already calcified into that circular but catchy assertion: "what will be, will be"' ('Let Them Be: Dickens's Stupid Politics', p. 334).
39. Castiglia, *Interior States*, p. 67.
40. In *The Body Economic*, Catherine Gallagher surprisingly reveals that the problem with industrialism is not the chaos or poverty it creates, but labour itself. Rendering subjects 'deaf to the call of time' is another way of suggesting that they are only labourers (p. 63).
41. In 'The Reader in *Hard Times*', Raymond Williams also uses the phrase 'divided time' (p. 174). For him, this division maps onto ideology and genre, revealing the extent to which *Hard Times* uneasily merges realism and naturalism as it seeks to represent characters as both individuals and products of a system.
42. Miller, *The Novel and the Police*, p. 98. Miller suggests that any apparent outside to power ultimately becomes reintegrated into disciplinary power.
43. Foucault, *The History of Sexuality*, p. 92.
44. Ferguson, *The Reorder of Things*, p. 18.

45. Edelman, *No Future,* pp. 44–5.
46. Muñoz, 'Cruising the Toilet', p. 364. In this article, Muñoz suggests that Edelman's critique of reproductive futurity does not engage with race or class, arguing that Edelman 'accepts and reproduces this monolithic figure of the child that is indeed always already white' (p. 364).
47. In fact, it can be argued that institutions produce a form of what Lauren Berlant calls 'cruel optimism', which exists 'when something you desire is actually an obstacle to your flourishing' (*Cruel Optimism,* p. 1).
48. Ruth, *Novel Professions,* p. 59.
49. Robbins, 'Telescopic philanthropy', pp. 213–30.
50. Miller, *The Novel and the Police,* p. 93.
51. Ibid. p. 90.
52. In '*Bleak House:* Pastoral', Rae Greiner indicates that the novel is divided between 'real, historical time – the past tense of Esther's narrative – and the perpetual present tense of third-person narration' (p. 88). I argue that this division replicates the difference between institutional time ('perpetual present tense' as it moves towards a known future) and historical time ('past tense').
53. Schor, *Dickens and the Daughter of the House,* p. 102. Importantly, however, Schor also claims that Esther is not separate from the Chancery plot, or positioned 'outside the law', but included within it (p. 99).
54. For this reason, Caroline Levine calls her a 'hub' in the novel's networks, 'Narrative Networks', p. 520.
55. As Nasser Mufti argues in 'Walking in *Bleak House*', Sir Leicester Dedlock, often not taken seriously, helps show that 'the very institutions that are meant to ground English society turn out to be self-destructive' (p. 66). Mufti's argument about social cohesion always dissolving into difference precisely because it is premised upon colonial difference shows that institutions are not threatened so much by the external forces that Sir Leicester fears as by the internal contradictions of the institutions he inhabits.
56. Morris, '*Bleak House* and the Struggle for the State Domain', p. 685. Pam Morris continues to argue that 'Their small enclosed world is perceived as the nation . . . the effect of this self-absorption, the text insists, is to seal them off from the realities of the larger world' (p. 685).
57. Or in the Miller's words, 'the anachronism of Chancery' (*The Novel and the Police,* p. 64).
58. In 'On the Genealogy of "Deportment"', Jonathan Farina also notes the productive reforms enabled through George Rouncewell's presence and the untimely temporalities it cultivates: 'Through his presence, that is to say, through his bearing, he makes present circumstances appear closer to his ideal temporality and structure of feeling. His presence, then, as a sort of regulative fiction, contests his

present reality as he and George concurrently revisit the past in their minds and manners.'

59. Ruskin, 'The Nature of the Gothic', pp. 166–7.
60. Kate Flint suggests that Dickens adopts 'a nationalism posited on looking inward' in *The Transatlantic Indian*, p. 143. Also see Amanda Claybaugh, who argues that Dickens's visit to the United States turned him 'into one of the few nineteenth-century novelists to argue for an exclusively national conception of reform' (*The Novel of Purpose*, p. 54).
61. Dickens, *Great Expectations*, p. 380. Hereafter cited parenthetically in the text, abbreviated as *GE*.
62. As Patrick Brantlinger demonstrates in *Rule of Darkness*, these departures, themselves, fit an imperial pattern: 'the Empire may intrude as a shadowy realm of escape, renewal, banishment, or return for characters who for one reason or another need to enter or exit from the scenes of domestic conflict' (p. 12).
63. Quoted in Antoinette Burton, *Empire in Question*, p. 261.
64. Joseph, '"Saving British Natives"', p. 261. Joseph ultimately argues that Dickens's representation of emigration departs from this typical settler colonial logic.
65. Hensley, *Forms of Empire*, p. 90.
66. Dickens, 'The Noble Savage', p. 337.
67. Dickens reflects on the Indigenous peoples represented in paintings in George Catlin's show as well as Indigenous people who were part of live exhibits in England.
68. Ibid. p. 337. Throughout the essay, Dickens narrates these customs in order to juxtapose the animalistic practices he describes with modern institutional practices, focusing especially on marriage, war and medical practices.
69. Ibid. p. 339.
70. Ibid.
71. Gibbons, *Transformations in Irish Culture*, pp. 150–1.
72. Rattler, 'Of the Red Indian', p. 655.
73. Although I think it is important to study the ways in which Irish and Indigenous peoples are connected through analogies in the nineteenth century, we should not conflate their experience. As I argue in 'How the Irish Became Settlers', often Irish nationalists used these analogies to erase Indigenous peoples and perpetuate a settler colonial project, pp. 83–4.
74. Dickens, 'The Noble Savage', p. 339.
75. Gilmore, 'Fatal Couplings of Power and Difference', p. 16. Irene Tucker provocatively suggests that race operates 'as a mode of institutionalization' because it materialises ideas and formalises embodied practices (*The Moment of Racial Sight*, p. 13).

76. In 'Market Indicators', Gordon Bigelow claims that despite this emphasis on connection, the novel depends upon divisions (p. 590).

77. Emily Steinlight makes a similar argument, suggesting that Dickens does not contradict Mr Jellyby's pronouncement ('Dickens's "Supernumeraries" and the Biopolitical Imagination of Victorian Fiction', p. 232).

78. Byrd, 'Arriving on a Different Shore', p. 180.

79. Byrd, *The Transit of Empire*, p. xxxv.

80. As Rayna Green warns in 'The Tribe Called Wannabe', 'metaphor signs the real Indian's death warrant' (p. 37).

81. As Kate Flint argues in *The Transatlantic Indian*, 'Dickens's writing typifies the way in which Native Americans mattered less in their own right than because they readily provided rhetorical tropes, something that subordinated them as racial subjects' (p. 154). Of course, this is in the context of English writing – Native Americans did and do matter 'in their own right'.

82. Dickens, *American Notes*, p. 185.

83. Freedgood, *The Ideas in Things*, p. 97.

84. As Grace Moore concludes, 'The Native, then, constitutes the ultimate other – silent, elusive and compliant' (*Dickens and Empire*, p. 63). I also recommend Rajeswari Sunder Rajan's article, '"The Shadow of that Expatriated Prince"', which argues that 'The reference to and by his generic title, "the Native" denies the Indian the status of *sui generis* reality, without at the same time allowing him to be seen as wholly invented' (p. 93).

85. In 'Dickens and Ireland', John Hennig characterises Dickens's relationship to Ireland as a 'casual remoteness' (p. 254).

86. Bigelow, 'Market Indicators', p. 597. Bigelow, himself, reinforces this reading by suggesting that the novel raises the question of whether Ireland is outside of the 'signifying economies of metropolitan England' (p. 598).

87. 'Biddy' appears throughout Mrs S. C. Hall's *Sketches of Irish Character*. In America, 'Biddy' increasingly represented an Irish servant in cartoons and tales, and on the stage. For an extended discussion of the Stage Irish tradition in the Victorian period, see Mary Trotter, *Ireland's National Theaters*, pp. 35–72.

88. 'Her Majesty's Irish Mail', p. 283.

89. 'The "Irish Difficulty" Solved by Con Mc Nale', p. 210.

90. Brozyna, *Labour, Love, and Prayer*, p. 4.

91. Hall, 'The Irish in England', p. 3.

92. Brozyna, *Labour, Love, and Prayer*, p. 173.

93. Hall, 'The Irish in England', p. 3.

94. My reading of Biddy's characterisation thus differs from that of Woloch, who suggests that this emphasis on her 'extremities' demonstrates

how the novel draws attention to minor characters through descriptions that underscore their 'human exteriority' (*The One vs the Many*, p. 183). Biddy's physical description emphasises exteriority, but also symbolically evokes the imagined interiority associated with the Irish Biddy type.

95. Grossman, 'Global Transport Network in *Great Expectations*', p. 233.
96. Robbins, *Upward Mobility and the Common Good*, p. 77.

Chapter 5

George Moore's Untimely *Bildung*

'Has it never come to you to think differently about things, to find your mind in a ferment of contradiction?'[1]

George Moore's realism differs from the other realist novels that I have focused on in this book. While these earlier novels seek to reform institutions, Moore attempts to reject them and the social coherence they provide. Experimenting with the methods of Zola's naturalism before breaking with Zola in the late 1880s, Moore's writing adopts naturalism's narrative trajectory of decline as he depicts how institutions fail characters and characters fail to meet institutional expectations. *A Drama in Muslin* (1886), Moore's first novel set in Ireland, chronicles the failure of colonial institutions and *Esther Waters* (1894) powerfully demonstrates the failure of the law by insisting that there is 'one law for the rich and another for the poor'.[2] In turn, his tendency towards naturalist description – what Georg Lukács calls 'monographic detail' – represents competing anachronisms within an existing institutional landscape.[3] For Moore, anachronisms suggest the discordance of historical time not simply by evoking the continued presence of the past or moments of untimely irruptions, but by questioning the dominance of a single time frame. In his novels, Anglo-Irish institutions appear anachronistic, but so do the Irish institutions with which Irish nationalists want to replace them. Unsettling the social and temporal coherence of institutions, Moore shows that historical time is not uniform; it is startlingly heterogeneous.

And yet, surprisingly, even as Moore adopts naturalism's trajectory of decline and emphasises details, he does not reject realist development altogether. Instead, he rejects development governed by institutions. Institutions establish what Caroline Levine calls 'rhythms – patterns of duration and repetition over time'.[4]

Institutions thus define development as a process of synchronisation, of learning to accept institutional rhythms in the name of a shared, if deferred, future.

Many of Moore's characters achieve maturity, but few synchronise with institutional rhythms. Like Dickens, Moore imagines forms of untimely development that result from realism's divided time – its institutional rhythms and anachronistic irruptions. But while Dickens questions the narrow futures that institutions imagine, Moore interrogates institutions' seemingly coherent present tense. Instead of activating origin stories that institutions erase, as Dickens does, Moore makes the more radical claim that public institutions and private growth are at odds. In *A Modern Lover* (1883), Lewis Seymour's public recognition – the fact that his paintings are hung in the Academy – only confirms his mediocrity. In *The Lake* (1905), Father Oliver's self-development begins when he questions and then neglects his priestly responsibilities. He realises that his institutional role in the Catholic Church only masks his true self. In *Esther Waters*, Esther achieves growth despite the fact that she never learns to read, suggesting a form of maturation without formal education. Combining an anti-institutional impulse with an anachronistic narrative temporality, Moore's realism questions the institutionalised assumptions of what constitutes proper growth.

This merger of realism and naturalism and refusal to synchronise with institutions allows Moore to reimagine the *Bildungsroman* so that it produces a developmental narrative temporality that resists institutional integration. Scholars commonly understand the *Bildungsroman* to be what Bruce Robbins calls 'an exercise in social integration'.[5] Ideally imagined as a spiritual and aesthetic process, *Bildung* quickly becomes an institutional one. Nineteenth-century narratives of development narrate this process as they merge individuals with the institutions that govern them, synchronising individual processes and institutional rhythms. Just think of George Eliot's emphasis on the blending of institutional and individual desires in *Adam Bede*, which I discuss in Chapter 3. These narratives also produce institutions that govern development: schools, museums, universities. Gregory Castle questions this 'socially pragmatic' form of *Bildung* associated with nineteenth-century English novels in his book-length study of the modernist *Bildungsroman*, suggesting that modernism invents forms of development at odds with these institutional rhythms and trajectories.[6] In such accounts, nineteenth-century realist novels of development integrate with and even produce institutions while modernist novels of development reject them.[7]

However, Moore's realist novels of development share many of the formal features that Castle identifies with the modernist *Bildungsroman* – dissent, disjunction, ambivalence, even failure. Instead of suggesting institutional integration or synchronised development, time in Moore's novels is messy, defined through dispersal and contradiction. *A Drama in Muslin*, a colonial *Bildungsroman*, grapples with the strange temporality of Ireland, a colonial nation, trying to define itself against the imperial British state and unsettles an easy distinction between old and new, English realism and French naturalism. In turn Moore's 'English' novel, *Esther Waters*, questions the extent to which Esther is an agent in control of time as it refuses to define development through institutions such as schools, hospitals or even the realist novel itself. Acting as an anachronistic figure of the untimely, Esther grows in opposition to institutions.

Although critics often read Moore's Irish and English novels separately, they both reimagine development through a distinct narrative form defined through discordant temporalities that celebrate anachronisms as a mode of institutional refusal.[8] *Esther Waters* and *A Drama in Muslin* redefine development as at odds with institutional integration. By resisting a trajectory of improvement that synchronises individuals and institutions, Moore's novels produce an anachronistic aesthetics that refuse to allow institutional rhythms to delimit the present. The fact that these anachronistic aesthetics both highlight the strange temporalities of Ireland's colonial position and underscore the discordant temporalities at work in England demonstrates that Moore's 'Irish' realism helps us better understand his 'English' realism. Together, Moore's novels create a form of untimely development where prevalent, competing anachronisms remain at odds with institutional time.

Realism and Naturalism, England and Ireland

In Georg Lukács's famous essay on naturalism, 'Narrate or Describe?', he contrasts realism and naturalism through their dominant forms: narration and description. To illustrate how these forms represent reality differently, Lukács juxtaposes Zola's naturalist description of a theatre with Balzac's realist narration of a theatre. He argues that while Zola describes social facts, Balzac narrates 'the drama of the institution in which they work', producing a narrative 'of the things with which they live, of the setting in which they fight their battles, of the objects through which they express themselves and through which their interrelationships are determined'.[9] This contrast between naturalism's reliance on facts and realism's depiction of interrelationships demonstrates why Lukács prefers realist narration to naturalist description: narration articulates relationships as opposed to details, expresses causality rather than chance.

But by explaining narration as that which demonstrates 'the drama of the institution in which they work', Lukács suggests another opposition between naturalist description and realist narration: narration is institutional in scope, while description's dynamic movement between micro- and macroscopic scales focuses on social facts and social relationships that both escape and exceed institutions.[10] Tellingly, when celebrating the great practitioners of realist narration, he emphasises their 'public activity', mentioning that Goethe and Stendhal 'served as government officials' and Tolstoy participated 'in various social organizations'.[11] By contrast, Lukács argues that Flaubert and Zola, exemplars of naturalist description, refuse 'public activity' and institutional participation. Although Lukács contends that such differences are historically determined – Flaubert's and Zola's refusal results from the era of capitalism in which they live – he highlights an implicit difference between realism and naturalism: realism is institutional, while naturalism is decidedly not.

When juxtaposing realist narration and naturalist description, Lukács pairs institutional refusal with proliferating anachronisms. Associating narration with the depiction of a single anachronism, Lukács praises Walter Scott's *Old Mortality* because the narrative 'exposes the hopeless anachronism of the feudal institutions'.[12] Despite the campaign to revive these institutions within Scott's narrative, the novel concludes that they no longer have popular support. For Lukács, the identification of an explicit anachronism – here, obsolete feudal institutions – makes historical development visible. Realist narration thus uses necessary anachronisms to establish a sense of shared time and shared development – a shared rhythm – in complex social landscapes.

By contrast, description emphasises synchronic social landscapes rather than diachronic development. Description produces multiple, competing anachronisms and discordant rhythms rather than shared development. Such unnecessary anachronisms appear throughout Moore's novels. In *Esther Waters*, descriptions of London neighbourhoods and buildings note the transience of the present as timely locations proleptically fall behind the times. Avondale Road, the 'new' neighbourhood where Miss Rice lives, has 'just sprung into existence' and yet, Esther notes, it too will quickly become out of fashion, thinking, 'Hot joint to-day, cold the next' (*EW* 182). In *A Drama in Muslin*, Ireland appears as 'a land of echoes and shadows' populated with people, buildings and objects that suggest disparate historical moments and trajectories.[13] Moore describes the men of the Kildare Street Club, an old-fashioned Anglo-Irish institution, and 'the cries of a new Ireland' that 'awaken the dormant air' in a single sentence, complicating who is in decline and who is in ascendance (*DM* 159). By representing social landscapes with an overwhelming multiplicity of social rhythms, Moore highlights anachronisms that unsettle an understanding of a unified contemporary moment or a shared developmental path. Instead of depicting institutional rhythms that ultimately synchronise into a single historical development, Moore represents individual rhythms that remain at odds with modern institutionalism as they imagine forms of untimely development.

Naturalist description's asynchronies as opposed to unified historical developments, multiple anachronisms rather than a single anachronism, helps explain Moore's own discontinuous trajectory as an author. Performatively refusing institutions even when inhabiting them, Moore often put himself at odds with larger literary developments. Throughout his career, Moore would identify with literary movements, people, even institutions only to repudiate them publicly. An Irish landlord from County Mayo who lived in London, Paris and Dublin respectively, Moore transformed himself from an art student in Paris who hobnobbed with Impressionists, to a disciple of Zola in England, to a collaborator with W. B. Yeats in Ireland. As he articulates it in *Confessions of a Young Man*, he had 'no enemy except the logical consequences of my past life and education'.[14] In other words, as Moore invents and reinvents himself to perform his opposition to institutions, his only obstacle is the way in which institutions have already shaped him.

Moore's shifting relationship to Ireland is a central component of his politics of institutional refusal. His scathing and satirical *Parnell and His Island* (1887) criticises Ireland for being backward, perpetuating 'a worn-out system' that cannot endure.[15] But, at the end of the century, he returned to Ireland and became a vocal supporter of the Irish Literary Revival. In this period, Moore celebrated Ireland as a place of artistic opportunity, dreaming of 'an old language revived and sharpened to literary usage for the first time' as he supported the efforts of the Gaelic League and collaborated with W. B. Yeats.[16] His return to Ireland and identification with the Revivalists also did not last and Moore published *Hail and Farewell* (1911–14), a humorous, gossipy account of the Revival that angered his friends. This memoir notably ends with a description of his departure for England, once again breaking ties. After Moore's death, George Russell declared Moore to be 'one of the most talented and unfilial of Ireland's children'.[17] Like the social landscapes that he depicts, Moore, the man, does not follow a single or coherent developmental path.

Moore's depiction of discordant social landscapes and own discontinuous self makes him difficult to place within literary history.[18] As I demonstrate in Chapter 1, literary history, like the forms of realism that Lukács favours, tends to be narrated in terms of a single developmental path – the rise of the novel.[19] But Moore's movement between nations and national traditions as well as his embrace of realism and naturalism makes him an outlier. In English literary histories, Moore's early naturalism, coupled with his sustained rejection of institutions, tends to make him an exception – a footnote to larger trends or a strange peculiarity.[20] Meanwhile, Irish literary histories view Moore as a precursor to James Joyce but often at odds with his own contemporaries.[21] His realist experiments influence later developments, but cannot easily be characterised *as* a development because they remain too at odds with the larger literary landscape, which scholars tend to define in national terms.[22] In this way, although Moore has a more complicated relationship to Irish realism and Irish writing than the previous Irish authors that I have studied, he most clearly demonstrates the necessity of a transnational history of realism that includes Ireland. His novels – whether set in England or Ireland, whether naturalist or realist – demonstrate how the tension between institutions and anachronisms becomes metacritical at the end of the nineteenth century. Moore imagines new forms of untimely development to question the apparent coherence of social institutions and ensure that realism remains a dynamic.

Moore's early writing tends to be directed against English institutions because he was writing at a time when realism was solidifying as an institution in England. The ongoing discussion about 'The Art of Fiction', for instance, begins with Walter Besant's claim that the best way to assess the success of a novel is to measure the extent to which it 'has drawn the story to the life'.[23] Although this lecture and subsequent pamphlet sparked discussions about whether the novel should or should not be realist, and should or should not be moral, it also reveals the extent to which realism was in the process of being institutionalised. As Henry James argues in his contribution to the discussion, 'The only reason for the existence of a novel is that it *does* compete with life.'[24] In other words, the novel has become a serious art form, worthy of a theory, precisely because it is realist. Tellingly, Besant identifies a canon, describes publishing practices, advises would-be novelists how to navigate them, and develops standards for judging the novel's success as an art form as he seeks to identify the novel's 'general laws'.[25] Quickly shifting from a theory of the realist novel to the institutionalised structures that produce this novel, Besant shows how for many Victorian critics, taking the novel seriously as an art form depended upon understanding it as an institution.

Actively resisting many of these 'general laws', Moore began his writing career by attacking one of the primary institutions shaping the production of the novel at the time: the circulating libraries. These libraries would not carry his first two novels, *A Modern Lover* (1883) and *A Mummer's Wife* (1885), despite the fact that these novels received favourable reviews. Positioning itself against Mr Mudie, the head of Mudie's Circulating Library, Moore's polemical *Literature at Nurse; or, Circulating Morals* (1885) famously attacked the censorship of novels. The problem, according to Moore, is that Mudie's library has become such a dominant institution that it actually restricts art: the librarian, not the novelist, is responsible for the shape and content of novels. In his words, 'The struggle for existence, therefore, no longer exists; the librarian rules the roost; he crows, and every chanticleer pitches his note in the same key. He, not the ladies and gentlemen who place their names on the title-pages, is the author of modern English fiction.'[26] Tellingly, in place of institutional control, Moore seeks the 'struggle for existence' – something that his early naturalistic novels might represent as an utterly bleak prospect, but here he associates with the opportunity for authorship and art.

By challenging the institutions that governed the production of the novel, Moore also challenged realism as it had been institutionalised in England. As Arthur Waugh suggests in a 1916 article on the 'New Realism', Moore broke away from the 'realist of the last generation' who desired to use writing in the service of 'the general improvement of social and human conditions'.[27] For Moore, established realist conventions mediated and sanitised reality. He reflects, 'Though adultery is as frequent in England as in any other country, our literary convention is that people of novels are chaste and never miss church, and any violation of this code will assuredly cause the book to be banned by the libraries.'[28] Not surprisingly, Moore's depiction of conventional realism shows how it implicitly defines morality in terms of participation in institutions: here, marriage and church attendance. By contrast, Moore's characters are not chaste and often question institutionalised religion. In *A Drama in Muslin*, Alice Barton – who does not believe in God – laments that Catholicism has become mere 'Sunday mummery' (71). In *Esther Waters*, Esther has an illegitimate child and does not attend church throughout most of the novel despite the fact that she is religious. Moore was not the only writer using realism to challenge realist social conventions: George Gissing, Thomas Hardy, Olive Schreiner similarly depicted social reality that exceeds realist conventions in order to depict social landscapes that cannot be easily reformed.

Irish settings intensified Moore's anti-institutionalism because Ireland's competing anachronisms could not resolve into a coherent institutional landscape. Although Moore often repudiated his national identity – he famously declares his 'original hatred of my native country' in *Confessions of a Young Man* – he made use of his native land to show the discordant rates of historical change that institutions obscure.[29] Representing Ireland in the midst of the Land Wars in *Parnell and His Island*, he depicts a country where Anglo-Irish institutions slowly dissolve, becoming more and more anachronistic each day. The alternative – native Irish institutions – is just as untimely for Moore. He portrays the Irish peasants rising up as part of 'a degenerate race – a race that has been left behind – and should perish, like the black rat perished before the brown and more ferocious species'.[30] Depicting institutional decay and evolutionary backwardness, Moore suggests that Ireland requires naturalism's shifting temporal scales precisely because it cannot resolve into either a shared present tense or a single anachronism.

In Ireland, modernity does not replace an anachronistic past; it joins it and produces additional anachronisms. Reflecting on the new awakening of Irish literature as he walks through London in *Hail and Farewell*, Moore declares Ireland to be a land of ruins, writing: 'And noiselessly, like a ghost, modern Ireland glided into my thoughts, ruinous as ancient Ireland, more so, for she is clothed not only with the ruins of the thirteenth century, but with the ruins of every succeeding century. In Ireland we have ruins of several centuries standing side by side, from the fifth to the eighteenth'.[31] Progressing forward in time means the accumulation of alternative times, ruins upon ruins.[32] Thus, although Moore's return to Ireland to participate in the Irish Revival marks a shift in his thinking, it also builds on his earlier, more critical writing about Ireland by suggesting that Ireland's anachronisms can disrupt modern institutionalism. Tellingly, Moore's public call for the revival of the Irish language – which he could not speak himself – associated the English language with the 'monotony of empire'.[33] For him, multiple, competing anachronisms were not only a formal feature of his writing, but a political response to imperial institutions that sought conformity and monotony.

I focus on naturalist description in Moore's novels and the proliferating anachronisms it produces not to stabilise Moore as a naturalist writer, but to show how naturalist techniques – description, an emphasis on decline rather than growth, dramatically shifting timescales – shape realism's contradictory movement between anachronisms and institutions at the end of the century.[34] After all, long after Moore publicly broke with Zola in 1886, he continued to use description to depict discordant social landscapes. Moore's novels are important precisely because he combines naturalist description with the realist *Bildungsroman*, a rejection of English institutions with representations of untimely Irish social landscapes. He challenges realism as it had been institutionalised in England, using anachronisms to unsettle the conventional rhythms of realist development. In turn, he draws on Ireland's anachronisms to indicate that there is no stable rhythm – no shared present tense – to produce the synchronised social integration typically associated with *Bildung*. As he moves between England and Ireland and draws upon his experience in France, Moore shows that literary history itself often requires description as well as narration.

Untimely Development: *A Drama In Muslin*

Moore wrote *A Drama in Muslin*, his first novel set in Ireland, when he was still working to promote Zola's naturalism in England. When publicly evaluating the novel, Moore declared, 'The best test whereby to judge a novelist is by his power of accounting for time.'[35] Insisting that time is the 'most corrosive of the world's acids', Moore objects to novelists 'who suppress it' by failing to chronicle its destructive force.[36] Such a statement reveals Moore's difference from the English realists for whom the passage of time brings progressive change and reform. Moore – 'Zola's ricochet in England' – favoured the new French naturalism, which was grittier, more scientific, and tended towards a more tragic trajectory of decay and decline.[37] In these naturalist novels, 'time's ravages are irreparable': they break down bodies and crush naïve illusions.[38]

Chronicling the lives of 'the Galway girls' as they leave their English convent, enter society and venture to Dublin to seek husbands in a ruthless marriage mart, *A Drama in Muslin* painstakingly portrays time's destructive force (15). The passage of time traps many female characters in narrow, meaningless lives – the older they get, the less likely they are to escape by finding a husband or breaking from convention. Time also destroys the Land League's collective 'struggle for nationhood' – by splintering it into groups and reinstating the discordant rhythms of everyday life.[39] As Dr Reed pessimistically concludes at the end of the novel, 'And when one thinks of the high hopes and noble ambitions that were lavished for the redemption of these base creatures, one is disposed to admit in despair the fatality of all human effort [. . .] all here is vileness and degradation' (*DM* 24). Most reviewers questioned Moore's taste in part because he so comprehensively described characters' failure to achieve growth. In the words of one critic, it was 'daringly and disgustingly suggestive, and descriptive of what writers of fiction commonly leave undescribed'.[40]

But the novel is not simply the 'tragedy of enforced, stagnant celibacy' that Victorian reviewers made it out to be – it is also a successful *Bildungsroman*.[41] In the midst of the decline of the landlord economy, the failure of the tenants to seize power, and the more personal struggles of 'the Galway girls', the protagonist, Alice Barton, achieves an independent and fulfilling life. She matures, takes up writing as a profession, marries the modest Dr Reed, and moves to a suburb of London. Given the pervasive failure and decline within the novel, her success is surprising. Scholars debate whether it is hopeful or ambivalent, whether it reflects Moore's own rejection of Ireland, and what enables Alice Barton's growth – her profession and practice as a writer.[42] At stake in these discussions is the question of how to connect Moore's critique of both the obsolete landlord system and the tenants who rise against it with the *Bildung* narrative of Alice Barton.

Suggesting that time expresses both aesthetics and politics, I argue that the novel's tension between two temporalities – slow decay and progressive growth – does not resolve or synchronise, but rather invites us to consider the political possibilities of untimeliness and anachronism. To be at odds with the historical moment, to be tied to residual or emergent forms, is to be opposed to the present arrangement of power. Such an embrace of untimeliness makes sense given Moore's own oppositional stance to his contemporary moment. As he told Geraint Goodwin, 'a great artist [. . .] is either before his time or behind it'.[43] But I claim that the novel's recurring trope of anachronism suggests more than an individual stance or authorial position – it is a statement about historical time itself. Discordant, uneven and messy, historical time is hardly uniform and certainly not linear within the novel – it expresses uneven power relations. As is the case with many postcolonial histories that emerge in the twentieth century, such discordance can open up space for new kinds of historical agency and new forms of power.[44]

George Moore is a theorist of historical time precisely because he rejects the national-historical time of the *Bildungsroman* to imagine a form of untimely development that resists both the imperial state and the imagined nation. This untimely development expands the political potential of what Jed Esty calls the 'colonial *Bildungsroman*'.[45] Unlike the *Bildungsroman*, which narrates an individual's progress through national-historical time, the colonial *Bildungsroman* registers the distance between imperial narratives of progress and untimely colonial experiences through the trope of 'frozen youth'.[46] In Olive Schreiner's *The Story of an African Farm*, for example, time passes without leading to progress. In the novel's opening scene, titled 'The Watch', Waldo listens to the loud, methodical ticking of a watch, wishing it would 'leave off'.[47] The novel closes with Waldo's death rather than straightforward development. But *A Drama in Muslin*'s colonial narrative does more than measure distance from the imperial centre or reflect differences; it constructs a politics of institutional dissent. Instead of choosing between development and death, Moore suggests that development is always untimely; it accompanies decay. By representing discordant synchronic time and untimely diachronic development, the novel reveals that the colonial *Bildungsroman* imagines political processes – negotiation, dissent, conflict – rather than solidifying institutional forms – the nation or the state. Time is a corrosive acid, but its uneven force, which both underwrites and dissolves social forms, creates spaces for productive political change.

Untimely Ireland

In quite different ways, both M. M. Bakhtin and Franco Moretti contend that the protagonist's successful *Bildung* hinges on his ability to integrate into, or in temporal terms, to synchronise with the nation. Bakhtin suggests that the personal development of the protagonist parallels the historical development of the nation, claiming that the genre portrays 'man growing in national-historical time'.[48] In turn, Moretti argues that the future-oriented trajectory of the *Bildungsroman* upholds the value of the nation, arguing that in this genre, 'time must be used to find a homeland'.[49] In his conception of the genre, the narrative cannot find closure and the protagonist cannot achieve maturity unless the protagonist finds a national homeland. In both accounts, narrative time implies national time: for Bakhtin, narrative time is 'national-historical time' and, for Moretti, the protagonist's integration into national-historical time is one of the ends of the narrative.

But *A Drama in Muslin* rejects national-historical time as uniform or synchronous, even as it carefully chronicles the contemporary moment. Historical events and historical people populate the narrative – talk of Gladstone, Griffith's valuation and the possibility of a new Coercion Act pepper the local gossip, and the news of the Phoenix Park murders dramatically interrupts a dinner party at Brookfield.[50] As Sara Maurer indicates, the novel has a 'journalistic immediacy' – it thrusts readers into the conflicts of the land wars and the dramas of the drawing rooms, repeating the newspaper headlines of the day.[51] Moore marketed the novel by celebrating its historical timeliness in advertisements that declared, 'The story will depict with photographic realism the TRUE CONDITION of IRELAND as IT IS NOW.'[52] In turn, reviewers noted the novel's clear temporal framework, writing: 'The story is solidly planted, so to speak, both in place and time. The state of Ireland between 1881 and 1884 is sketched so vividly that the book will one day be recognized as a valuable document in socio-political history.'[53]

Because of the political unrest of the Irish land wars, national-historical time becomes visible not as a uniform progression or as a shared space into which the protagonist integrates, but rather through disparate perspectives that uncover the discordant rates of historical change. Anachronisms abound and what it means to be contemporary is precisely what is up for debate. From the perspective of the Irish tenants who attempt to establish continuity with Ireland's Celtic past, the Anglo-Irish Big House appears as a 'strange anachronism' (*DM* 40).[54] By contrast, from the perspective of the imperial state that values stability, routine and monotony, the Irish peasants are anachronistic remnants of a previous historical era – 'as incapable of thinking as of dressing up to the ideas of the present generation' (*DM* 68).[55] Each perspective has a historical narrative – one of cultural continuity that legitimates national independence, the other of modernisation and stability that legitimates the state – but these narratives cannot be reconciled or synchronised. Thus, the 'historical plotting' that Maurer suggests drives the narrative does not simply create a linear sequence of dates – it creates conflict, disagreement and political posturing about what it means to live in Ireland in 1881–4.[56]

Importantly for Moore, the anachronisms that proliferate are not errors or historical mistakes that need correction or further historical development; they productively resist the dominance of a single time frame. In this way, his portrayal of the Irish Land Wars is far more ambivalent than many found in the newspapers and periodicals of the day. Tending towards partisanship, these accounts used anachronism as a way of solidifying one historical narrative.[57] Those who opposed the Land League insisted that the Irish people were too anachronistic and too underdeveloped to become agents in their own right. Arguing against peasant proprietary, W. Glenny-Crory declared, 'The United Kingdom has progressed beyond the condition in which a peasant proprietary in land would be for the interests of the State, the good of the tillers of the soil, and the ends of economic progress.'[58] Implicitly understanding history as economic development, Glenny-Crory insists that the British state should control time and history. But the Irish Land League argued the very opposite, depicting the system of land tenure and the landowners as anachronistic vestiges of feudalism. They also understood history as progress, but saw themselves rather than the state as the proper agents who would guarantee it. Tellingly, Michael Davitt's history of the Land League, *The Fall of Feudalism in Ireland*, recounts how the actions of the Land League sought to abolish 'anachronism in the control of Irish rural affairs'.[59] Moore betrays his own identification with the landlord class throughout the novel, but does not legitimate its history, choosing instead to emphasise discordance and disagreement.

In a location defined through proliferating anachronisms, there is hardly a stable communal space that allows for social integration. Ireland appears as 'a land of echoes and shadows' – haunted by the untimeliness of historical change (*DM* 159). The traditional acts of the Castle season seem ghostly – holdovers from the past that are out of place in the present. The girls wait in line to kiss the Lord Lieutenant: 'a lingering survival of the terrible Droit de Siegneur – diminished and attenuated, but still circulating through our modern years – this ceremony, a pale ghost of its former self, is performed' (*DM* 175). The 'muslin martyrs' belatedly repeat the fashions of England: 'How their London fashions sit upon them; how they strive to strut and lisp like those they saw last year in Hyde Park' (*DM* 159). Irish-Americans, and the threat of emigration to America, haunt the street scene: 'their sinister faces' reveal Ireland's porous boundaries (*DM* 171). The present is out of joint because the old customs, institutions and economic orders seem out-of-date and ghostly, and the future they promise no longer seems viable: 'the city lay mysteriously dead – immovable and mute beneath the moon, like a starved vagrant in the last act of a melodrama' (*DM* 203).

Perceptible change is precisely what the state seeks to suppress. Following Henri LeFebvre, many theorists of the state argue that it attempts to foster an endless present by converting time into space. Suggesting that the state is 'born in and with a space',[60] LeFebvre articulates the three ways in which the state uses space to perpetuate its power: first, by creating a national territory; second, by governing the creation of social spaces – institutions that 'acquire a quasi-natural self-evidence in everyday life'; and third, by managing representations of space – the way that people conceive themselves in space.[61] Set in a historical moment when the national territory is contested, *A Drama in Muslin* highlights how the social spaces that once served the interests of the state, such as 'the colonnades of the Bank of Ireland' and 'the long grey line that is Trinity College', no longer appear as natural and self-evident as they once had (*DM* 218). Despite their seeming permanence, they are merely temporary bastions of power – the Marquis realises that they too 'would perish before the triumphant and avenging peasant' (*DM* 218).

The Anglo-Irish seem to recognise for the first time that their way of life – like the life of the tenants who oppose them – is subject to historical forces that they cannot control. Seemingly permanent institutions dissolve as they become subject to time's 'corrosive' force. In Moore's words: 'And now they saw that which they had taken to be eternal, vanishing from them' (*DM* 95). Tellingly, the Marquis acknowledges his fear of the future after looking at the Daniel O'Connell statue – the first memorial to a Catholic man in Dublin – recognising that this material marker points to 'a new power established' that would eventually render his class and his social position obsolete (*DM* 218). In other words, the creation of new social spaces forces the Anglo-Irish landowners to confront the fragility of state power and recognise their own untimely presence in the Irish landscape, even as they continue to ask the state to suppress the Land League by passing a Coercion Act.

By contrast, the collective struggle for nationhood transforms the Irish tenants from anachronisms to agents as they create a national time that opposes the state. Talking in Irish amongst themselves, resisting the threat of state intervention, and refusing to be placated by the meagre appeals of the land agent, the Irish tenants appear committed to the idea of a nation that will restore the continuity between Ireland's past and its future. Unlike the Anglo-Irish landowners who confront the increasing obsolescence of their class as individuals, the tenants are 'united by one thought, organized by one determination to resist the oppressor, marching firmly to nationhood' (*DM* 324). Moore rarely explores events from their perspective, but rather shows their increasing control over time and history by transforming them from 'vague forms' (86) who scramble through the landscape to solid groups and crowds: 'twenty or thirty peasants who, with heads set against the wild gusts, advanced steadily' (*DM* 124). This transformation shows how they become historical actors in a social landscape as opposed to ghostly elements of a natural landscape.

Such solidity and solidarity make the landowners confront their foreign origins and attachments. As Catherine Gallagher suggests in her reading of *Castle Rackrent*, this is precisely what the Anglo-Irish did not want to do. Knowing the 'shaky historical grounds of their tenure', they preferred to justify their power within Ireland 'on the basis of their present actions'.[62] In Moore's novel, we see just how shaky these historical grounds are. When the landowners attempt to distinguish between those families who were in Ireland before Cromwell and those who acquired land in the land courts in order to assert their ties to Ireland, 'the heavy jaws and flabby cheeks of age and middle-age grew hopelessly dejected, and their vision of poverty had become so intolerably distinct that they saw not the name of the entrée on the menu' (*DM* 44). Such dejection results from the recognition that they will never be able to legitimate their ownership of the land in terms of national-historical time. Instead, they begin to face the possibility of a future outside of Ireland – 'America rose above the horizon of their vision, and the plunge into its shadowy arms threatened' (*DM* 95).

By the end of the novel, the Land League has accomplished very little – the landowners return to their daily routines, and the tenants return to their poor, 'animal' existence – and yet, through their brief tenure in power, they have undermined the state control of temporality (*DM* 322). Alice Barton's school friend who marries the Marquis – Violet Scully – symbolises the precarious plight of the Anglo-Irish even after the state reasserts control. Having gained everything she wanted – a husband with a title, the dissolution of the Land League – her days in power are nevertheless numbered: she knows that 'she will be sold up in a year. But the present is the present, and she enjoys it' (*DM* 268). No longer believing that the present is eternal, the Anglo-Irish cling to the present because it will soon become past. Moore's far more cynical *Parnell and His Island* – written just after

A Drama in Muslin – captures this plight well when it ventriloquises an Irish landlord saying:

> I am an Irish landlord. I have done this, I do this, and I shall continue to do this, for it is as impossible for me as for the rest of my class to do otherwise; but that doesn't prevent me from recognising the fact that it is a worn-out system, no longer possible in the nineteenth century, and one whose end is nigh.[63]

In other words, the state re-establishes control by the close of the novel, but cannot resume its control over time. Neither the Anglo-Irish nor the Irish tenants appear to be the agents of history; they seem instead to be waiting for what comes next.

Given the pervasive decay and the ongoing conflicts that resist historical consensus and unsettle the expectation for a shared future, Alice Barton's successful development is surprising. Should not she, like her class, be doomed to destruction? If time is a 'corrosive' force, how does she find a way to mature? 'A girl who silently but firmly declined to acquiesce', Alice does not integrate into a shared national space or grow in 'national-historical time' but rather achieves maturity precisely because she remains at odds with the expectations of her class, her community, her gender and her religion.[64] Moore declared Alice Barton 'the best thing in the book', because she was 'representative of the modern idea'. 'The modern idea' that Alice Barton represents celebrates discordant rates of change within modernity. Her untimely development imagines a heterogeneous historical time that opens up spaces for political agency at odds with the nation and the state.

Precisely because Alice Barton successfully develops, *A Drama in Muslin* is more radical than the colonial *Bildungsroman* that Esty examines. While these novels contain the trope of 'frozen youth' – or prolonged adolescence punctuated by death – to suggest that social integration into the nation is impossible in a colonial setting, Moore shows how the very discordance between the nation and the state can enable new forms of untimely development. For example, Esty's interpretation of Elizabeth Bowen's *The Last September* helpfully reveals how the ambivalence of Bowen's novel is not necessarily nostalgia for an old way of life, but rather a way of accounting for the uneven and untimely realities of colonial existence. Understanding the protagonist, Lois Farquar, as a 'living figure of a cultural death', Esty reveals how she resists maturity and adulthood because she represents the anachronistic position of her class.[65] In the process, he suggests that narratives of development will always fail in a colonial setting. For Esty, the colonial *Bildungsroman* reveals the unbounded temporalities of global capitalism without imagining new forms of untimely development or modes of resistance.

By contrast, *A Drama in Muslin* forges new narratives of development that, as the novel's English ending suggests, can circulate in both Ireland and England. Like Bowen, Moore conveys ambivalence towards the decline of the Anglo-Irish culture, but in this novel, prolonged adolescence is a threat that Alice fears but ultimately avoids. Recognising how unfair social constraints limit the scope of women's lives, Alice worries that she will never be able to achieve maturity and live an active life. In her worst moments, she imagines a protracted girlhood replaced by ignorant old age:

> And from this awful mummery in muslin there was no escape. It would continue until the comedy became tragedy; until, with aching hearts and worn faces, they would be forced aside by the crush of the younger generation; and, looking aghast in the face of their five and thirty years, read there their sentence to die, as they had lived, ignorant of life and its meaning. (*DM* 99)

In many ways, Alice's fears are justified, for the Irish landscape is populated with figures of frozen youth. Her sister, Olive, remains stuck in 'the perpetual trying to make up matches' (*DM* 328), as do most of the women on the marriage market. These women 'remain' and 'wither' rather than develop and progress. But, despite this fear, Alice achieves maturity. Rejecting her mother's advice, she speaks in 'her own individual right', decides to marry the modest Dr Reed, and moves to England where she continues to pursue her writing (*DM* 314). In the process, she achieves adulthood, recognising that 'the last few sands of girl-life were [. . .] disappearing into the obscure void of the past' (*DM* 316).

How does Alice Barton escape the fate of her class and her friends? She succeeds precisely because she is a figure of the untimely. Most of the characters in the novel imagine a future that ensures historical continuity and institutional integration: the Anglo-Irish desire the state to re-establish 'order' so that they can return to the timeless rhythms of everyday life, the Irish tenants desire the nation to re-establish continuity with the past, and the 'muslin martyrs' desire a husband so that they can fulfil their mothers' dreams of social mobility. But Alice Barton does not allow the state, the emerging nation or even her gender to determine her understanding of the future.

Instead, she embraces her anachronistic and anatopistic position – the ways she is at odds with her historical moment and her cultural location – as that which allow her to develop as a person and an artist. In a novel where there are stark contrasts between landlords and tenants, men and women, Catholics and Protestants, Alice does not easily fit in any of these social categories: she questions the landlord economic structure, does not believe in a Catholic or Protestant god and resists the social constraints on women by pursuing a writing career. She seems to have no future – 'there was no end for her to attain, no height for her to climb; and now looking into the future she could see no issue for the love and energy which throbbed within her' (*DM* 98). Yet, precisely because she understands that such lack is a problem of the institutions that govern her life – they imagine futurity too narrowly – she succeeds.

Moore quantifies Alice's untimeliness as he declares her to be a representative woman of 1885 in 1882 Ireland. In a confusing reference to Eduard von Hartmann, Moore claims that Alice adopts Hartmann's ideas. Since an English translation of Hartmann's *Philosophy of the Unconscious* did not appear until 1884 – in 1882 he was almost completely unknown in Ireland – this brief scene appears to engage with the novel's moment of production rather than the moment it attempts to represent.[66] But the narrator insists that Alice Barton expresses 'ideas not yet in existence, but which are quickening in the womb of the world' (*DM* 228). He then goes further, claiming that William Wordsworth anticipated Schopenhauer and concluding with the question: 'Is it therefore unnatural or even extraordinary that Alice Barton, who is if anything a representative woman of 1885, should have, in an obscure and formless way, divined the doctrines of Eduard van Hartman' (*DM* 228–9)? Like Maggie Tulliver before her, Alice Barton's reading and thinking is at odds with a coherent inherited tradition and thus allows her to make untimely connections. Alice is associated with artists from the past – Wordsworth – and thinkers who will affect Ireland in the future – Hartmann.

The question that remains, however, is why does Moore quantify Alice's alienation by explicitly telling the reader that she is a woman of 1885 in 1882 Ireland? For Elizabeth Grubgeld, such a reference might function as an instance of the 'ahistorical' emergence of the individual artist.[67] But, as Grubgeld herself admits, Moore hardly recognises Alice as an artist. His narrator repeatedly undermines her writing, representing it as too sentimental, too provincial and too businesslike to have any lasting value. In fact, Moore suggests that

Alice's anticipation of Hartmann's philosophy actually undermines the apparent agency of the individual artist by revealing 'ideas which we believe to have been the invention of individuals, are but the intellectual atmosphere of that epoch breathed in greater or less quantities by all' (*DM* 228). Shifting the locus of agency away from the artist and towards the 'intellectual atmosphere', Moore emphasises history's discordant rates of change.

By explicitly noting Alice's untimeliness, Moore disrupts a politics grounded in continuity. Unlike the state and nation, which both desire continuity, Alice is a figure of discontinuity. She anticipates ideas and exemplifies the non-linear nature of inheritance. As Maurer argues, the novel reveals how inheritance – both inherited traits and inherited property – is not traceable within the novel.[68] Alice inherits 'her love of books' from her grandfather, her 'clear logical intelligence' from her mother, but 'of her father's brain she had nothing' (*DM* 38). Heredity matters as much for the ruptures it engenders as for the continuities it assures. Thus, unlike Dickens, who shows the political possibilities of English origins that reanimate the past only to deny colonised people pasts, Moore suggests that origins cannot be recovered or reanimated. For Moore, inheritance is always discontinuous and discordant, and thus one does not need to return to the past to activate anachronism, one only has to acknowledge the multiplicity of the present.

Accessing ideas that do not easily fit into a narrative of national development or contribute to the perpetuation of state power, Alice repeatedly resists the nation's and the state's control over time. Alice's marriage – the very thing that allows her to achieve maturity – does not serve either the nation or the state. In order to marry Dr Reed, who 'was educated at the National School, and [. . .] used to run there without shoes', Alice must disobey her mother, accept a more economical way of life and move to a London suburb, Ashbourne Crescent (*DM* 314). Even within England, her supposed 'connatural' home, Alice is slightly out of place: the character of her house 'is therefore essentially provincial, and shows that its occupants have not always lived amid the complex influences of London life, viz., is not even suburban. Nevertheless here and there traces of new artistic impulses are seen' (*DM* 327). Combining the provincial with 'new artistic impulses', Alice Barton embodies the multiple temporalities necessary for historical change even after she has achieved maturity.

Scholars tend to argue that this English ending undermines Moore's nuanced portrait of Ireland, as they tend to overlook the discordant time within England. Some scholars read the ending biographically, claiming that Alice's decision to leave Ireland reflects Moore's own renunciation of the land of his birth.[69] For them, the novel juxtaposes Ireland's discordant temporalities with stable, civilised England in order to suggest that England productively reinstates homogeneous, empty time. Even Grubgeld, who questions whether the ending is as positive a portrayal of England as most scholars suggest, claims that the ending 'seems to exist outside of time'.[70] For these scholars, the ending closes down the narrative's radical potential because it replaces the untimely realities of colonial experience with the stable, 'civilised' life in the imperial centre.[71]

At first glance, Ashbourne Crescent's monotonous life certainly seems to offer a stable alternative to the discordant temporalities at work in Ireland. In his depiction of Ashbourne Crescent, Moore maps the endless present that the state promises onto the nation, insisting that this place where 'life flows monotonously' is 'typical England' (*DM* 326). Here, routine reigns without any apparent fear for the future: 'there is neither Dissent nor Radicalism, but general aversion to all considerations which might disturb belief in all the routine of existence' (*DM* 325). Yet Moore suggests that even Ashbourne Crescent contains the seeds of revolution:

> And that Ashbourne Crescent, with its bright brass knockers, its white-capped maidservant, and spotless oilcloths, will in the dim future pass away before some great tide of revolution that is now gathering strength far away, deep down and out of sight in the heart of the nation, is probable enough. (*DM* 325–6)

In England then, where the nation and the state seem to merge into one continuous present – one shared institutional rhythm – there are still shifting timescales that express temporal contradiction: the monotony of the present, and the slow, gathering strength of a revolution 'in the heart of the nation'.

By concluding the novel in England, where the nation and state cohere rather than antagonise one another, Moore offers a critique of the nation-state and its control of temporality. For Moore, the possibility of revolution is not threatening; it 'renews the tired life of man' in part by activating temporal rhythms at odds with institutions (*DM* 326). Tellingly, Moore returns to the notion of the 'atmospheric', describing political revolution as 'those sempiternal storms which, like atmospheric convulsions, by destroying, renew the tired life of man' (*DM* 325). In this account, revolution does not serve the nation, as the Irish land league desires, because as a 'sempiternal storm', revolution does not necessarily lead to stability or a new control over temporality. But that does not mean that Moore encourages 'the failed nationalist to embrace the virtues and values of the centre', as Patrick Ward claims.[72] Rather the novel seems to celebrate the failure of the nation, the landlord economy, and Ashbourne Crescent's 'fund of materialism' in order to acknowledge the political possibilities of asynchronicity (*DM* 325). Ensuring the continued proliferation of anachronism and discordant rates of change, the fact that these institutions fail to reassert control over time creates the possibility of untimely development.

As a figure of discontinuity, Alice Barton certainly disrupts the 'larger narrative of the civilizing process'.[73] Moore celebrates Alice's untimely development without necessarily wanting to generalise it – he does not teach readers how to anticipate ideas not yet in existence, or make Ashbourne Crescent represent a national community. Instead, Moore highlights how Alice resists the narratives of the nation, the state, her class and even her gender – in order to celebrate her successful development as a form of radical dissent. Moore's contemporaries often noticed the novel's violation of dominant narratives, praising the novel as one of the 'most original novels of the year' only to complain about its disruptive narrative form.[74] One reviewer was so disappointed with Moore's 'melancholy' characters that he found consolation in the fact that *A Drama in Muslin*'s characters are not 'complete pictures of typical personages'.[75] Another reviewer complained that *A Drama in Muslin* failed to celebrate 'virtuous' characters, writing, 'It would be refreshing to feel at the close of the chapter that virtue, whether in life or death, is its own reward'.[76] I suggest that these complaints express unease about a novel that traces an individual's successful development but consistently refuses the dominant narrative of 'the civilizing process'.

Returning to the question of the colonial *Bildungsroman*, then, the Irish setting shapes the peculiar model of development that Alice follows. In Ireland, a site of contested time, synchronisation is not the mark of maturity or the goal of development. Integration into a uniform temporality would merely obscure continued oppositions within the nation, between genders, religions and classes, and against the state. Alice's untimely development reveals the limits of the traditional *Bildungsroman*, not just to register distance or express difference, but to show how exploiting oppositions rather than reconciling them creates change. In order to develop, grow and mature in a land of echoes and shadows, one must embrace untimeliness.

Illiteracy in an Age of Improvement: *Esther Waters*

Esther Waters, by contrast, is a self-consciously English book. As Molly Youngkin argues, this story of Esther's fight to raise her illegitimate son was Moore's attempt to insert himself into the English canon 'by applying a softer, more English form of realism to the woman-centred subject matter he had already used in his earlier, more naturalist novels'.[77] The novel sympathetically portrays Esther's protracted struggles against institutions that fail and, in some cases, actively oppress, working-class women. Victorian critics celebrated Moore's apparent shift towards this 'softer' realism and the morality it implies, claiming that 'the realism of "Esther Waters" is redeemed from offensiveness – and therefore from the reproach of bad art – by the moral lessons it teaches'[78] and reviewing it as 'a tract against betting'.[79] Moore notes that although the novel is 'pure of all intention to do good', it is 'a thoroughly healthy book'.[80] He comically laments the social reforms that the novel inspired, including the foundation of an 'Esther Waters Home' for homeless children, suggesting that the success of the book will actually impede his art.

Recent critics tend to reinforce the sense that *Esther Waters* departs from both Moore's naturalism and his Irish fiction. Simon Joyce contends that *Esther Waters* differs from *A Drama in Muslin*, claiming that Esther Waters' Englishness 'enables her to shift from the determined subject of naturalism to the self-determining agency required by realism'.[81] Joyce juxtaposes Esther's decision-making with Alice's self-revelations to suggest that national setting ultimately shapes character. But character and setting are actually formally similar in these two novels: both settings are temporally discordant, and both Esther and Alice develop because of their own untimeliness. *Esther Waters* shares *A Drama in Muslin*'s rejection of institutions and its depiction of proliferating anachronisms as it chronicles Esther's struggle to survive and, ultimately, thrive. Reading the two novels together demonstrates that even after Moore moved away from Zola's naturalism and self-consciously wrote a form of English realism, he continued to rethink the *Bildungsroman* as a structure of untimely development rather than institutional integration. As an anachronism, Esther questions the temporal rhythms of realist narrative as she models a form of development through regression.

In *Esther Waters*, descriptions of setting emphasise the disjunction between the entropy of natural life and the artificial order of social institutions. Moore's descriptions of Woodview, the rural estate where the novel begins and ends, show how nature's dynamism tends towards decline. At the end of the novel, Esther confronts the ruin of the once elegant estate and concludes, 'Nature does not take long – a few years, a very few years' (*EW* 391). Descriptions of urban scenes indicate that nature is also at work in the city. As Esther makes her way to Queen Charlotte's Hospital, the narrator notes the 'beautiful weather' and indicates that 'wherever nature could find roothold, a spray of green met the eye' (*EW* 116). By contrast, social institutions seek to impose order that keeps nature and its rhythms at bay. Moore describes the hospital as gray, 'square, forbidding' – 'an ugly desert place' (*EW* 117). The natural metaphor, 'ugly desert place', suggests stasis – a place where nothing grows – but also implies that nature is at work in this bounded social space. As is the case with the ending of *A Drama in Muslin*, moments of apparent stability and shared time mask the ongoing historical changes occurring at disparate temporal scales.

Esther, like Alice, grows and develops by remaining at odds with institutional rhythms. In *Esther Waters*, events typically associated with maturation are startlingly out of order.[82] Esther prematurely quits school to protect her mother from her abusive stepfather; goes into service at Woodview; picks up her schooling with her mistress, Mrs Barfield; in a moment of weakness, has sex with her fellow servant, William Latch; becomes pregnant and leaves service; becomes a mother; becomes a wet nurse; returns to service; leaves service to move in with William; returns to service with Mrs Barfield at Woodview after William dies. Esther's return to Woodview is a regression – a 'returning to former conditions' (*EW* 381). But it is also a sign of successful *Bildung* as it allows her to practice her religion, support her son and, most importantly, act as an individual as opposed to a mere servant.

At each stage of her development, Esther opposes institutions such as the legal system, the patriarchal family structure, the hospital. As the narrator declares in the middle of the novel, 'Hers is a heroic adventure if one considers it – a mother's fight for the life of her child against all the forces that civilization arrays against the lowly and the illegitimate' (*EW* 172). 'The forces that civilization arrays' are institutional forces: the legal system punishes the poor and protects the rich, the family structure exploits women while giving men power and freedom, the hospital prioritises its subscribers over its patients. Esther recognises this inequality but refuses to allow it to diminish the value of her or her child's life. For Moore, this struggle connects her to Alice Barton despite their class and national differences. He indicates that 'both represent the personal conscience striving against the communal'.[83]

Instead of being ahead of the time, like Alice, Esther is decidedly behind it.[84] Her inability to read marks her as an anachronism
in an era of universal education. While other servants engage with
the news and culture of the day through print – Sarah Tucker 'has
read every story that has come out in Bow Bells for the last three
years' and the men at Woodview defend their predictions for upcom-
ing horse races by citing the recent *Bell's Life* and the *Sportsman* –
Esther gets her news belatedly, through oral sources (*EW* 4). She
arrives at Woodview carrying a bundle of her mother's books, which
draw attention to her illiteracy. For her, they are mementos of a past
life and 'mysteries' that prompt wonder, rather than literary texts to
read (*EW* 22). Moore frequently mentions these books to highlight
generational change that is not progressive – Esther's mother can
read, but Esther cannot – as well as to underscore Esther's untimely
relationship to a social landscape increasingly mediated by print.

Esther's illiteracy also unsettles realist conventions by moving
realist tropes associated with minor characters and minor plots to
the centre of the novel to indicate that development occurs alongside stasis. As I discuss in Chapter 3, George Eliot's realist fiction
uses literacy to distinguish between the present tense of characters
and readers: illiteracy marks characters, like Hetty Sorrel, as anachronisms who will not continue into the present. Literacy works
similarly in Dickens's novels, showing that realism's emphasis on
improvement does not extend to everyone. In *Bleak House*, Esther
Summerson tries to teach her servant, Charley, grammar and writing, but Charley is 'not at all grammatical' at the novel's end.[85]
Esther concludes that Charley's grammar 'never did any credit to
my educational powers'.[86] Charley's persistent bad grammar questions the progressive trajectory of realist plots on the one hand and
educational initiatives on the other, showing that life often unfolds
through repetition rather than growth. Unlike Hetty Sorrel and
Charley, who, in different ways, are minor characters, Esther Waters
is the protagonist of the novel. Her illiteracy at a moment when
literacy was even more widespread reinforces the fact that she struggles against institutions instead of being aided by them. Mrs Barfield
tries to teach her how to read, but 'Esther did not make much progress, nor did her diligence seem to help her' (*EW* 31). Even in a
novel that celebrates Esther's untimely development, she ends the
novel as she begins it, unable to read her son's letters.

The fact that Esther does not learn how to read even as she learns
to adapt herself to different social roles produces narrative repetition
rather than incremental growth. Every time she encounters a new

institution – the hospital where she gives birth, the registry office where she seeks employment – she also encounters new effects of her inability to read. She cannot communicate with her son's nurse, she cannot reply to print advertisements for jobs and she shares letters with her employers that should be kept secret. Over the course of the novel, this repetition reinforces the fact that knowledge of reading and writing is required to be able to synchronise with institutions.

Moore uses Esther's untimeliness to imagine a story of maturation at odds with the institutional rhythms of schooling. In Esther's narrative, repetition does not lead to synchronicity, and *Bildung* suggests return and regression as opposed to slow improvement over time. According to the standards of the educational initiatives that Moore deplores, Esther does not progress. And yet, Esther succeeds in her 'heroic adventure' to raise her son by finding both community and spiritual fulfilment (*EW* 172). At the close of the novel, she returns to Woodview and peacefully settles with Mrs Barfield. The house is nearly a ruin, the land is let, and yet this return to a decaying Woodview marks Esther's growth. For the first time, 'she was content in the peaceful present' (*EW* 388). Importantly, this 'peaceful present' is distinctly anachronistic – at odds with the institutions that Esther struggled against for so long. Hosting religious meetings of the Plymouth Brethren, Mrs Barfield and Esther attempt 'to live like the Early Christians' (*EW* 22) and reanimate the time of miracles (*EW* 387). The culmination of Esther's *Bildung* is thus defined through an explicitly anachronistic religious practice that celebrates spiritual communion rather than institutionalised community.

While *A Drama in Muslin* concludes by depicting the divided time of routine and revolution in Alice Barton's suburban home, *Esther Waters* represents the divisions between the 'peaceful present' and ongoing decay at Woodview. Esther's hard-won peace is transient: the 'long ruins of stables, coach-houses, granaries, rick-yards' reveal Woodview's persistent decline (*EW* 391). But such decline, however inevitable, is not necessarily sad. Through this contrast between Esther's peace and the estate's decay, Moore signals historical change that will thwart existing institutions and enable new political possibilities. Tellingly, the dissolution of stark social hierarchies accompanies the decline of the house. Living in an estate that seems to have no future, 'the two women came to live more and more like friends and less like mistress and maid' (*EW* 388). When institutions are no longer the horizon of political imagining, the present becomes a site of practising the very woman-centred, cross-class politics that seem impossible throughout the rest of the novel.

Esther's inability to read not only makes her an anachronism within the social landscape that Moore represents, but also at odds with the novel form in which she appears. Like *Adam Bede*'s Hetty Sorrel, Esther lives her life unmediated by novels. But, because Esther is the centre of the novel, she functions more like Thady Quirk, the illiterate narrator from *Castle Rackrent* that I discuss in Chapter 1. Esther, like Thady, does not know what a novel is, even as the narrative of her experience takes the form of a novel. For instance, when Esther works for the novelist, Miss Rice, Esther asserts 'I don't know what she writes' (*EW* 187). Such a statement implies that although Esther knows that Miss Rice writes novels, Esther does not understand what distinguishes the novel as a genre. Parroting the voice of morality, Fred Parsons, the upright stationer who desires to marry Esther, warns her that novels 'are very often stories about the loves of men for other men's wives. Such books can serve no good purpose' (*EW* 188). Moore dismisses Fred's perspective by repeatedly insisting that novels are tame in contrast with Esther's life (*EW* 188). Listening to Esther tell her story, Miss Rice thinks 'for a moment to the novel she was writing, so pale and conventional did it seem compared with this rough page torn out of life' (*EW* 245).[87] Representing Esther as a 'rough page torn out of life' whose story is both more real and more compelling than the novels that Miss Rice writes, Moore makes a claim for his heightened realism by questioning the conventionality of novels.

In these references to novel writing, the novel form appears like the hospital: 'square, forbidding' as it mediates and sanitises life (*EW* 117). The stark juxtapositions between Esther's immersion in ongoing conflicts and Miss Rice's safe distance from any trouble shows that the novelist, however disposed to representing real life, reproduces conventions. As Moore contrasts Esther's experience with the serial fiction that her fellow servants read, the novel that the medical students discuss and the novels that Miss Rice writes, he contributes to ongoing debates about the novel form, suggesting, as Henry James puts it, that the novel works 'to alter and arrange the things that surround us, to translate them into conventional, traditional moulds'.[88] By contrast, Moore implies that *his* novel is utterly original because it chronicles an untimely story that refuses to be translated into the 'traditional mould'. As an anachronism, Esther represents an immediacy that education or novel-reading necessarily eradicate. Reading novels – or actively opposing the reading of novels – assimilates people like Miss Rice and Fred Parsons into established institutional rhythms and, in the process, necessarily distances them from the more discordant and dynamic rhythms of Esther's unconventional life.

I argue this contrast between Esther's seemingly unmediated life and the mediations of the novel form demonstrate how the contradictions between realism's institutional and anachronistic aesthetics become metacritical at the end of the century. As late nineteenth-century writers like Moore reflect on the institutionalisation of realism, they both consolidate and undermine realism's institutional effects. For George Levine, these metacritical moves are a sign of realism's breakdown, while Lauren Goodlad, drawing on René Wellek, contends that they are crucial to the emergence of a 'self-identified realist movement'.[89] I suggest that as realism becomes institutionalised at the end of the century, it adds another layer to the dynamic movement between institutions and anachronisms within realist fiction: temporal contradictions within the text implicitly refer to literary developments outside of the text.

George Gissing's novels demonstrate that these metacritical reflections on realism do not all reach the same conclusion even as they grapple with similar contradictions. Like Moore, Gissing reflects on the anachronisms that emerge alongside the increasing institutionalisation of realist conventions. But while Moore celebrates the anachronisms that expose realist mediation, Gissing suggests that realist conventions are necessary to mediate the tedium and monotony of real life. *New Grub Street* dramatises how Harold Biffen's commitment to the realist project leads him to defy realist conventions in his novel, 'Mr Bailey, Grocer'.[90] But precisely because Biffen's text departs from the conventional narrative temporality of realist novels, it does not find readers. The critics understand it as a novel without 'story': 'a warning to all men who propose drawing from life'.[91] In turn, in *The Odd Women*, Rhoda Nunn claims that novels perpetuate a vulgar, idealised version of love because depicting real relationships would be too boring. She asks, 'What is more vulgar than the ideal of novelists? They won't represent the actual world; it would be too dull for their readers.'[92] Acknowledging that realist mediation is 'vulgar', Gissing nevertheless suggests such mediation is necessary in order to create a compelling story. Both Moore and Gissing reflect on how realist conventions mediate real life, but while Moore suggests that realism produces normative rhythms that are in themselves monotonous, Gissing suggests that such conventions provide trajectories for stories that otherwise 'would be too dull'.[93] Both writers show that the tension between anachronisms and institutions in realist fiction of the late nineteenth century becomes self-referential as they question the solidification of realist forms.

I suggest that Moore's metacritical reflections on the realist novel are another instance of his refusal of institutional integration. Esther's immediacy, crucial to her untimely development, questions the established conventions of realist narrative by disrupting the rhythms and the order of established plots. In turn, as a character who cannot read in an era of nearly universal literacy, she rejects the institutional rhythms of school. Esther develops by regressing, and, like Alice Barton before her, suggests that personal growth occurs through refusal rather than integration. At odds with institutional rhythms at both the beginning and the end of the novel, Esther shows that rejecting institutions' shared social time in favour of temporal discordance is a way to dissent from institutions' control over both time and social life. Such dissent changes the ends of realist novels of development – they do not solidify institutions such as the nation or the state as the culmination of *Bildung* – but also transforms the form of realist development. Instead of narrating the synchronisation of individual and institutional rhythms, Moore's novels insist on multiple, competing temporal rhythms that allow readers to imagine the politics and history otherwise.

Like Dickens, George Moore uses anachronism to imagine developmental paths at odds with modern institutionalism's emphasis on shared temporality and a fixed future. But while Dickens's anachronisms reanimate the past to reform institutions, Moore's anachronisms highlight the temporal discordance within the present in order to attempt to reject institutions altogether. Merging naturalist description with realist narration and moving between English and Irish settings, Moore's proliferating anachronisms create a form of untimely development that celebrates history's multiple, competing temporal rhythms. Ultimately, Moore's novels show that the contradiction between anachronisms and institutions within the realist novel can be a way to refuse institutions even while inhabiting them.

Notes

1. Moore, 'My Impressions of Zola', p. 481.
2. Moore, *Esther Waters*, p. 306. Hereafter cited parenthetically in the text, abbreviated as *EW*.
3. Lukács, 'Narrate or Describe?', p. 113.
4. Levine, *Forms*, p. 56.

5. Robbins, *Upward Mobility and the Common Good*, p. 58. Jesse Rosenthal makes a more recent version of this argument, claiming: 'the *Bildungsroman*, more generally, produces a narrative that works toward both development and social inclusion' in *Good Form*, p. 140.

6. Castle, *Reading the Modernist Bildungsroman*, p. 18.

7. As Pieter Vermeulen and Ortwin de Graef argue, '*Bildung* is not merely a spiritual process: its attempt to blend matter and form has given rise to institutions – museums, universities, philosophies, monuments, books, buildings – whose dynamics no longer obeys the wishful logic of self-manifestation' in '*Bildung* and the State in the Long Nineteenth Century' p. 245. In turn, Christiane Gannon argues that the 'democratic bildungsroman' at the end of the century 'inspired the creation of actual institutions of aesthetic education' in 'Walter Besant's Democratic Bildungsroman', p. 377. Gannon argues that this subgenre of the *Bildungsroman* shifts its focus from inner spiritual development to collective nation-building.

8. As John Wilson Foster argues, 'a discussion of George Moore by an Irish critic will typically concentrate on *A Drama in Muslin* (1886) and *The Untilled Field* (1903) and ignore say, *A Mummer's Wife* (1885) and *The Brook Kerith* (1916), though these are indubitably works by an Irish novelist of the period' in *Irish Novels 1890-1940*, p. 9. A notable exception is Simon Joyce's chapter 'A Naturalism for Ireland' from *Modernism and Naturalism in British and Irish Fiction* which considers both *Esther Waters* and *A Drama in Muslin*. He argues that 'Moore retained from his naturalist years a suspicion of literary style, and he continued to value a directness of language that led him to champion Gaelic for Irish writing against what he came to see as an increasingly artificial and debased English' (*Modernism and Naturalism in British and Irish Fiction*, p. 87).

9. Lukács, 'Narrate or Describe?', p. 114.

10. Later in the essay, Lukács reinforces this argument by claiming that realist narration is preferable because it is retrospective, writing, 'Only in practical activity, only in the complicated intercatenation of varied acts and passions is it possible to determine what objects, what institutions, etc., significantly influence men's lives and how and when this influence is effected' (Narrate or Describe?', p. 128).

11. Lukács, 'Narrate or Describe?', p. 118.

12. Lukács, 'Narrate or Describe?', p. 114.

13. Moore, *A Drama in Muslin*, p. 159. Hereafter cited parenthetically in the text, abbreviated as *DM*.

14. Moore, *Confessions of a Young Man*, p. 140. Here, it is easy to see how George Moore's narratives of development push against Jesse Rosenthal's understanding of the *Bildungsroman* as a narrative form that 'depends on unifying oneself with that law-giving self in the past'

(*Good Form*, p. 125). Moore narrates his personal development to celebrate – and often exaggerate – his discontinuity from his past self.

15. Moore, *Parnell and his Island*, p. 3.

16. Moore, *Hail and Farewell*, p. 56.

17. Quoted in Carla King, 'Introduction', p. xxvii.

18. For example, Lauren Goodlad begins 'Introduction' by portraying Moore as an anti-realist critic but concludes by claiming that *Esther Waters* exemplifies the hybridity of late-Victorian realism, pp. 183-201.

19 .Joe Cleary reflects on how the forms we use to narrate literary history limits our understanding the nineteenth-century Irish novel as he questions the 'preoccupation with identifying a single, continuous linear model of novelistic evolution' in *Outrageous Fortune*, p. 50. In turn, Katie Trumpener models a form of literary history that resists this narrative as she maps 'the national and transnational lineages of nationalist fiction in the early nineteenth century' in *Bardic Nationalism*, p. xiv.

20. P. J. Keating goes so far as to claim that *Esther Waters* is 'the only English working-class novel of this period that can be said to be profoundly influenced by French naturalism belongs in many ways to a purely English tradition' in *The Working-Classes in Victorian Fiction*, p. 134. John Plotz also presents Moore as anomalous, writing: 'British naturalism is (a debatable novel or two by George Moore or George Gissing aside) the dog that did not bark' in 'Speculative Naturalism and the Problem of Scale', p. 36. George Levine argues that 'the later realism, as an alternative to the earlier and apparently conventionalized realism, had few serious exponents in England, where there are no Maupassants or Zolas or Goncourts. Gissing, Hardy, James, Conrad, Moore himself – they all rejected the "experimental novel": and, despite their great differences, they wrote recognizably within the English tradition' (*The Realistic Imagination*, p. 6). David Baguley considers the absence of naturalism in England and English literary histories, concluding that the reception of English and foreign naturalist novels shows that naturalism thwarted readerly expectations in *Naturalist Fiction*, p. 35.

21. Joe Cleary, for instance, argues that Moore's most important contributions to naturalism 'are situated in England' in order to make the case that Irish naturalism truly begins with James Joyce and other counter-revival writers (*Outrageous Fortune*, p. 131). Unlike Cleary, who seeks to rethink Irish modernism – that is, what comes *after* Moore – I am interested the Irish novel's relationship to naturalism to rethink Irish realism and what precedes Moore. John Wilson Foster makes a similar claim as Cleary, suggesting that 'Moore anticipated the relocated experiments of the young Joyce who began to compose *Dubliners* a decade later and drew on realist and naturalist predecessors such as Moore' in *Fictions of the Irish Revival*, p. 121.

James H. Murphy suggests that George Moore introduces naturalism to England, but had little impact on Ireland until his participation in the Irish Revival in *Irish Novelists and the Victorian Age*, pp. 215–17. By contrast, Derek Hand argues that 'George Moore's *A Drama in Muslin* encapsulates perfectly the anxieties central to the Irish novel form in the nineteenth century' in *A History of the Irish Novel*, p. 150.

22. As Caroline Levine argues, nation-based literary histories and literary criticism is 'an institutional effect' in 'From Nation to Network', p. 647.

23. Walter Besant, 'The Art of Fiction', p. 19. As Homer Brown argues, 'This late-nineteenth-century conjecture is, effectively, the moment when the novel "began" for the modernist New Criticism, and the enabling, foundational origin in what seems to me the most crucial institutional history of the novel' in 'Prologue', p. 21.

24. Henry James, 'The Art of Fiction', p. 54.

25. Ibid. p. 3.

26. Moore, *Literature at Nurse*, p. 20.

27. Waugh, 'The New Realism', p. 850. Also, Forest Reid claims in 1909, 'From the beginning he has been a reactionary, while his attitude has been one of pugnacious, contemptuous defiance of all that does not interest him, including, I need hardly say, the traditions of English fiction' in 'The Novels of George Moore', p. 201.

28. Moore, 'Apologia Pro Scriptis Meis', p. 534.

29. In *George Moore and the Autogenous Self*, Elizabeth Grubgeld studies what she calls 'his discourse of repudiation' (p. 3), claiming that 'he recognized early in his career a need to disclaim his Irish heritage (and the very principle of heredity) in order to affirm later that he was truly a man who 'made himself because he imagined himself" (p. 2).

30. Moore, *Parnell and His Island*, p. 36.

31. Moore, *Hail and Farewell*, pp. 57–8.

32. While Moore suggests this temporal landscape is peculiar to Ireland, English modernity can also be understood as the accumulation of disparate temporalities – especially through Thomas Hardy's novels. For instance, Andrew Radford argues that Hardy uses Stonehenge 'as an opportunity imaginatively to revisit several different bygone periods and to contrive that the modern moment is seen in relation to them' in *Thomas Hardy and the Survivals of Time*, p. 3.

33. Moore, 'A Plea for the Soul of the Irish People', p. 293.

34. Here, I am building on John Plotz who argues that understanding naturalism as a set of formal features allows us to recognise the prevalence of naturalist elements in English fiction that is not straightforwardly naturalist ('Speculative Naturalism and the Problem of Scale', p. 32).

35. Moore, 'Defensio Pro Scriptis Meis', p. 283.

36. Ibid. p. 282.
37. Frazier, *George Moore*, p. 95.
38. Moore, 'Defensio Pro Scriptis Meis', p. 283.
39. Ibid. p. 283
40. Wallace, 'Two Pinches of Snuff', pp. 39–40.
41. 'Review', p. 5. Alice Barton's development is perhaps one reason why Judith Mitchell calls the novel 'Victorian' rather than naturalist in 'A Drama in Muslin', pp. 211–24
42. Judith Mitchell is hopeful about the ending, Alexander Gonzalez claims that Alice offers a way out of paralysis in 'Paralysis and Exile in George Moore's *A Drama in Muslin*', p. 152; Paul Goetsch argues that the ending shows Alice's resignation in 'The Country House in George Moore's *A Drama in Muslin*', p. 91; Mª Elena Jaime De Pablos suggests that Alice Barton achieves liberty but only because she renounces the confining environment of Ireland in 'George Moore: The Committed Feminist', p. 193.
43. Goodwin, *Conversations with George Moore*, p. 27.
44. Simon Gikandi argues that this is what postcolonial studies contributes to globalization: an understanding of historical time and historical agency that disrupts the temporality of modernization 'Globalization and the Claims of Postcoloniality', p. 636.
45. Esty, *Unseasonable Youth*, p. 2.
46. Ibid. p. 2.
47. Schreiner, *The Story of an African Farm*, p. 3. Esty suggests that Waldo is 'not subject to everyday realist temporality' (*Unseasonable Youth*, p. 78); I suggest instead that the novel dramatises the disparate and contradictory temporalities that comprise realism. Moore was friends with Schreiner, and he wrote *A Drama in Muslin* with *The Story of an African Farm* in mind.
48. Bakhtin, 'The *Bildungsroman* and Its Significance in the History of Realism (Toward a Historical Typology of the Novel)', p. 25.
49. Moretti, *The Way of the World*, p. 19.
50. This particular scene is important because it contrasts the feeling that the murders inspire – shock, terror, a sense of crisis – with the consequences of the murders – the Coercion Act that the landlords desire (Moore, *A Drama in Muslin*, pp. 240–1).
51. Maurer, *The Dispossessed State*, p. 181.
52. 'The Condition of Ireland', p. 16.
53. 'Review', p. 5.
54. Of course, the land wars originated from far more complex causes than nationalist desire for a 'nativist' nation. An 1878 agricultural crisis intensified demands for land reform by mobilising diverse populations. But one of the effects of the land war was the solidification of 'a collectively held notion of the land for the people, as opposed to the "alien"

landowners, an idea imbued with the sense of "native" dispossession'
Alan O'Day, *Irish Home Rule,* p. 17.

55. Historically, these divisions were not so stark. As Paul A. Townend
    argues, the land league's nationalism was not necessarily anti-empire
    and not always opposed to the British state. What is telling, though, is
    that within the novel Moore represents a relatively simple opposition
    between peasant nationalists and Anglo-Irish landlords associated with
    the state, even as he represents the diversity of each group. 'Between
    Two Worlds', p. 144.
56. Maurer, *The Dispossessed State,* p. 181.
57. D. George Boyce suggests that one of the dominant question of nine-
    teenth-century Ireland was, 'If Ireland were to have self-government,
    which of the major groups in Ireland was to inherit the future?'
    Moore shows that one of the ways that this question played itself
    out was debates over who is part of the present (*Nineteenth-Century
    Ireland,* p. 8).
58. Glenny-Crory, 'The Irish Land Question', p. 538.
59. Davitt, *The Fall of Feudalism in Ireland,* p. 687.
60. LeFebvre, 'Space and the State', p. 224. Also see Ian Baucom who
    claims that the state has a 'thinner grammar of time' in 'Afterword',
    p. 713.
61. LeFebvre, 'Space and the State', p. 225.
62. Gallagher, *Nobody's Story,* p. 289.
63. Moore, *Parnell and His Island,* p. 3.
64. Moore, 'Defensio Pro Scriptis Meis', p. 278.
65. Esty, 'Virgins of Empire', p. 271.
66. See Patrick Bridgewater's *George Moore and German Pessimism,*
    p. 34 who claims that Moore probably read this 1884 translation,
    although Bridgewater does not think that Moore engaged seriously
    with Hartmann's ideas.
67. Grubgeld, *George Moore and the Autogenous Self,* p. 4.
68. Maurer, *The Dispossessed State,* p. 186.
69. While Patrick Ward claims that this resolution to the novel juxtaposes
    the barbarous Ireland with the civilised England in *Exile, Emigration
    and Irish Writing,* p. 195. John Wilson Foster suggests that Moore's
    heroes discover their 'Protestant' selves in *Fictions of the Irish Literary
    Revival,* p. 124.
70. Grubgeld, *George Moore and the Autogenous Self,* p. 15.
71. Patrick Ward suggests this (see note above). In a slightly different, but
    related vein, John Cronin writes, 'The move is from overblown Anglo-
    Irish decadence to British materialism and there is a curious sense
    of loss and diminution at the work's end which is hardly altogether
    appropriate to the central satirical purpose of Moore's novel' in *The
    Anglo-Irish Novel,* p. 132.

72. Ward, *Emigration and Irish Writing*, p. 195.
73. Lloyd, *Anomalous States*, p. 127.
74. 'The Courting of Mary Smith', p. 110.
75. 'Literature', p. 6.
76. 'The New Realism', p. 3.
77. Youngkin, 'George Moore's Quest for Canonization and Esther Waters as Female Helpmate', p. 119. In his 1913 study of the 1890s, Holbrook Jackson suggests that *Esther Waters* accomplishes this goal. He argues: 'the realistic novel came complete with *Esther Waters* and *Jude the Obscure*' ('The New Fiction', p. 228).
78. 'Esther Waters', p. 10.
79. Miller, 'Books Worth Reading', p. 296.
80. Moore, *Hail and Farewell*, p. 101.
81. Joyce, *Modernism and Naturalism in British and Irish Fiction*, p. 99. Terry Eagleton reaches a similar conclusion, writing: '*Esther Waters* transcends the demeaning naturalism of *A Mummer's Wife* into genuine realism: it is social forces, not some genetic inheritance or psychological flaw, which impels its heroine's downward trajectory' in *Heathcliff and the Great Hunger*, p. 221.
82. Rachel Bowlby writes, 'This narrative oddness adds to the effect of Moore's social critique as well as the shock he wants to inflict on his readers: all the proper elements are present, but they are out of order' (*A Child of One's Own*, p. 180).
83. Moore, *Hail and Farewell*, p. 275.
84. Jules Law and Bruce Robbins help convey the extent of Esther's position within the narrative. Law suggests that wet-nursing – which Esther does after the birth of her son – is a 'dying or anachronistic labor practice' in *The Social Life of Fluids*, p. 130. In turn, reading representations of servants in English fiction, Robbins argues: 'Aggressively vestigial, reminders of earlier literature and earlier society, servants might be described in general terms as repetitions of the premodern within and against the novel's modernity' in *The Servant's Hand*, p. 42.
85. Dickens, *Bleak House*, p. 911.
86. Ibid. 642.
87. Rachel Bowlby argues that this passage shows how 'Moore boasts of the superior truth to "life" of his own novel by loudly dismissing the "conventional" literary novels it is not' (*A Child of One's Own*, p. 177).
88. James, 'The Art of Fiction', p. 74.
89. Levine, *The Realistic Imagination*, p. 6; Goodlad, 'Introduction', p. 185.
90. For Aaron Matz, many of Gissing's metacritical moves – especially his reference to Biffen as 'the realist' – lead to satire. He argues that *New Grub Street* 'simultaneously inhabits and critiques the idea of realism itself' in *Satire in an Age of Realism*, p. 76.

91. Gissing, *New Grub Street,* p. 486.
92. Gissing, *The Odd Women*, p. 67.
93. Joshua Taft argues that by questioning Biffen's realism, Gissing endorses realism as opposed to naturalism, contending 'The distinction between Biffen and Gissing can thus be phrased quite simply: Biffen is a naturalist, while Gissing remains committed to Victorian realism' in '*New Grub Street* and the Survival of Realism', p. 368.

Coda: Inhabiting Institutions

'It is that university that is itself a contradictory institution, in part because we inhabit it, because we insist upon surviving in it, because and in spite of it.'[1]

This book has argued that nineteenth-century realist novels offer strategies for inhabiting institutions while imagining both politics and history otherwise. Although these novels shore up modern institutionalism insofar as they work to define both modernity and futurity in institutional terms, their prevalent anachronisms restore the full range of historical and political possibilities. Such anachronisms are more prevalent and pronounced in realist novels from Ireland, where modern institutionalism violently tried to replace traditional Irish community formations with colonial institutions. But, as I have argued throughout this book, the explicit anachronisms that produce Irish realism's contradictory dynamic are not anomalous: they make the tension between modern institutionalism and the unruly politics of anachronisms visible in British realist novels. Whether Maria Edgeworth's Thady Quirk, who shows that traditional pasts, seemingly useless within modern Ireland, can inspire new futures, or George Eliot's Maggie Tulliver, who collapses the distance between past and present to unsettle the sense of historical inevitability that results from path-dependent historicism, characters within realist novels demonstrate the radical potential of untimeliness. Capturing the contradictions that accompany everyday life governed by institutions, realist novels suggest that we must refuse institutional time in order to imagine a future that does not simply extend existing social arrangements.

My desire to challenge the shared time of modern institutionalism emerges in part from my own experience inhabiting the twenty-first-century university. In my everyday life as a faculty member,

I want more from the university as an institution. But there is a great deal of political and social pressure to defend – even argue for – the compromised future that the contemporary university promises. As a result, there is a distinct gap between my lived experiences of the university and public defences of it. Universities endlessly defer their progressive ideals to the future, failing to hire and support minority faculty members, serve minority students, address the university's reliance on contingent labour, ensure that college is affordable for all students. Everyday life in the university thus is one of struggle: to support students, often in opposition to official university policies; to think and write, frequently in ways that the university will not recognise; to cultivate social relationships that work against the narrow structure of professionalism and the emphasis on social reproduction at a time when there are fewer and fewer sustainable jobs.

But defences of the university – especially defences of humanities education within the university – often encourage scholars to forget the daily struggles within their own institutions and not only accept, but actively seek to maintain, existing institutional arrangements as an ideal present and desired future.[2] We see this impulse in defences of the humanities that insist that humanistic study is necessary for democracy, that it produces good citizens, that it fosters the common good without grappling with the question of who has access to universities.[3] This impulse is also present within defences of academic freedom that do not acknowledge its inherent limits or uneven protections.[4] It is even visible in the university's drive to integrate what Roderick Ferguson calls 'minority difference' as the university promotes 'disembodied and abstract' minority representation without changing material conditions.[5] People and fields of study that desire to transform existing institutional arrangements – that imagine the university otherwise – often become assimilated into existing arrangements under the rubric of 'diversity'.

Against the grain of such defences of the university that view the future as an extension of the present, I find political inspiration in postcolonial and queer theory's untimely presence in the academy. Failing to create the chrononormativity of more traditional fields of study, their 'end' and 'death' proclaim their arrival to academic institutions.[6] Postcolonial theory is plagued by premature endings and early deaths. In fact, debating whether postcolonial theory is over has become one of the liveliest discussions in the field. A 2007 roundtable in the *PMLA*, 'The End of Postcolonial Theory?', considers whether postcolonial theory continues to be relevant after 'the institutional consolidation of postcolonial studies'.[7] Partly arguing that the world has changed and postcolonial theory fails to address these changes, partly questioning how postcolonial theory is institutionalised within the academy, this roundtable reveals the extent to which postcolonial studies' arrival is also its demise.[8] The ghostly metaphors of 'ruins' and 'remains' that Ato Quayson focuses on in *New Literary History*'s discussion of postcolonial studies' lasting relevance suggest that while one of the field's great theoretical contributions is a new approach to anachronism, the field itself has become an anachronism in the twenty-first century.[9]

The rise of queer theory similarly accompanies its death, for as Lauren Berlant and Michael Warner argue, people accused the theory of having 'only academic – which is to say, dead – politics', even in its very early years.[10] Although queerness as a stance, form of activism and mode of sexuality is contested and diverse, queer theory, as institutionalised by the university, appears to have 'a stable referential content and pragmatic force'.[11] José Esteban Muñoz pushes against these supposedly 'dead' politics with a different form of untimeliness, arguing that 'queerness is not yet here . . . the future is queerness's domain'.[12] The queer futurity that Muñoz articulates fundamentally differs from modern institutionalism's foreclosed futurity. While queerness opens up otherwise possibilities that reject the present organisation of power, institutional futurity limits the horizon of possibility to narrow, institutional terms. Either dead on arrival or requiring a new temporal structure altogether, queer theory's anachronistic relationship with the academy shows how institutions produce anachronisms by relegating that which will change the institution to either an anachronistic past or an untimely future.

Celebrating the inherent untimeliness of these fields, I contend that the repeated discussions of whether these fields are over or dead do not highlight problems within the theoretical approaches themselves, but rather demonstrate that these two theoretical approaches – both within and outside of the university – refuse the temporal logic of modern institutionalism. Despite the claims that postcolonial theory has moved 'from the margin to the center of' the academy and the importance of queer theory, they are both largely absent from public defences of the humanities.[13] They are part of the university but seemingly unnecessary when it comes time to defend the future of the university as an institution. To adopt Nick Mitchell's language, which I use as an epigraph to this coda, these fields render the university a 'contradictory institution' by encouraging social and historical relationships and modes of political thinking that live on 'because and in spite of' the university's institutional organization.[14]

Taking inspiration from postcolonial and queer theory's anachronistic presence within the academy, *Novel Institutions* argues that in order to inhabit institutions without foreclosing futurity, we must refuse institutional time. Resisting modern institutionalism's work to define the future as an extension of the present, anachronisms insist that social and historical relationality is not simply a form of social reproduction. In realist novels, these anachronisms show that even path-dependent narratives activate otherwise possibilities. In the contemporary university, they demonstrate the political possibility of being out of sync with the institution's vision of the future, present within but at odds with existing institutional arrangements. Because institutions necessarily create anachronisms, they create relations that undercut the institution's desire for a coherent, homogeneous form, abstract agency and shared time. Legitimising anachronisms thus acknowledges how institutions shape our lives while refusing to allow existing institutions to define our futures.

Notes

1. Mitchell, '(Critical Ethnic Studies) Intellectual', p. 92.
2. Abigail Boggs and Nick Mitchell call this *'the crisis consensus'* or arguments that invoke 'the university as a good in itself, as an institution defined ultimately by the progressive nature at its core' in 'Critical University Studies and the Crisis Consensus', p. 234.
3. By this I mean not only who can afford to attend university or who has access to university support, but also, who is and is not included in humanistic knowledge and conceptions of citizenship. As Walter Mignolo warns in 'Citizenship, Knowledge, and the Limits of Humanity', 'The conditions for citizenship are still tied to a racialized hierarchy of human beings that depends on universal categories of thought created and enacted from the identitarian perspectives of European Christianity and by white males' (p. 313).
4. For this reason, Piya Chatterjee and Sunaina Maira deliberately shift away from focusing on the question of academic freedom and towards 'the logics of racism, warfare, and nationalism that undergird U.S. imperialism and also the architecture of the U.S. academy' in 'The Imperial University', p. 6. Also see Fred Moten who argues that 'Academic freedom is the condition under which the intellectual submits herself to the normative model of the settler. Academic freedom is a form of violence perpetrated by academic bosses who operate under the protection and in the interest of racial state capitalism. Recognize that as a form of violence it is *reactive and reactionary* in its brutality'

in 'Fred Moten's Statement in Support of a Boycott of Israeli Academic Institutions'.

5. Roderick Ferguson, *The Reorder of Things,* p. 8. Also see Kandice Chuh, who argues 'Debates about canonicity and curriculum in relation to multicultural literary studies in this sense are symptomatic of the structural barriers to attending to difference in light of the university's liberal mission to abstract and universalize' in *Imagine Otherwise,* p. 17.

6. Freeman, *Time Binds,* p. 3.

7. Wenzel, 'Editor's Column: The End of Postcolonial Theory?', p. 634.

8. As Simon Gikandi writes, this very conversation 'seems to designate, on the one hand, an arrival into the institution of interpretation and, on the other hand, an evacuation from the same edifice'. 'Editor's Column: The End of Postcolonial Theory?', p. 635.

9. Quayson, 'The Sighs of History', p. 360. Of course, postcolonial theorists do not always use the term 'anachronism' to describe their rethinking of historical time. In the words of Vilashini Cooppan, postcolonial analysis 'finds its central method . . . [in] the uncovering of 'intertwined and overlapping histories' precisely where there seems to be only a single one; only empire, say, or only resistance, only the national or only the global' 'The Double Politics of Double Consciousness', p. 301.

10. Lauren Berlant and Michael Warner, 'What does Queer Theory Teach us about X', p. 344. Michael Warner returns to this question more recently in 'Queer and Then?'

11. Berlant and Warner, 'What does Queer Theory Teach us about X', p. 344.

12. Muñoz, *Cruising Utopia,* p. 1.

13. Pillai, 'Gaging the Postcolonial Hegemonic', p. 232. Also see Elizabeth Freeman, *'Monsters, Inc',* where she reflects on the 'absence of discussion about feminist and queer theory and sexuality studies in so many of the essays on the crisis of the humanities' (p. 83).

14. Mitchell uses the idea of the university as a contradictory institution to think about the role of critique in critical ethnic studies: how it both works to oppose the university and expresses desire for the university ('(Critical Ethnic Studies) Intellectual', p. 92).

Bibliography

Abel, Elizabeth, Marianne Hirsch and Elizabeth Langland, *The Voyage In: Fictions of Female Development* (Hanover, NH: University Press of New England, 1983).

Agathocleous, Tanya, *Urban Realism and the Cosmopolitan Imagination in the Nineteenth Century: Visible City, Invisible World* (Cambridge: Cambridge University Press, 2011).

Ahmed, Sara, 'The Nonperformativity of Antiracism', *Meridians: feminism, race, transnationalism* 7:1 (2006), pp. 104–26.

Ahmed, Sara, 'Willful Parts: Problem Characters or the Problem of Character', *New Literary History* 42:2 (Spring 2011), pp. 231–53.

Ahmed, Sara, *On Being Included: Racism and Diversity in Institutional Life* (Durham, NC: Duke University Press, 2012).

Ahmed, Sara, *Living a Feminist Life* (Durham, NC: Duke University Press, 2017).

Allison, Sarah, *Reductive Reading: A Syntax of Victorian Moralizing* (Baltimore: Johns Hopkins University Press, 2018).

Anderson, Amanda, *The Powers of Distance: Cosmopolitanism and the Cultivation of Detachment* (Princeton: Princeton University Press, 2001).

Anderson, Amanda, *Bleak Liberalism* (Chicago: The University of Chicago Press, 2016).

Aravamudan, Srinivas, 'The Return of Anachronism', *MLQ: Modern Language Quarterly* 62:4 (2001), pp. 331–53.

Armstrong, Nancy, *Desire and Domestic Fiction: A Political History of the Novel* (Oxford: Oxford University Press, 1990).

Armstrong, Nancy, *Fiction in the Age of Photography: The Legacy of British Realism* (Cambridge, MA: Harvard University Press, 2002).

Arnold, Matthew, *The Study of Celtic Literature* (London: Smith, Elder, & Co., 1905).

'Art. XI. Orange Societies in Great Britain – Their Illegality and Criminality', *Westminster Review* (January 1836), pp. 480–513.

'Article XIV. Reports from the Select Committees appointed to inquire . . .', *The British and Foreign Review: or European Quarterly Journal* (January 1836), pp. 328–94.

Austen, Jane, *Emma*, ed. Fiona Stafford (London: Penguin Books, 1996).

Backus, Margot, *The Gothic Family Romance: Heterosexuality, Child Sacrifice, and the Anglo-Irish Colonial Order* (Durham, NC: Duke University Press, 1999).

Baguley, David, *Naturalist Fiction: The Entropic Vision* (Cambridge: Cambridge University Press, 1990).

Bakhtin, M. M., 'Epic and Novel: Toward a Methodology for the Study of the Novel', in Michael Holquist (ed.), *The Dialogic Imagination*, trans. Caryl Emerson and Michael Holquist (Austin: University of Texas Press, 1981), pp. 3–40.

Bakhtin, M. M., 'The *Bildungsroman* and Its Significance in the History of Realism (Toward a Historical Typology of the Novel)', in Caryl Emerson and Michael Holquist (eds), *Speech Genres and Other Late Essays*, trans. Vern W. McGee (Austin: University of Texas Press, 1986), pp. 10–59.

'Banim and the Irish Novelists', in R. H. Horne (ed.), *A New Spirit of the Age* (New York: Harper and Brothers, 1844), pp. 271–7.

Barbauld, Anna Letitia, 'On the Origin and Progress of Novel-Writing', *The Library of Congress*, <https://archive.org/details/onoriginprogress-00barb> (last accessed 28 February 2019).

Baucom, Ian, 'Afterword: States of Time', *Contemporary Literature* 49:4 (Winter 2008), pp. 712–17.

Beer, Gillian, 'Beyond Determinism: George Eliot and Virginia Woolf', in Mary Jacobus (ed.), *Women Writing and Writing About Women* (London: Croom Helm, 1979), pp. 80–99.

Belanger, Jacqueline, '"Le vrai n'est pas toujours vraisemblable": the Evaluation of Realism in Edgeworth's Irish Tales', in Heidi Kaufman and Chris Fauske (eds), *An Uncomfortable Authority: Maria Edgeworth and Her Contexts* (Newark: University of Delaware Press, 2004), pp. 105–26.

Belanger, Jacqueline, 'Introduction', in Jacqueline Belanger (ed.), *The Irish Novel in the Nineteenth Century: Facts and Fictions* (Dublin: Four Courts Press, 2005), pp. 11–33.

Belich, James, *Replenishing the Earth: The Settler Revolution and the Rise of the Anglo-World, 1783–1939* (Oxford: Oxford University Press, 2009).

Bentley, Nancy, *The Ethnography of Manners: Hawthorne, James, Wharton* (Cambridge: Cambridge University Press, 1995).

Berlant, Lauren, *Cruel Optimism* (Durham, NC: Duke University Press, 2011).

Berlant, Lauren, and Michael Warner, 'What Does Queer Theory Teach Us about X?', *PMLA* 110:3 (1995), pp. 343–9.

Besant, Walter, 'The Art of Fiction: A Lecture Delivered at the Royal Institution, April 25, 1884', in Walter Besant and Henry James, *The Art of Fiction* (Boston: Cupples and Hurd, 1884), pp. 3–48.

Bigelow, Gordon, 'Market Indicators: Banking and Domesticity in Dickens's *Bleak House*', *ELH* 67:2 (Summer 2000), pp. 589–615.

Bigelow, Gordon, 'Form and Violence in Trollope's *The Macdermots of Ballycloran*', *Novel: A Forum on Fiction* 46:3 (Fall 2013), pp. 386–405.

Black, Scott, 'Quixotic Realism and the Romance of the Novel', *Novel: A Forum on Fiction* 42:2 (Summer 2009), pp. 239–44.

Boggs, Abigail, and Nick Mitchell, 'Critical University Studies and the Crisis Consensus', *Feminist Studies* 44:2 (2018), pp. 432–63.

Bourdieu, Pierre, *The Logic of Practice*, trans. Richard Nice (Stanford: Stanford University Press, 1990).

Bowlby, Rachel, 'Versions of Realism in George Eliot's *Adam Bede*', *Textual Practice* 25:3 (2011), pp. 417–36.

Bowlby, Rachel, *A Child of One's Own: Parental Stories* (Oxford: Oxford University Press, 2013).

Boyce, D. George, *Nineteenth-Century Ireland: The Search for Stability* (Dublin: Gill & Macmillan Ltd., 2005).

Braddon, Mary Elizabeth, *Lady Audley's Secret*, ed. David Skilton (Oxford: Oxford University Press, 1987).

Brantlinger, Patrick, *Rule of Darkness: British Literature and Imperialism, 1830–1914* (Ithaca: Cornell University Press, 1990).

Brantlinger, Patrick, *Dark Vanishings: Discourse on the Extinction of the Primitive Races, 1800–1930* (Ithaca: Cornell University Press, 2003).

Bridgewater, Patrick, *George Moore and German Pessimism* (Durham: University of Durham, 1988).

Brontë, Charlotte, *Jane Eyre*, ed. Richard J. Dunn (New York: W. W. Norton & Company, 2001).

Brown, Homer Obed, 'Why the Story of the Origin of the (English) Novel is an American Romance (If Not the Great American Novel)' in Deidre Lynch and William B. Warner (eds), *Cultural Institutions of the Novel* (Durham, NC: Duke University Press, 1996), pp. 11–43.

Brown, Homer Obed, *Institutions of the English Novel from Defoe to Scott* (Philadelphia: University of Pennsylvania Press, 1998).

Brozyna, Andrea Ebel, *Labour, Love, and Prayer: Female Piety in Ulster Religious Literature, 1850–1914* (Montreal: McGill-Queen's University Press, 1999).

Bryan, Dominic, *Orange Parades: The Politics of Ritual, Tradition and Control* (London: Pluto Press, 2000).

Burton, Antoinette, *Empire in Question: Reading, Writing, and Teaching British Imperialism* (Durham, NC: Duke University Press, 2011).

Butler, Marilyn, *Maria Edgeworth: A Literary Biography* (Oxford: Clarendon Press, 1972).

Buzard, James, *Disorienting Fiction: The Autoethnographic Work of Nineteenth-Century British Novels* (Princeton: Princeton University Press, 2005).

Byrd, Jodi A., *The Transit of Empire: Indigenous Critiques of Colonialism* (Minneapolis: University of Minnesota Press, 2011).

Byrd, Jodi A., 'Arriving on a Different Shore: US Empire at Its Horizons', *College Literature* 41:1 (2014), pp. 174–81.

Campbell, John L., *Institutional Change and Globalization* (Princeton: Princeton University Press, 2004).

Carleton, William, *Traits and Stories of the Irish Peasantry* (Dublin: William Curry, Jun. and Co., 1843).

Carleton, William, *The Black Prophet: A Tale of Irish Famine* (London: Simms and M'Intire, 1847).

Carleton, William, *Valentine M'Clutchy, The Irish Agent; or, the Chronicles of Caster Cumber; Together with the Pious Aspirations, Permissions, Vouchsafements and other Sanctified Privileges of Solomon M'Slime, A Religious Attorney* (Dublin: James Duffy, 1848).

Carlyle, Thomas, *Chartism*, 2nd edn (London: Chapman & Hall, Strand, 1842).

Carlyle, Thomas, *Past and Present*, ed. Richard D. Altick (New York: New York University Press, 1965).

Carlyle, Thomas, 'Signs of the Times', in G. B. Tennyson (ed.), *A Carlyle Reader: Selections from the Writings of Thomas Carlyle* (Acton: Copley Publishing Group, 1999), pp. 3–24.

Castiglia, Christopher, *Interior States: Institutional Consciousness and the Inner Life of Democracy in the Antebellum United States* (Durham, NC: Duke University Press, 2008).

Castle, Gregory, *Reading the Modernist Bildungsroman* (Gainesville: University Press of Florida, 2006).

Certeau, Michel de, *The Practice of Everyday Life*, trans. Steven Rendall (Berkeley: University of California Press, 1984).

Chakrabarty, Dipesh, *Provincializing Europe: Postcolonial Thought and Historical Difference* (Princeton: Princeton University Press, 2000).

'Charles Kickham's Career', *Irish Independent*, 30 August 1928, p. 5.

Chatterjee, Piya, and Sunaina Maira, 'The Imperial University: Race, War, and the Nation-State', in Piya Chatterjee and Sunaina Maira (eds), *The Imperial University: Academic Repression and Scholarly Dissent* (Minneapolis: University of Minnesota Press, 2014), pp. 1–50.

Chuh, Kandice, *Imagine Otherwise: On Asian Americanist Critique* (Durham, NC: Duke University Press, 2003).

Claybaugh, Amanda, *The Novel of Purpose: Literature and Social Reform in the Anglo-American World* (Ithaca: Cornell University Press, 2007).

Cleary, Joe, *Literature, Partition and the Nation State: Culture and Conflict in Ireland, Israel and Palestine* (Cambridge: Cambridge University Press, 2002).

Cleary, Joe, 'Introduction: Ireland and Modernity', in Joe Cleary and Claire Connolly (eds), *The Cambridge Companion to Modern Irish Culture* (Cambridge: Cambridge University Press, 2005), pp. 1–21.

Cleary, Joe, 'The Nineteenth-Century Irish Novel: Notes and Speculations on Literary Historiography', in Jacqueline Belanger (ed.), *The Irish Novel in the Nineteenth Century: Facts and Fictions* (Dublin: Four Courts Press, 2005), pp. 202–21.

Cleary, Joe, *Outrageous Fortune: Capital and Culture in Modern Ireland* (Dublin: Field Day Publications, 2007).

Cleary, Joe, 'Realism after Modernism and the Literary World-System', *Modern Language Quarterly* 73:3 (September 2012), pp. 255–68.

Clifford, James, 'On Ethnographic Allegory', in James Clifford and George E. Marcus (eds), *Writing Culture: the Poetics and Politics of Ethnography* (Berkeley: University of California Press, 1986), pp. 98–121.

Comerford, R. V., *Charles J. Kickham: A Study in Irish Nationalism and Literature* (Dublin: Wolfhound Press, 1979).

Conary, Jennifer, '"Whether we like it or not": *Bleak House* and the Limits of Liberalism', *Dickens Studies Annual* 45 (2014), pp. 205–28.

'The Condition of Ireland', *The Pall Mall Gazette*, 21 December 1885, p. 16.

Connolly, Claire, *A Cultural History of the Irish Novel, 1790–1829* (Cambridge: Cambridge University Press, 2012).

Cooper, Frederick, *Colonialism in Question: Theory, Knowledge, History* (Los Angeles: University of California Press, 2005).

Cooppan, Vilashini, 'The Double Politics of Double Consciousness: Nationalism and Globalism in *The Souls of Black Folk*', *Public Culture* 17:2 (Spring 2005), pp. 299–318.

Corbett, Mary Jean, *Allegories of the Union in Irish and English Writing, 1790–1870: Politics, History, and the Family from Edgeworth to Arnold* (Cambridge: Cambridge University Press, 2000).

Coulthard, Glen S., 'Subjects of Empire: Indigenous Peoples and the "Politics of Recognition" in Canada', *Contemporary Political Theory* 6:4 (November 2007), pp. 437–60.

Coundouriotis, Eleni, *Claiming History: Colonialism, Ethnography, and the Novel* (New York: Columbia University Press, 1999).

'The Courting of Mary Smith', *The Athenaeum*, 24 July 1886, pp. 109–10.

Crawley, Ashon, 'Otherwise, Instituting', *Performance Research* 20:4 (2015), pp. 85–9.

Crawley, Ashon, *Blackpentecostal Breath: The Aesthetics of Possibility* (New York: Fordham University Press, 2017).

Cronin, John, *The Anglo-Irish Novel: The Nineteenth Century* (Totowa, NJ: Barnes & Noble Books, 1980).

'The Croppy, a Tale of 1798', *The Edinburgh Review* (January 1831), pp. 410–31.

Dames, Nicholas, 'Realism and Theories of the Novel', in John Kucich and Jenny Bourne Taylor (eds), *Oxford History of the Novel in English: Volume Three: The Nineteenth-Century Novel, 1820–1880* (Oxford: Oxford University Press: 2012), pp. 289–305.

Davitt, Michael, *The Fall of Feudalism in Ireland: Or, the Story of the Land League Revolution* (London: Harper & Brothers Publishers, 1904).

Deane, Seamus, *Strange Country: Modernity and Nationhood in Irish Writing since 1790* (Oxford: Clarendon Press, 1997).

Devon, Lord, 'The Apprehended Irish Famine', *The Times*, 27 November 1845, p. 5.

Dickens, Charles, 'The Noble Savage', *Household Words*, 11 June 1853, pp. 337–9.

Dickens, Charles, *Hard Times*, ed. Kate Flint (London: Penguin Books, 1995).

Dickens, Charles, *Great Expectations*, ed. Janice Carlisle (New York: Bedford Books, 1996).

Dickens, Charles, *Our Mutual Friend*, ed. Adrian Poole (New York: Penguin Books, 1997).

Dickens, Charles, *Bleak House*, ed. Stephen Gill (Oxford: Oxford University Press, 1998).

Dickens, Charles, *Little Dorrit*, ed. Stephen Wall and Helen Small (London: Penguin Books, 1998).

Dickens, Charles, *Martin Chuzzlewit*, ed. Margaret Cardwell (Oxford: Oxford University Press, 1998).

Dickens, Charles, *Dombey and Son*, ed. Alan Horsman (Oxford: Oxford University Press, 1999).

Dickens, Charles, *American Notes*, ed. Patricia Ingham (London: Penguin Books, 2004).

Dames, Nicholas, *Amnesiac Selves: Nostalgia, Forgetting, and British Fiction, 1810–1870* (Oxford: Oxford University Press, 2001).

Dougherty, Jane Elizabeth, 'An Angel in the House: The Act of Union and Anthony Trollope's Irish Hero', *Victorian Literature and Culture* 32:1 (2004), pp. 133–45.

Duffy, Charles Gavan, *Young Ireland: A Fragment of Irish History 1840–1845* (Dublin: M. H. Gill & Son, 1884).

Duncan, Ian, *Modern Romance and Transformations of the Novel: The Gothic, Scott, Dickens* (Cambridge: Cambridge University Press, 1992).

Duncan, Ian, 'The Provincial or Regional Novel', in Patrick Brantlinger and William B. Thesing (eds), *A Companion to the Victorian Novel* (Oxford: Blackwell Publishers Ltd., 2005), pp. 318–35.

Duncan, Ian, *Scott's Shadows: The Novel in Romantic Edinburgh* (Princeton: Princeton University Press, 2007).

Eagleton, Terry, *Criticism and Ideology: A Study in Marxist Literary Theory* (London: Verso, 1976).

Eagleton, Terry, *Heathcliff and the Great Hunger: Studies in Irish Culture* (New York: Verso, 1995).

Edgeworth, Maria, *Patronage* (London: Pandora Press, 1986).

Edgeworth, Maria, *Castle Rackrent* and *Ennui*, ed. Marilyn Butler (London: Penguin Books, 1992).

Edelman, Lee, *No Future: Queer Theory and the Death Drive* (Durham, NC: Duke University Press, 2004).

Eliot, George, *Daniel Deronda*, ed. Barbara Hardy (London: Penguin Books, 1986).

Eliot, George, 'Margaret Fuller and Mary Wollstonecraft', in A. S. Byatt and Nicholas Warren (eds), *Selected Essays, Poems and Other Writings* (London: Penguin Books, 1990), pp. 332–8.

Eliot, George, 'The Natural History of German Life', in A. S. Byatt and Nicholas Warren (eds), *Selected Essays, Poems and Other Writings* (London: Penguin Books, 1990), pp. 107–39.

Eliot, George, 'Silly Novels by Lady Novelists', in A. S. Byatt and Nicholas Warren (eds), *Selected Essays, Poems and Other Writings* (London: Penguin Books, 1990), pp. 140–63.

Eliot, George, *Felix Holt, The Radical*, ed. Lynda Mugglestone (London: Penguin Books, 1995).

Eliot, George, *Adam Bede*, ed. Valentine Cunningham (Oxford: Oxford University Press, 1996).

Eliot, George, *Middlemarch*, ed. David Carroll (Oxford: Oxford University Press, 1996).

Eliot, George, *Romola*, ed. Dorothea Barrett (London: Penguin Books, 1996).

Eliot, George, *The Mill on the Floss*, ed. Gordon Haight (Oxford: Oxford University Press, 1998).

Elliot, Michael, 'Other Times: Herman Melville, Lewis Henry Morgan, and Ethnographic Writing in the Antebellum United States', *Criticism* 49:4 (Fall 2007), pp. 481–503.

'English Books for Irish Children', *Irish Independent*, 12 September 1973, p. 12.

Ermarth, Elizabeth Deeds, *Realism and Consensus in the English Novel* (Princeton: Princeton University Press, 1983).

'Esther Waters', *The Times*, 15 May 1894, p. 10.

Esty, Jed, *Unseasonable Youth: Modernism, Colonialism, and the Fiction of Development* (Oxford: Oxford University Press, 2012).

Esty, Jed, and Colleen Lye, 'Peripheral Realisms Now', *Modern Language Quarterly* 73:3 (September 2012), pp. 269–88.

Fabian, Johannes, *Time and the Other: How Anthropology Makes its Object* (New York: Columbia University Press, 1983).

Farina, Jonathan, 'On David Masson's *British Novelists and their Styles* (1859) and the Establishment of Novels as an Object of Academic Study', ed. Dino Franco Felluga, *BRANCH: Britain, Representation and Nineteenth-Century History*, extension of *Romanticism and Victorianism on the Net* (May 2012), <http://www.branchcollective.org/?ps_articles=jonathan-farina-on-david-massons-british-novelists-and-their-styles-1859-and-the-establishment-of-novels-as-an-object-of-academic-study> (last accessed 28 February 2019).

Farina, Jonathan, 'On the Genealogy of "Deportment": Being Present in *Bleak House*', *b2O: An Online Journal* (October 2016), <http://www.boundary2.org/2016/10/jonathan-farina-on-the-genealogy-of-deport-ment-being-present-in-bleak-house/> (last accessed 28 February 2019).

Fegan, Melissa, *Literature and the Irish Famine, 1845–1919* (Oxford: Oxford University Press, 2002).

Felski, Rita, *The Gender of Modernity* (Cambridge, MA: Harvard University Press, 1995).

Fergus, Jan, '"Pictures of Domestic Life in Country Villages": Jane Austen and the "Realist" Novel', in J. A. Downie (ed.), *Oxford Handbook of the Eighteenth-Century Novel* (Oxford: Oxford University Press, 2016), pp. 536–50.

Ferguson, Roderick, *The Reorder of Things: The University and Its Pedagogies of Minority of Difference* (Minneapolis: University of Minnesota Press, 2012).

Ferris, Ina, *The Achievement of Literary Authority: Gender, History, and the Waverley Novels* (Ithaca: Cornell University Press, 1991).

Ferris, Ina, *The Romantic National Tale and the Question of Ireland* (Cambridge: Cambridge University Press, 2002).

Flint, Kate, *The Woman Reader, 1837–1914* (Oxford: Clarendon Press, 1993).

Flint, Kate, 'Dickens and the Native American', in Wendy S. Jacobson (ed.), *Dickens and the Children of Empire* (New York: Palgrave, 2000), pp. 94–104.

Flint, Kate, *The Transatlantic Indian, 1776–1930* (Princeton: Princeton University Press, 2009).

Foster, John Wilson, *Fictions of the Irish Literary Revival: A Changeling Art* (Syracuse, NY: Syracuse University Press, 1993).

Foster, John Wilson, *Irish Novels 1890–1940: New Bearings in Culture and Fiction* (Oxford: Oxford University Press, 2008).

Foster, R. F., *Irish Story: Telling Tales and Making it up in Ireland* (Oxford: Oxford University Press, 2002).

Foucault, Michel, *The History of Sexuality, Volume I: An Introduction*, trans, Robert Hurley (New York: Vintage Books, 1990).

Foucault, Michel, *Discipline and Punish: The Birth of the Prison*, trans. Alan Sheridan (New York: Vintage Books, 1995).

Fraiman, Susan, *Unbecoming Women: British Women Writers and the Novel of Development* (New York: Columbia University Press, 1993).

Frazier, Adrian, *George Moore, 1852–1933* (New Haven: Yale University Press, 2000).

Freedgood, Elaine, *The Ideas in Things: Fugitive Meaning in the Victorian Novel* (Chicago: University of Chicago Press, 2006).

Freedgood, Elaine, 'Fictional Settlements: Footnotes, Metalepsis, the Colonial Effect', *New Literary History* 41:2 (Spring 2010), pp. 393–411.

Freedgood, Elaine, 'Hetero-ontologicality, or Against Realism', *English Studies in Africa* 57:1 (2014), pp. 92–100.

Freeman, Elizabeth, '*Monsters, Inc.*: Notes on the Neoliberal Arts Education', *New Literary History* 36:1 (Winter 2005), pp. 83–95.

Freeman, Elizabeth, 'Theorizing Queer Temporalities: A Roundtable', *GLQ: A Journal of Lesbian and Gay Studies* 13:2–3 (2007), pp. 177–95.

Freeman, Elizabeth, *Time Binds: Queer Temporalities, Queer Histories* (Durham, NC: Duke University Press, 2010).

Gallagher, Catherine, *Nobody's Story: The Vanishing Acts of Women Writers in the Marketplace, 1670–1820* (Berkeley: University of California Press, 1994).

Gallagher, Catherine, 'The Potato in the Materialist Imagination', in Catherine Gallagher and Stephen Greenblatt (eds), *Practicing New Historicism* (Chicago: The University of Chicago Press, 2000), pp. 110–35.

Gallagher, Catherine, *The Body Economic: Life, Death, and Sensation in Political Economy and The Victorian Novel* (Princeton: Princeton University Press, 2006).

Gamer, Michael, 'Maria Edgeworth and the Romance of Real Life', *Novel: A Forum on Fiction* 34:2 (Spring 2001), pp. 232–66.

Gannon, Christiane, 'Walter Besant's Democratic Bildungsroman', *Narrative* 22:3 (October 2014), pp. 372–94.

'Garden Party and Reception', *Irish Independent*, 26 June 1939, pp.10.

Gaskell, Elizabeth, *North and South*, ed. Angus Easson (Oxford: Oxford University Press, 1998).

Gaskell, Elizabeth, *Wives and Daughters*, ed. Pam Morris (New York: Penguin Books, 2001).

Gaskell, Elizabeth, *Mary Barton*, ed. Shirley Foster (Oxford: Oxford University Press, 2006).

Genette, Gérard, *Narrative Discourse: An Essay in Method*, trans. Jane E. Lewin (Ithaca: Cornell University Press, 1980).

Gibbons, Luke, *Transformations in Irish Culture* (Cork: Cork University Press, 1996).

Gikandi, Simon, 'Globalization and the Claims of Postcoloniality', *South Atlantic Quarterly* 100:3 (2001), pp. 627–58.

Gikandi, Simon, 'Editor's Column: The End of Postcolonial Theory?' *PMLA* 122:3 (May 2007), pp. 633–51.

Gilbert, Sandra M., and Susan Gubar, *The Madwoman in the Attic: The Woman Writer and the Nineteenth-Century Literary Imagination* (New Haven: Yale University Press, 1979).

Gilmore, Ruth Wilson, 'Fatal Couplings of Power and Difference: Notes on Racism and Geography', *The Professional Geographer* 54:1 (2002), pp. 15–24.

Gissing, George, *New Grub Street*, ed. John Goode (Oxford: Oxford University Press, 1999).

Gissing, George, *The Odd Women*, ed. Patricia Ingham (Oxford: Oxford University Press, 2008).

Glenny-Crory, W., 'The Irish Land Question', *Time: A Monthly Magazine* (1887), pp. 535–43.

Goetsch, Paul, 'The Country House in George Moore's *A Drama in Muslin*', in Otto Rauchbauer (ed.), *Ancestral Voices: The Big House in Anglo-Irish Literature: A Collection of Interpretations* (Dublin: Lilliput Press Ltd, 1992), pp. 79–92.

Gonzalez, Alexander, 'Paralysis and Exile in George Moore's *A Drama in Muslin*', *Colby Library Quarterly* 20:3 (1984), pp. 152–63.

Goodlad, Lauren M. E., *Victorian Literature and the Victorian State: Character and Governance in a Liberal Society* (Baltimore: The Johns Hopkins University Press, 2003).

Goodlad, Lauren M. E., *The Victorian Geopolitical Aesthetic: Realism, Sovereignty, and Transnational Experience* (Oxford: Oxford University Press, 2015).

Goodlad, Lauren M. E., 'Worlding Realism Now', *Novel: A Forum on Fiction* 49:2 (August 2016), pp. 183–201.

Goodwin, Geraint, *Conversations with George Moore* (London: Ernest Benn Limited, 1929).

'The Grand Orange Lodge of Ireland', *Freemans Journal*, 22 November 1798, pp. 1.

Green, Rayna, 'The Tribe Called Wannabe: Playing Indian in America and Europe', *Folklore* 99:1 (1988), pp. 30–55.

Greiner, Rae, '*Bleak House*: Pastoral', *Critical Quarterly* 55:1 (2013), pp. 75–93.

Grossman, Jonathan H., *Charles Dickens's Networks: Public Transport and the Novel* (Oxford: Oxford University Press, 2012).

Grossman, Jonathan H., 'Living the Global Transport Network in *Great Expectations*', *Victorian Studies* 57:2 (2015), pp. 225–50.

Grosz, Elizabeth, *The Nick of Time: Politics, Evolution, and the Untimely* (Crows Nest, NSW: Allen & Unwin, 2004).

Grosz, Elizabeth, 'The Untimeliness of Feminist Theory', *NORA-Nordic Journal of Feminist and Gender Research* 18:1 (March 2010), pp. 48–51.

Grubgeld, Elizabeth, *George Moore and the Autogenous Self: The Autobiography and Fiction* (Syracuse, NY: Syracuse University Press, 1994).

Hack, Daniel, 'Inter-Nationalism: "Castle Rackrent" and Anglo-Irish Union', *Novel: A Forum on Fiction* 29:2 (Winter 1996), pp. 145–64.

Hack, Daniel, 'Close Reading at a Distance: The African Americanization of *Bleak House*', *Critical Inquiry* 34:4 (2008), pp. 729–3.

Haddon, A. C., 'The Aran Islands, County Galway: A Study in Irish Ethnography', *The Irish Naturalist* (December 1893), pp. 303–8.

Hadley, Elaine, *Living Liberalism: Practical Citizenship in Mid-Victorian Britain* (Chicago: University of Chicago Press, 2010).

Hall, Catherine, *Civilising Subjects: Metropole and Colony in the English Imagination 1830–1867* (Chicago: University of Chicago Press, 2002).

Hall, S. C., 'The Irish in England: The Washerwoman', *The Irish Penny Journal* (1840), pp. 2–4.

Hall, S. C., *Sketches of Irish Character* (London: Nattali and Bond, 1855).

Hand, Derek, *A History of the Irish Novel* (Cambridge: Cambridge University Press, 2011).

Harrison, Frederic, 'A Pedantic Nuisance', *The Nineteenth-Century: A Monthly Review* 19 (January 1886), pp. 87–105.

Haydu, Jeffrey, 'Reversals of Fortune: Path Dependency, Problem Solving, and Temporal Cases', *Theory and Society* 39:1 (January 2010), pp. 25–48.

Helsinger, Elizabeth, *Rural Scenes and National Representation* (Princeton: Princeton University Press, 1997).

Hennig, John, 'Dickens and Ireland', *The Irish Monthly* (1947), pp. 248–55.

Hensley, Nathan, *Forms of Empire: Poetics of Victorian Sovereignty* (Oxford: Oxford University Press, 2017).

'Her Majesty's Irish Mail', *All the Year Round*, 16 July 1859, pp. 283–8.

Herbert, Christopher, *Culture and Anomie: Ethnographic Imagination in the Nineteenth Century* (Chicago: University of Chicago Press, 1991).

Hervey, Alison, 'Irish Aestheticism in Fin-de-Siècle Women's Writing: Art, Realism, and the Nation', *Modernism/modernity* 21:3 (September 2014), pp. 805–26.

Higney, Robert, '"Law, Good Faith, Order, Security": Joseph Conrad's Institutions', *Novel: A Forum on Fiction* 48:1 (May 2015), pp. 85–102.

Hodgson, Geoffrey, 'What Are Institutions?' *Journal of Economic Issues* 40:1 (March 2006), pp. 1–25.

Homans, Margaret, *Bearing the Word: Language and Female Experience in Nineteenth-Century Women's Writing* (Chicago: The University of Chicago Press, 1986).

Houlihan, Con, 'Kickham's work up there with the great Irish novels', *Sunday Independent*, 28 October 2007, p. 20.

Howes, Marjorie Elizabeth, 'William Carleton's Literary Religion', in James H. Murphy (ed.), *Evangelicals and Catholics in Nineteenth-Century Ireland* (Dublin: Four Courts Press, 2005), pp. 107–22.

Howes, Marjorie Elizabeth, *Colonial Crossings: Figures in Irish Literary History* (Dublin: Field Day Publications, 2006).

'inhabitation, n.', *OED Online*, <http://www.oed.com/> (last accessed 28 February 2019).

'The "Irish Difficulty" Solved by Con Mc Nale', *Household Words*, 25 May 1850, pp. 207–10.

Jackson, Holbrook, 'The New Fiction', in *The Eighteen Nineties: A Review of Art and Ideas at the Close of the Nineteenth Century* (Atlantic Highlands, NJ: Humanities Press, Inc., 1976), pp. 216–30.

Jaime De Pablos, Mᵃ Elena, 'George Moore: The Committed Feminist', in Mary Pierse (ed.), *George Moore: Artistic Visions and Literary Worlds* (Newcastle: Cambridge Scholars Press, 2006), pp. 184–96.

James, Henry, 'The Art of Fiction', in Walter Besant and Henry James, *The Art of Fiction* (Boston: Cupples and Hurd, 1884), pp. 49–85.

Jameson, Fredric, 'The Realist Floor-Plan', in Marshall Blonsky (ed.), *On Signs* (Baltimore: The Johns Hopkins University Press, 1985), pp. 373–83.

Jameson, Fredric, *The Antinomies of Realism* (New York: Verso, 2013).

Jenkins, Brian, *The Fenian Problem: Insurgency and Terrorism in a Liberal State* (Montreal: McGill-Queen's University Press, 2008).

Joseph, Terra Walston, '"Saving British Natives": Family Emigration and the Logic of Settler Colonialism in Charles Dickens and Caroline Chisholm', *Victorian Literature and Culture* 43:2 (2015), pp. 261–80.

Joyce, Simon, *Modernism and Naturalism in British and Irish Fiction, 1880–1930* (Cambridge: Cambridge University Press, 2015).

K.T., 'A Literary Causerie', *The Speaker: The Liberal Review*, 17 September 1892, pp. 352–4.

Keating, P. J., *The Working Classes in Victorian Fiction* (London: Routledge, 2016).

Kiberd, Declan, *Inventing Ireland: The Literature of the Modern Nation* (London: Vintage, 1996).

Kickham, Charles J., 'A Retrospect', *Irish People*, 2 January 1864, p. 89.

Kickham, Charles J., *For the Old Land: A Tale of Twenty Years Ago* (Dublin: M. H. Gill and Son, 1886).

Kickham, Charles J., *Knocknagow; or The Homes of Tipperary* (Dublin: M. H. Gill and Son Ltd., 1953).

Kilfeather, Siobhán, 'Terrific Register: The Gothicization of Atrocity in Irish Romanticism', *boundary 2* 31:1 (2004), pp. 49–71.

Kinealy, Christine, *This Great Calamity: The Irish Famine, 1845–52* (Dublin: Gill & MacMillan Ltd., 1994).

King, Carla, 'Introduction', in Carla King (ed.), *Parnell and his Island* (Dublin: University College Dublin Press, 2004), pp. vii–xxvii.

Korobkin, Laura, 'Avoiding "Aunt Tomasina": Charles Dickens Responds to Harriet Beecher Stowe's Black American Reader, Mary Webb', *ELH* 82:1 (Spring 2015), pp. 115–40.

Kornbluh, Anna, *Realizing Capital: Financial and Psychic Economies in Victorian Form* (New York: Fordham University Press, 2014).

Kristeva, Julia, 'Women's Time', in Kelly Oliver (ed.), *The Portable Kristeva* (New York: Columbia University Press, 1997), pp. 349–68.

Laird, Heather, *Subversive Law in Ireland, 1879–1920: From 'Unwritten Law' to the Dáil Courts* (Dublin: Four Courts Press, 2005).

Langbauer, Laurie, *Novels of Everyday Life: The Series in English Fiction, 1850–1930* (Ithaca: Cornell University Press, 1999).

Law, Jules, *The Social Life of Fluids: Blood, Milk, and Water in the Victorian Novel* (Ithaca: Cornell University Press, 2010).

'Leader Page Parade', *Irish Independent*, 22 December 1954, p. 4.

Lecours, André, 'New Institutionalism: Issues and Questions', in André Lecours (ed.), *New Institutionalism: Theory and Analysis* (Toronto: University of Toronto Press, 2005), pp. 3–26.

Lee, Yoon Sun, 'Bad Plots and Objectivity', *Representations* 139:1 (Summer 2017), pp. 34–59.

LeFebvre, Henri, *State, Space, World: Selected Essays*, ed. Neil Brenner and Stuart Elden, trans. Gerald Moore, Neil Brenner and Stuart Elden (Minneapolis: University of Minnesota Press, 2009).

Levine, Caroline, *The Serious Pleasures of Suspense: Victorian Realism and Narrative Doubt* (Charlottesville: University of Virginia Press, 2003).

Levine, Caroline, 'Narrative Networks: *Bleak House* and the Affordances of Form', *Novel: A Forum on Fiction* 42:3 (2009), pp. 517–23.

Levine, Caroline, 'From Nation to Network', *Victorian Studies* (Summer 2013), pp. 647–6.

Levine, Caroline, *Forms: Whole, Rhythm, Hierarchy, Network* (Princeton: Princeton University Press, 2015).

Levine, George, *The Realistic Imagination: English Fiction from Frankenstein to Lady Chatterley* (Chicago: University of Chicago Press, 1981).

'The Life and Letters of Maria Edgeworth', *The Quarterly Review* (October 1895), pp. 305–23.

Lim, Bliss Cua, *Translating Time: Cinema, the Fantastic, and Temporal Critique* (Durham, NC: Duke University Press, 2009).

'Literature', *Glasgow Herald*, 20 July 1886, p. 6.

Lloyd, David, *Anomalous States: Irish Writing and the Post-Colonial Moment* (Durham, NC: Duke University Press, 1993).

Lloyd, David, 'Afterword: Hardress Cregan's dream – for another history of the Irish novel', in Jacqueline Belanger (ed.), *The Irish Novel in the Nineteenth Century: Facts and Fictions* (Dublin: Four Courts Press, Ltd., 2005), pp. 229–37.

Lloyd, David, *Irish Times: Temporalities of Modernity* (Dublin: Keough-Naughton Institute for Irish Studies, University of Notre Dame/Field Day, 2008).

Lloyd, David, *Irish Culture and Colonial Modernity 1800–2000: The Transformation of Oral Space* (Cambridge: Cambridge University Press, 2011).

Lootens, Tricia, *The Political Poetess: Victorian Femininity, Race, and the Legacy of Separate Spheres* (Princeton: Princeton University Press, 2017).

Lowe, Lisa, *The Intimacies of Four Continents* (Durham, NC: Duke University Press, 2015).

Luciano, Dana, *Arranging Grief: Sacred Time and the Body in Nineteenth-Century America* (New York: New York University Press, 2007).

Lukács, Georg, 'Narrate or Describe?', in Arthur D. Kahn (ed. and trans.), *Writer & Critic and Other Essays* (New York: Universal Library, 1971), pp. 110–48.

Lukács, Georg, *The Historical Novel*, Hannah and Stanley Mitchell (translators) (Lincoln: University of Nebraska Press, 1983).

Maher, James, 'Tale of a Stamp', *Irish Independent*, 24 August 1953, pp. 4.

Maine, Henry Sumner, *Lectures on the Early History of Institutions* (New York: H. Holt and Company, 1875), <https://archive.org/details/lecturesonearly11maingoog> (last accessed 28 February 2019).

Malachuk, Daniel S., *Perfection, the State and Victorian Liberalism* (New York: Palgrave Macmillan, 2005).

Marcus, Sharon, *Between Women: Friendship, Desire, and Marriage in Victorian England* (Princeton: Princeton University Press, 2007).

Markovits, Stefanie, 'George Eliot's Problem with Action', *SEL Studies in English Literature 1500–1900* 41:4 (Autumn 2001), pp. 785–803.

Martin, Amy E., *Alter-nations: Nationalisms, Terror, and the State in Nineteenth-Century Britain and Ireland* (Columbus: The Ohio State University Press, 2012).

Martineau, Harriet, *Life in the Sick-Room*, ed. Maria H. Frawley (Peterborough: Broadview Press Ltd., 2003).

Masson, David, *British Novelists and Their Styles: Being a Critical Sketch of the History of British Prose Fiction* (Cambridge: Macmillan and Co., 1859).

Matus, Jill, 'Proxy and Proximity: Metonymic Signing', *University of Toronto Quarterly: A Canadian Journal of the Humanities* (1988–9), pp. 305–26.

Matz, Aaron, *Satire in an Age of Realism* (Cambridge: Cambridge University Press, 2010).

Maurer, Sara, *The Dispossessed State: Narratives of Ownership in 19th-Century Britain and Ireland* (Baltimore: Johns Hopkins Press, 2012).

McClintock, Anne, *Imperial Leather: Race, Gender and Sexuality in the Colonial Context* (New York: Routledge, 1995).

McGurl, Mark, *The Program Era: Postwar Fiction and the Rise of Creative Writing* (Cambridge, MA: Harvard University Press, 2011).

Mehta, Uday Singh, *Liberalism and Empire: A Study in Nineteenth-Century British Liberal Thought* (Chicago: University of Chicago Press, 1999).

Michie, Helena, 'Hard Times, Global Times: Simultaneity in Anthony Trollope and Elizabeth Gaskell', *SEL: Studies in English Literature 1500–1900* 56:3 (Summer 2016), pp. 605–26.

Mighall, Robert, *A Geography of Victorian Gothic Fiction: Mapping History's Nightmares* (Oxford: Oxford University Press, 1999).

Mignolo, Walter, 'Citizenship, Knowledge, and the Limits of Humanity', *American Literary History* 18:2 (2006), pp. 312–31.

Mill, John Stuart, 'England and Ireland', in John M. Robson (ed.), *Essays on England, Ireland, and the Empire* (Toronto: University of Toronto Press, 1982), pp. 505–32.

Mill, John Stuart, 'Considerations on Representative Government', in John Gray (ed.), *On Liberty and Other Essays* (Oxford: Oxford University Press, 1991), pp. 205–470.

Mill, John Stuart, 'The Subjection of Women', in John Gray (ed.), *On Liberty and Other Essays* (Oxford: Oxford University Press, 1991), pp. 471–582.

Miller, D. A., *The Novel and the Police* (Berkeley: University of California Press, 1988).

Miller, Fenwick, Mrs, 'Books Worth Reading: "Esther Waters"', *The Woman's Signal*, 3 May 1894, pp. 296–7.

Miller, J. Hillis, 'Narrative and History', *ELH* 41:3 (August 1974), pp. 455–73.

Miller, J. Hillis, *Reading for Our Time:* Adam Bede *and* Middlemarch *Revisited* (Edinburgh: Edinburgh University Press, 2012).

Mitchel, John, *The Last Conquest of Ireland (Perhaps)* (Glasgow: R. & T. Washbourne, Ltd., 1882).

Mitchel, John, *Jail Journal* (Dublin: The University Press of Ireland, 1982).

Mitchell, Judith, '*A Drama in Muslin*: George Moore's Victorian Novel', *English Literature in Transition (1880–1920)* 25:4 (1982), pp. 211–24.

Mitchell, Nick, '(Critical Ethnic Studies) Intellectual', *Critical Ethnic Studies* 1:1 (Spring 2015), pp. 86–94.

Moore, George, *Literature at Nurse, or, Circulating Morals* (London: Vizetelly & Co., 1885).

Moore, George, 'Defensio Pro Scriptis Meis', *Time: A Monthly Magazine* (1887), pp. 277–84.

Moore, George, 'Is Education Worth Having?', *London St James Gazette*, 10 September 1890, p. 6.

Moore, George. 'My Impressions of Zola', *The English Illustrated Magazine* (February 1894), pp. 477–89.

Moore, George, 'A Plea for the Soul of the Irish People', *The Nineteenth Century and After: A Monthly Review* (February 1901), pp. 285–95.

Moore, George, *Confessions of a Young Man* (New York: Press of J. J. Little & Co., 1901).

Moore, George, 'Apologia Pro Scriptis Meis', *Fortnightly Review* 112 (1922), pp. 529–44.

Moore, George, *A Drama in Muslin: A Realistic Novel* (Gerrards Cross: Colin Smythe Ltd., 1981).

Moore, George, *Hail and Farewell: Ave, Salve, and Vale*, ed. Richard Allen Cave (Gerrards Cross: Colin Smythe Ltd., 1985).

Moore, George, *Esther Waters*, ed. David Skilton (Oxford: Oxford University Press, 1995).

Moore, George, *Parnell and His Island*, ed. Carla King (Dublin: University College Dublin Press, 2004).

Moore, Grace, *Dickens and Empire: Discourses of Class, Race and Colonialism in the Works of Charles Dickens* (Farnham: Ashgate Publishing Company, 2004).

Moretti, Franco, *The Way of the World: The Bildungsroman in European Culture* (London: Verso, 1987).

Moretti, Franco, *Atlas of the European Novel, 1800–1900* (London: Verso, 1999).

Morris, Pam, '*Bleak House* and the Struggle for the State Domain', *ELH* 68.3 (2001), pp. 679–98.

Morris, William, *News from Nowhere*, ed. Stephen Arata (New York: Broadview, 2003).

Moten, Fred, 'Fred Moten's Statement in Support of a Boycott of Israeli Academic Institutions', *MLA Members for Justice in Palestine: The Modern Language Association and the Movement for the Boycott of Israeli Academic Institutions*, 7 September 2016, <https://mlaboycott. wordpress.com/2016/09/07/fred-motens-statement-in-support-of-a-boycott-of-israeli-academic-institutions/> (last accessed 28 February 2019).

'Mr William Carleton', *The London Review of Politics, Society, Literature, Art, and Science*, 6 February 1869, pp. 126–7.

Mufti, Nasser, 'Walking in *Bleak House*', *Novel: A Forum on Fiction* 49:1 (2016), pp. 65–81.

Muñoz, José Esteban, 'Cruising the Toilet: LeRoi Jones/Amiri Baraka, Radical Black Traditions, and Queer Futurity', *GLQ: A Journal of Lesbian and Gay Studies* 13:2–3 (2007), pp. 353–67.

Muñoz, José Esteban, *Cruising Utopia: The Then and There of Queer Futurity* (New York: New York University Press, 2009).

Mullen, Mary, 'Anachronistic Aesthetics: Maria Edgeworth and the "Uses" of History', *Eighteenth-Century Fiction* 26:2 (Winter 2013–14), pp. 233–59.

Mullen, Mary, 'In Search of Shared Time: National Imaginings in Elizabeth Gaskell's *North and South*', in Lesa Scholl, Emily Morris and Sarina Gruver Moore (eds), *Place and Progress in the Works of Elizabeth Gaskell* (Farnham: Ashgate Publishing Ltd., 2015), pp. 107–19.

Mullen, Mary L., 'Empire and Unfielding: Charles Kickham's *Knocknagow: Or, the Homes of Tipperary*', *b2o: an online journal* (October 2016), <http://www.boundary2.org/2016/10/mary-l-mullen-empire-and-unfielding-charles-kickhams-knocknagow-or-the-homes-of-tipperary/> (last accessed 28 February 2019).

Mullen, Mary L., 'How the Irish Became Settlers: Metaphors of Indigeneity and the Erasure of Indigenous Peoples', *New Hibernia Review* 20.3 (Autumn 2016), pp. 81–96.

Murphy, James H., 'Canonicity: The Literature of Nineteenth-Century Ireland', *New Hibernia Review* 7.2 (2003), pp. 45–54.

Murphy, James H., *Irish Novelists and the Victorian Age* (Oxford: Oxford University Press, 2011).

Myers, Janet C., *Antipodal England: Emigration and Portable Domesticity in the Victorian Imagination* (Albany: State University of New York Press, 2009).

Myers, Mitzi, 'Shot from Canons: Or, Maria Edgeworth and the Cultural Production and Consumption of the Late Eighteenth-Century Woman Writer', in Ann Birmingham and John Brewer (eds), *The Consumption of Culture, 1600–1800: Image, Object, Text* (London: Routledge, 1995), pp. 193–214.

'The New Realism', *Northern Echo*, 6 March 1893, p. 3.

Nolan, Emer, *Catholic Emancipations: Irish Fiction from Thomas Moore to James Joyce* (Syracuse, NY: Syracuse University Press, 2007).

'North and South', *The Athenaeum*, 7 April 1855, p. 403.

'The Novels of Mr Anthony Trollope', *The Dublin Review*, October 1872, pp. 393–430.

O'Connell, Helen, *Ireland and the Fiction of Improvement* (Oxford: Oxford University Press, 2006).

O'Day, Alan, *Irish Home Rule: 1867–1921* (Manchester: Manchester University Press, 1998).

O'Donnell, Katherine, 'Castle Stopgap: Historical Reality, Literary Realism, and Oral Culture', *Eighteenth-Century Fiction* 22:1 (2009), pp. 115–30.

O'Donoghue, David J., *The Life of William Carleton* (London: Downey & Co., 1896).

Ó Gallchoir, Clíona, *Maria Edgeworth: Women, Enlightenment and Nation* (Dublin: University College Dublin Press, 2005).

O'Leary, John, *Recollections of Fenians and Fenianism*, vol. 1 (London: Downey & Co., Limited, 1896).

O'Malley, Patrick, '"The length, breadth, and depth, of the wound": Irish Historical Violence and *Ennui's* Amnesiac Aesthetics', *ELH* 84.1 (Spring 2017), pp. 143–70.

O'Malley, Patrick, *Liffey and Lethe: Paramnesiac History in Nineteenth-Century Anglo-Ireland* (Oxford: Oxford University Press, 2017).

Oliphant, Margaret, *Hester*, ed. Philip Davis and Brian Nellist (Oxford: Oxford University Press, 2003).

'The Orange Institution', *Dublin University Magazine* (April 1836), pp. 400–8.

Orwell, George, 'Charles Dickens', in *A Collection of Essays* (New York: Mariner Books, 1970), pp. 48–103.

Perera, Suvendrini, *Reaches of Empire: The English Novel from Edgeworth to Dickens* (New York: Columbia University Press, 1991).

Peters, Laura, *Dickens and Race* (Manchester: Manchester University Press, 2013).

Pillai, Sharon, 'Gaging the Postcolonial Hegemonic: Three Contributions to Rethinking the Norms at Play', *Studies in the Novel* 44.2 (Summer 2012), pp. 231–9.

Plotz, John, 'The Semi-Detached Provincial Novel', *Victorian Studies* 53:3 (Spring 2011), pp. 405–16.

Plotz, John, 'Speculative Naturalism and the Problem of Scale: Richard Jeffries's *After London*, after Darwin', *Modern Language Quarterly: A Journal of Literary History* 76:1 (March 2015), pp. 31–56.

'Popular Tales by Maria Edgeworth', *The Annual Review of History and Literature* (January 1804), pp. 461–3.

Povinelli, Elizabeth A., 'The Will to Be Otherwise/The Effort of Endurance', *The South Atlantic Quarterly* 111:3 (Summer 2012), pp. 453–75.

Price, Leah, 'Reader's Block: Response', *Victorian Studies* 46:2 (2004), pp. 231–42.

Quayson, Ato, 'The Sighs of History: Postcolonial Debris and the Questions of (Literary) History', *New Literary History* 43:2 (2012), pp. 359–70.

Radford, Andrew, *Thomas Hardy and the Survivals of Time* (New York: Routledge, 2016).

Rajan, Rajeswari Sundar, '"The Shadow of that Expatriated Prince": The Exorbitant Native of Dombey and Son', *Victorian Literature and Culture* 19 (1991), pp. 85–106.

Rancière, Jacques, 'The Concept of Anachronism and the Historian's Truth', *InPrint* 3:1 (June 2015), pp. 21–48.

Rattler, Morgan, 'Of the Red Indian', *Fraser's Magazine for Town and Country* (1844), pp. 655–76.

Reid, Forest, 'The Novels of George Moore', *Westminster Review* (August 1909), pp. 200–8.

'Review', *The Pall Mall Gazette*, 14 July 1886, pp. 5–6.

Rezek, Joseph, *London and the Making of Provincial Literature* (Philadelphia: University of Pennsylvania Press, 2015).

Rifkin, Mark, *Beyond Settler Time: Temporal Sovereignty and Indigenous Self-Determination* (Durham, NC: Duke University Press, 2017).

Robbins, Bruce, *The Servant's Hand: English Fiction from Below* (New York: Columbia University Press, 1986).

Robbins, Bruce, 'Telescopic Philanthropy: Professionalism and Responsibility in *Bleak House*', in Homi K. Bhabha (ed.), *Nation and Narration* (London: Routledge, 1990), pp. 213–30.

Robbins, Bruce, 'The Smell of Infrastructure: Notes toward an Archive', *Boundary 2* (Spring 2007), pp. 25–33.

Robbins, Bruce, *Upward Mobility and the Common Good: Toward a Literary History of the Welfare State* (Princeton: Princeton University Press, 2007).

Rohy, Valerie, 'Ahistorical', *GLQ: A Journal of Lesbian and Gay Studies* 12:1 (2006), pp. 61–83.

Rohy, Valerie, *Anachronism and its Others: Sexuality, Race, Temporality* (Albany: State University of New York Press, 2009).

Rosenthal, Jesse, *Good Form: The Ethical Experience of the Victorian Novel* (Princeton: Princeton University Press, 2017).

Rubenstein, Michael, *Public Works: Infrastructure, Irish Modernism, and the Postcolonial* (Notre Dame: University of Notre Dame Press, 2010).

Ruskin, John, *Sesame and Lilies* (London: Smith, Elder & Co., 1871).

Ruskin, John, 'The Nature of the Gothic', in J. G. Links (ed.), *The Stones of Venice* (New York: Da Capo Press, 2003), pp. 157–90.

Russell, Matthew, 'A Few More Relics of Charles Kickham', *The Irish Monthly* (March 1888), pp. 131–7.

Ruth, Jennifer, *Novel Professions: Interested Disinterest and the Making of the Professional in the Victorian Novel* (Columbus: The Ohio State University Press, 2006).

Ryan, W. P., 'The Best Irish Books', *The New Century Review* (August 1898), pp. 90–100.

Ryder, Sean, 'Literature in English', in Laurence M. Geary and Margaret Kelleher (eds), *Nineteenth-Century Ireland: A Guide to Recent Research* (Dublin: University College Dublin Press, 2005), pp. 118–35.

Said, Edward, *The Question of Palestine* (New York: Vintage Books, 1992).

Said, Edward, *Culture and Imperialism* (New York: Vintage Books, 1994).

Sanders, Andrew, *Dickens and the Spirit of the Age* (Oxford: Clarendon Press, 1999).

Schor, Hilary M., *Dickens and the Daughter of the House* (Cambridge: Cambridge University Press, 2004).

Schor, Hilary M., *Curious Subjects: Women and the Trials of Realism* (Oxford: Oxford University Press, 2013).

Scott, Joan Wallach, *The Fantasy of Feminist History* (Durham, NC: Duke University Press, 2012).

Scott, Walter, 'General Preface,' in *Waverley; or, 'Tis Sixty Years Since*, ed. Claire Lamont (Oxford: Oxford University Press, 1986), pp. 349–61.

Scott, Walter, *Waverley; or, 'Tis Sixty Years Since*, ed. Claire Lamont (Oxford: Oxford University Press, 1986).

Schreiner, Olive, *The Story of an African Farm*, ed. Joseph Bristow (Oxford: Oxford University Press, 1992).

Sedgwick, Eve Kosofsky, *Between Men: English Literature and Male Homosocial Desire* (New York: Columbia University Press, 1985).

Sedgwick, Eve Kosofsky, 'Queer and Now', in *Tendencies* (Durham, NC: Duke University Press, 1993), pp. 1–20.

Seeley, J. R., *The Expansion of England: Two Courses of Lectures* (Boston: Little, Brown and Company, 1905).

Shaw, Harry E., *Narrating Reality: Austen, Scott, Eliot* (Ithaca: Cornell University Press, 1999).

Smith, G. Barnett, 'A Brilliant Irish Novelist', *Fortnightly Review*, 1 January 1897, pp. 104–16.

St Clair, William, *The Reading Nation in the Romantic Period* (Cambridge: Cambridge University Press, 2004).

Spencer, Herbert, *The Study of Sociology* (Ann Arbor: The University of Michigan Press, 1969).

Spencer, Herbert, 'Political Institutions', in J. D. Y. Peel (ed.), *On Social Evolution: Selected Writings* (Chicago: University of Chicago Press, 1972), pp. 185–205.

'St Clair of the Isles: Or, the Outlaws of Barra, a Scottish Tradition', *Annual Review and History of Literature* (January 1803), pp. 606.

Stasiulis, Daiva, and Nira Yuval-Davis, 'Introduction: Beyond Dichotomies – Gender, Race, Ethnicity and Class in Settler Societies', in Daiva Stasiulis and Nira Yuval-Davis (eds), *Unsettling Settler Societies: Articulations of Gender, Race, Ethnicity and Class* (London: Sage Publications, 1995), pp. 1–38.

Steinlight, Emily, 'Dickens's "Supernumeraries" and the Biopolitical Imagination of Victorian Fiction', *Novel: A Forum on Fiction* 43:2 (2010), pp. 227–50.

Stockton, Kathryn Bond, *The Queer Child, or Growing Sideways in the Twentieth Century* (Durham, NC: Duke University Press, 2009).

Stoler, Ann Laura, *Race and the Education of Desire: Foucault's History of Sexuality and the Colonial Order of Things* (Durham, NC: Duke University Press, 1995).

Taft, Joshua, '*New Grub Street* and the Survival of Realism', *English Literature in Transition, 1880–1920* 54:3 (2011), pp. 362–81.

'Tales of Fashionable Life', *The Dublin Review* (April 1838), pp. 45–543.

Taylor, Christopher, *Empire of Neglect: The West Indies in the Wake of British Liberalism* (Durham, NC: Duke University Press, 2018).

Taylor, Jenny Bourne, '"Received, a Blank Child": John Brownlow, Charles Dickens, and the London Foundling Hospital – Archives and Fictions', *Nineteenth-Century Literature* 56:3 (December 2001), pp. 293–363.

Teves, Stephanie Nohelani, Andrea Smith and Michelle H. Raheja, 'Tradition', in Stephanie Nohelani Teves, Andrea Smith and Michelle H. Raheja (eds), *Native Studies Keywords* (Tucson: University of Arizona Press, 2015), pp. 233–42.

Townend, Paul A., 'Between Two Worlds: Irish Nationalists and Imperial Crisis 1878–80', *Past and Present: A Journal of Historical Studies* 194 (1 February 2007), pp. 139–74.

Townsend, Sarah L., 'The Drama of Peripheralized Bildung: An Irish Genre Study', *New Literary History* 48:2 (Spring 2017), pp. 337–62.

Trevelyan, Charles Edward, *The Irish Crisis* (London: Longman, Brown, Green & Longmans, 1848).

Trollope, Anthony, *An Autobiography*, ed. Michael Sadleir and Frederick Page (Oxford: Oxford University Press, 1950).

Trollope, Anthony, *Phineas Finn: The Irish Member*, ed. Jacques Berthoud (Oxford: Oxford University Press, 1982).

Trollope, Anthony, *Castle Richmond*, ed. Mary Hamer (Oxford: Oxford University Press, 1989).

Trotter, Mary, *Ireland's National Theaters: Political Performance and the Origins of the Irish Dramatic Movement* (Syracuse: Syracuse University Press, 2001).

Trumpener, Katie, *Bardic Nationalism: The Romantic Novel and the British Empire* (Princeton: Princeton University Press, 1997).

Tucker, Irene, *The Moment of Racial Sight: A History* (Chicago: University of Chicago Press, 2013).

Vimalassery, Manu, Juliana Hu Pegues and Aloysha Goldstein, 'Introduction: On Colonial Unknowing', *Theory and Event* 19:4 (1 October 2016).

Vermeulen, Pieter, and Ortwin de Graef, 'Bildung and the State in the Long Nineteenth Century', *Partial Answers: Journal of Literature and the History of Ideas* 10:2 (June 2012), pp. 241–50.

Wagner, Tamara, *Victorian Narratives of Failed Emigration: Settlers, Returnees, and Nineteenth-Century Literature in English* (London: Routledge, 2016).

Wallace, William, 'Two Pinches of Snuff', *The Academy* (17 July 1886), pp. 39–40.

Ward, Megan, 'Our Posthuman Past: Victorian Realism, Cybernetics, and the Problem of Information', *Configurations* 20:3 (Fall 2012), pp. 279–97.

Ward, Patrick, *Exile, Emigration, and Irish Writing* (Dublin: Irish Academic Press, 2002).

Warhol, Robyn, 'Toward a Theory of the Engaging Narrator: Earnest Interventions in Gaskell, Stowe, and Eliot', *PMLA* 101:5 (October 1986), pp. 811–18.

Warner, Michael, 'Queer and Then?' *The Chronicle of Higher Education*, 1 January 2012, <http://chronicle.com/article/QueerThen-/130161/> (last accessed 28 February 2019).

Waugh, Arthur, 'The New Realism', *Fortnightly Review*, 1 May 1916, pp. 849–58.

Wellek, René, 'The Concept of Realism in Literary Scholarship', in Stephen G. Nichols, Jr. (ed.), *Concepts of Criticism* (New Haven: Yale University Press, 1963), pp. 222–52.

Wenzel, Jennifer, 'Editor's Column: The End of Postcolonial Theory?', *PMLA* 122:3 (May 2007), pp. 633–51.

'What Has Scott Done for Scotland?', *The Leisure Hour: A Family Journal of Instruction and Recreation*, 5 August 1871, pp. 491–2.

Whelan, Kevin, 'The Other Within: Ireland, Britain and the Act of Union', in Dáire Keogh and Kevin Whelan (eds), *Acts of Union: The Causes, Contexts and Consequences of the Act of Union* (Dublin: Four Courts Press Ltd., 2001), pp. 13–33.

Williams, Raymond, *The Country and the City* (London: Chatto and Windus, 1973).

Williams, Raymond, *Marxism and Literature* (Oxford: Oxford University Press, 1977).

Williams, Raymond, 'The Reader in *Hard Times*,' *Writing in Society* (London: Verso, 1991), pp. 166–76.

Wolfe, Patrick, *Settler Colonialism and the Transformation of Anthropology: The Politics and Poetics of an Ethnographic Event* (London: Cassell, 1999).

Woloch, Alex, *The One vs the Many: Minor Characters and the Space of the Protagonist in the Novel* (Princeton: Princeton University Press, 2003).

Wright, Daniel, 'Let Them Be: Dickens's Stupid Politics', *Dickens Studies Annual: Essays on Victorian Fiction* 46 (2015), pp. 339–56.

Vernon, James, *Distant Strangers: How Britain Became Modern* (Berkeley: University of California Press, 2014).

Yeats, W. B., 'Irish National Literature', *The Bookman* (August 1895), pp. 138–40.

Yeats, W. B., 'Introduction', in *Representative Irish Tales*, ed. Mary Helen Thuente (Gerrards Cross: Colin Smythe Ltd., 1979), pp. 25–32.

Youngkin, Molly, 'George Moore's Quest for Canonization and Esther Waters as Female Helpmate', *English Literature in Transition (1880–1920)*, 46:2 (2003), pp. 116–39.

Index

and institutions, 120
in Ireland, 37, 52, 55, 94
local particulars, 59
made historical, 44
and social difference, 51–2
state power over, 19
and state violence, 96
untimely, 53
women novelists and, 65n
exclusion, 3, 61n, 65n
    Austen and, 58
    Dickens and, 160, 168n
    Eliot and, 21, 117–18, 135n,
        136n
    and futurity, 8
    Gaskell and, 16
    settlement and, 158
experience
    authors', 76, 77, 103n, 183
    colonial, 185, 194
    English, 56
    of institutions, 18, 81–2, 85, 87,
        99, 102
    Irish, 62n, 94
    literature as imaginary, 22
    lived, 71, 72, 74, 75, 82,
        95, 97
    personal, 110–11, 124–5, 129,
        130, 135n, 147, 200
    transhistorical, 44, 46

Fabian, Johannes, 8, 104n, 107n
factories, 141, 153, 157, 160
family, 2
    Dickens and, 139, 140, 150–2,
        154, 155–6, 161–2
    Edgeworth and, 38, 45, 48–9, 56
    Eliot and, 119, 120, 126–7, 128,
        130, 131, 136n
    Kickham and, 96
    Moore and, 197
    Oliphant and, 50
famine, 74, 87–8, 90, 93, 106n;
    see also Great Famine
Farina, Jonathan, 171–2n
Fegan, Melissa, 91, 106n
Felski, Rita, 134n

Fenianism, 95, 103n
    Kickham and, 23, 72, 73, 79, 107n
Fergus, Jan, 62n
Ferguson, Roderick, 2, 51, 141,
    150, 212
Ferris, Ina, 60–1n, 62n, 64n
feudalism, 178, 187
Flint, Kate, 168n, 172n, 173n
forgetting, 23, 30n, 74, 93–4
formalism, 74, 104n
Foster, John Wilson, 203n, 204n,
    207n
Foster, R. F., 103n
Foucault, Michel, 2, 20, 25n, 28n,
    29n, 33n, 60n, 140, 150
Foundling Hospital, 144
Fraiman, Susan, 29n
France, 179, 183
Freedgood, Elaine, 26n, 54, 131,
    133n, 142
Freeman, Elizabeth, 21–2, 112–13,
    215n
frozen youth, 11, 185, 190–1
Fuller, (Sarah) Margaret, 112–13,
    116, 124, 136n
futurity, 4, 5–6, 12, 14, 24–5, 28n,
    170n
    alternative *see* otherwise
        possibilities
    Carleton and, 88–9
    Carleton and Kickham and, 74
    Charlotte Brontë and, 18
    Dickens and, 1, 139, 146–7, 151–2,
        153–5, 162
    Edgeworth and, 13, 45, 48,
        64n, 211
    Eliot and, 23, 118, 119, 122–3,
        124, 131
    fixed, 27n
    institutions as horizon of, 39, 43,
        50–1
    Kickham and, 80, 99, 100
    known, 32n
    Moore and, 176, 188, 190,
        191–2
    national tale and, 19
    reproductive, 171n

untimeliness, 2, 11, 22, 24–5,
40, 62n
of anachronism, 21, 184–5
Carleton and, 79
of development, 185
Dickens and, 56, 141, 150, 151,
158, 167, 171–2n
Edgeworth and, 42
Eliot and, 21, 111, 113–14, 125,
127, 132
of everyday life, 53
of Irish realism, 16
Moore and, 23, 176, 177, 180,
187–8, 191–2, 193, 195, 196,
198–9, 202
postcolonialism and queer theory
and, 213
Scott and, 45
women and, 134n
useless past, 8, 12, 211

*Valentine M'Clutchy, the Irish
Agent . . .* (Carleton)
changing character name, 105n
ethnography, 81–2, 83–4
ethos, 74
and liberalism, 82–3, 87
and nationalism, 85–6
vanishing primitive, 74, 88, 94,
102
Vermeulen, Pieter, 203n
Vernon, James, 26–7n
Vimalassery, Manu, 18
violence
of academic freedom, 214–15n
British forgetting, 74
British imperial, 31n
of colonialism, 6, 19, 21, 140,
141–2, 168n
of famine, 89
fictional, 88
historical, 64n
of law, 80–1
of liberalism, 10, 21, 33n
not in service of state, 61n
provoked by injustice, 83

sectarian, 85
state, 86, 96, 99, 101–2

Wagner, Tamara S., 169n
Ward, Megan, 11
Ward, Patrick, 195, 207n
Warhol, Robyn, 135n
Warner, Michael, 213, 215n
Waugh, Arthur, 181
Wellek, René, 41–2, 201
Whelan, Kevin, 64n
Williams, Raymond, 7, 28n, 170n
Wolfe, Patrick, 144
Wollstonecraft, Mary, 112–13, 115,
116, 124
Woloch, Alex, 14, 169n, 173–4n
women
belatedness in relation to men, 8
domestic, 59–60, 116, 117, 134n
and education, 110, 116–17,
125–6, 127, 132
and institutional futurity, 50–1,
124–5
oppressed, 196
relationship to institutionalism,
23, 136n
as servants, 208n
and slow reform, 113
transhistorical relationship
between, 21
untimeliness, 111, 113–14, 134n
as writers, 65n, 116, 192–3, 200
see also Fuller, (Sarah) Margaret;
gender; Wollstonecraft, Mary
workhouses, 3, 5, 79, 120, 139,
167n
Wright, Daniel, 170n

Yeats, W. B., 14–15, 30–1n, 76–7,
95, 103n, 179
Young Ireland movement, 79, 81
Youngkin, Molly, 196
Yuval-Davis, Nira, 170n

Zola, Émile, 175, 177, 178, 179,
183, 196